Alaska in the Progressive Age

ALASKA

IN THE **PROGRESSIVE** AGE

A POLITICAL HISTORY 1896 to 1916

THOMAS ALTON

UNIVERSITY OF ALASKA PRESS : FAIRBANKS

Text © 2019 University of Alaska Press

Published by
University of Alaska Press
P.O. Box 756240
Fairbanks, AK 99775-6240

Interior design by Kristina Kachele Design, llc

Cover image: Laying steel rails for construction of the Alaska Railroad. Once the route was determined, crews began working north from Seward and south from Fairbanks. The route was divided into three sections with a commissioner in charge of each section (UAF Rasmuson Library Archives UAF-1984-75-8).

Library of Congress Cataloging-in-Publication Data

Names: Alton, Thomas L., author.
Title: Alaska in the Progressive Age / by Tom Alton.
Description: Fairbanks, AK : University of Alaska Press, 2019. |
Includes bibliographical references and index. |
Identifiers: LCCN 2018061189 (print) | LCCN 2019001124 (ebook) |
ISBN 9781602233850 (e-book) | ISBN 9781602233843 (pbk. : alk. paper)
Subjects: LCSH: Alaska—History—1867-1959. |
Progressivism (United States politics)
Classification: LCC F909 (ebook) |LCC F909 .A47 2019 (print) |
DDC 979.8/03dc-23
LC record available at https://lccn.loc.gov/2018061189

To Kathy, with love, always and forever.

F ALASKA HOME RY, SEPT. 16-07.

CONTENTS

FOREWORD

-๛-

ON SEPTEMBER 3, 1938, Ernest Gruening paid a visit to James Wickersham at his home on a quiet street in the hills above Juneau. Gruening was then an official with the Interior Department, where he oversaw the administration of federal territories, including Alaska. A year later, he would be appointed governor of the territory. Wickersham, eighty-one years old and retired after a career as lawyer, federal judge, and Alaska's congressional delegate, spent his days dabbling in legal work and dictating letters to his wife, Grace, whose help he required since he was going blind. For an hour or so, the two men discussed current issues in Alaska. As was his habit, Wickersham grumbled about uninformed congressmen, government obstructionists, outside corporate interests, and everyone else he believed was holding Alaska back. A few weeks later, the former delegate fired off a thirty-page letter to the future governor, castigating what he called the "felonious" mining, logging, railway, and steamship trusts that epitomized "monopoly and greed." "I will write what I know to [Gruening]," Wickersham wrote in his diary that fall, "and let him work out the facts." Many years later, when Gruening was himself eighty-six years old, he remembered the tête-à-tête with Wickersham, writing in his memoir how the delegate spoke with vigor about his many fights against the "looting of Alaska" by J. P. Morgan, the Guggenheims, and other corporatists.

That James Wickersham remained a pugnacious advocate for Alaska even in his last days as a nearly blind octogenarian should surprise no one. As Tom Alton explains in this insightful and thoroughly researched book, the always-uncompromising Wickersham really came into his own as Alaska's congressional delegate, serving seven nonconsecutive terms between 1908 and 1933, during which he delivered countless stem-winders on the House floor and relished every fight, in part for what he could deliver to Alaska when he won but also for the mere sport of it all.

Alton notes that for all the political skills Wickersham possessed, he also had the good fortune to arrive in Washington at the height of the Progressive Era, a time when the federal government responded to the social and economic effects of industrialization by assuming a more active role in regulating big business, managing the nation's natural resources, and funding infrastructure projects for public benefit. It was Alaska's good fortune too. Wickersham leveraged those prevailing political winds to the long-term benefit of the territory and its residents. Major gold strikes in the Klondike, Nome, and Fairbanks had convinced Washington to begin paying attention to the nation's northernmost territory, and Wickersham was instrumental in establishing an elected legislature as well as Alaska's first college, its largest railroad, and Mt. McKinley National Park.

This book makes a remarkable contribution to Alaska history by bringing all those stories together under the umbrella of Progressivism, a widely studied movement in American history but one whose impact on Alaska has remained relatively unexplored. As Alton points out, the political, economic, and social development of Alaska in the early twentieth century was going to happen one way or another. The discovery of gold, stampede of settlers, and steamships full of tourists clamoring to see glaciers and totem poles would see to that. But if some degree of transformation was a given, there was still nothing inevitable about the nation's response, nothing preordained when it came to railroads, national parks, territorial legislatures, or any other mechanism by which the federal government might see to Alaska's future. To be sure, the legislative dynamo that was James Wickersham played a major role in steering that course, but the developments also occurred within a unique set of circumstances as Americans responded to the rapid modernization happening in their country. Historians are always mindful of the *post hoc, ergo propter hoc* fallacy, the misguided notion that because one event follows another, it must therefore have been caused by it. Alton is at his best when he distinguishes, with meticulous detail and carefully chosen words, that Progressivism did not *cause* Alaska's early territorial development but rather exerted a profound influence on what was already happening in the proverbial last frontier. National currents worked to establish the political foundation—as well as the literal foundation in the case of infrastructure projects such as the railroad—on which today's Alaska stands.

The author similarly brings a penetrating yet nuanced scrutiny to Wickersham's long-standing claim that the federal government consistently neglected to promote Alaska's development, a lament Gruening would advance throughout his own political career. The attention of Washington and the many gains of the Progressive Era complicate the narrative. It is to Alton's credit that he avoids trying to prove or disprove the theory of neglect, choosing instead to focus on how the politically potent idea functioned in public discourse at the time. When Gruening visited Wickersham on that late-summer day in 1938, he asked the former delegate whether he viewed his prized railroad bill as a victory against corporate control of Alaska. Although it operated at the margins of economic profitability, the federally owned railway still epitomized the progressive ideal of public resources managed for public benefit. Wickersham valued the railroad, he told Gruening, but wished he could have done more. "I hoped that the government would build not merely one but two railroads over different routes," he stated. "The legislation I sponsored and Congress approved authorized two routes, but only one was built." Neglect indeed!

The Progressive Era in Alaska was as complex, contradictory, and meaningful as any in the state's history. I hope readers enjoy Tom Alton's book as much as I did.

—*Ross Coen, University of Alaska Fairbanks Department of History*

Alaska in the Progressive Age

INTRODUCTION

Go north, young man, go north

—◊—

JAMES WICKERSHAM was prepared for a fight as he arrived on Capitol Hill on the morning of January 14, 1914. Opposition to his prized Alaska Railroad bill, he had noted in his diary, was "active and spiteful."[1] As Alaska's lone delegate to Congress, Wickersham had voice but no vote in the House of Representatives. His chance to raise that voice in support of the territory had arrived this day in a scheduled speech before a floor session of the full House, and he had every intention of working it to his best advantage. The prospect of a lively debate energized the combative former attorney and federal judge. He had stayed in Washington over the congressional holiday break and had spent most of the weeks since Christmas cloistered in his office, dictating to his stenographer.

For Wickersham, this speech was an opportunity to educate Congress about the wealth of resources present in Alaska and the unlimited potential for jobs and economic development that would be made possible by a government-owned railroad stretching from the southcentral coast to the Interior. But at the same time, it was the forum Wickersham needed to launch an attack against his sworn enemy—the "overshadowing evil"—which threatened the welfare of every struggling pioneer in the territory. The enemy was the Alaska Syndicate, a powerful business conglomerate controlled by New York financier J. P. Morgan in partnership with the Guggenheim family, also of New York, and the Close Brothers of London.[2]

1

The Alaska Syndicate was a political as well as an economic force, with a virtual monopoly on copper mining and steamship and railroad transportation in the territory. It owned the Kennecott copper mine, the Copper River and Northwestern Railway, and the Alaska Steamship Company. Operating in a market that lacked any level of meaningful oversight, the syndicate set its own freight rates, stifled competition, and sent teams of lobbyists to Washington to protect its interests. In 1914, the focus of those interests was the effort to block the Alaska Railroad bill.

Wickersham was incensed. The syndicate, in his view, was prepared to go to any lengths to preserve its monopoly in Alaska, clearly in violation of federal antitrust laws. Where he considered a federally financed railroad to be the key to success for independent miners and farmers working to make a go of it in a harsh but resource-rich new country, the Alaska Syndicate saw unfair government intrusion into the workings of a free and open market.

The House convened at noon and immediately called on the Alaska delegate to begin his remarks. Opening with a quote from President Woodrow Wilson's State of the Union speech given just the previous month, Wickersham focused on the current administration's endorsement of a federally funded railroad in Alaska. He cited Wilson's support for the role of government in enhancing resource development while ensuring wise use, conservation, and protection of the country and its people against the interests of any monopoly. "Alaska, as a storehouse, should be unlocked," Wilson had told Congress. A railroad was the means of "thrusting in the key to the storehouse and throwing back the lock and opening the door."

Wickersham now stood on firm footing as the full House settled in for the day's debate. "That," he declared in reference to Wilson's statement, "is progressive democracy, and I shall give it my approval and support."[3]

"Progressive democracy" was certainly the right term to describe the political movement that elected the Democrat Wilson and brought Democratic majorities to the House and Senate in the elections of 1912. Progressivism had grown as activists from across the political spectrum saw the need for social and economic reform. Corporate greed seemed out of hand, and the public demanded regulation and control. Reformers turned to government as the only force capable of

James Wickersham, appointed federal district court judge for Alaska and elected to seven terms as Alaska territorial delegate to congress (Alaska State Library ASL-Wickersham-James-1).

protecting the interests of the people against the power of the trusts. In the first years of the century, voters turned hopefully to President Theodore Roosevelt, who had promised to make his Republican Party a party of progressive conservatives in response to robber baron businessmen of the Gilded Age. Roosevelt built his trust-busting reputation by demanding that big business yield to the superior power of government. However, while Roosevelt was using the power of the presidency to bring corporate America to heel, it was another political leader, Robert La Follette, who became the voice of the Progressive movement. Elected governor of Wisconsin in 1900 and to the US Senate in 1906, La Follette represented a wing of the Republican Party that occupied a more radical place than Roosevelt was able to go. La Follette had accomplished much in his home state, shepherding through broad reform measures based largely on his stand against the powerful railroad trusts.

In these first years of the century, Progressive ideas reshaped the nation's economy, engendered broad social and political reforms, and ushered in a movement aimed at conserving natural resources from the excessive exploitation of corporate trusts. These too were the formative years of modern-day Alaska. The gold rush captured worldwide attention, and suddenly the nation's northern possession became a destination for every sort of pioneer, explorer, and settler. Southcentral and interior Alaska, especially the Tanana Valley, attracted a wide variety of newcomers, spurring Congress to enact regulatory codes and establish a judicial structure where virtually none had existed before. In the thirty-three years following the 1867 purchase of Alaska from Russia, it had been easy for the nation to ignore this little-known possession, and Congress did little else than organize customs districts and run a system of Native schools under the Bureau of Education while the president appointed a territorial governor. Now, however, prospectors pouring into the country were returning with news of fabulous untapped resources of gold, copper, and coal, as well as the excellent potential for agricultural development in the Interior. Suddenly, a progressive-minded Congress took note, and as a result, the federal government became a catalyst for development during the crucial years of discovery and settlement of the Alaska territory.

This book is a history of Alaska from 1896 to 1916, the two decades in which Alaska developed its mineral resources, birthed a structure of highway and railroad transportation, and founded modern cities, all encouraged and enabled by Progressive politicians and bureaucrats in Washington. The story focuses on interior and southcentral Alaska, but especially on Fairbanks, the adopted home of James Wickersham and the site of agricultural lands that were touted widely as having production value equal to the best areas of northern Europe.

By 1906, attention had shifted away from southeastern Alaska and the Klondike. Fairbanks, Kennecott, and Nome were the booming centers of mining activity while Sitka, Juneau, and Dawson began to decline.

In the 1860s and '70s, American exploration of Alaska had largely been a response by government to the need for some knowledge of the vast expanse of wild country it had purchased from the Russian empire. Newspapers critical of the purchase dubbed the area "Walrussia" and "Seward's Icebox," the latter in reference to Secretary of State William Seward, who was the chief proponent of the deal. In the public mind, Alaska was unimaginably distant, and the inland regions were especially unknowable. William Healey Dall, who by the time of the purchase had built a reputation as one of the most knowledgeable Americans alive on the geography of Alaska, referred to the broad Interior as "the *terra incognita* between the limit of Russian explorations and the Hudson Bay Territory."[4] Joining the Western Union Telegraph Expedition in 1866, Dall helped explore a route for a wire connecting America with Europe by crossing the Bering Strait and connecting to a line through Siberia. Though he reported extensively on coastal areas and landmasses of southcentral and southwestern Alaska, vast expanses of the Interior remained entirely unexplored. Of the Tanana River he wrote, "No white man has dipped his paddle into its waters, and we only know of its length and character from Indian reports."[5] Western Union abandoned its project when the competing transatlantic cable was completed in 1867, but the explorations of Dall and his predecessor, Robert Kennicott, provided the government and the general public with valuable data on Alaska climate, geography, flora, and fauna, and its Native inhabitants.

In 1867, the year of the purchase, Secretary of State William Seward ordered an official government exploration of Alaska headed by George Davidson of the US Coast Survey. After a four-month tour of the shoreline aboard the US Revenue Cutter *Lincoln*, Davidson returned with reports of Alaska's wealth of fur, fish, and mineral resources. But with 70 percent of the landmass still untouched by exploration, Americans expressed no enthusiasm for its potential as a place for permanent settlement and agricultural production.[6] Alfred Hulse Brooks concluded that in the thirty years following the acquisition, most of the knowledge gained about interior Alaska was due not to the work of the federal government but to the personal efforts of prospectors and fur traders. The US Coast and Geodetic Survey, and later the US Navy, conducted investigations of coastal areas, but few government-sanctioned explorers ventured into the unknown Interior. Public interest in Alaska had faded quickly after the purchase as the nation focused its attention on post–Civil War Reconstruction, industrial development including railroad construction, and on settling the Indian wars in the West.

There was, however, a late-century flurry of tourism in southeastern Alaska. Conservationist and author John Muir made his first trip to the Panhandle in 1879, and his effusive descriptions of mountains, glaciers, forests, and wildlife helped to launch numerous excursions of sightseers through the Inside Passage. Historian Robert Campbell has noted that these tourists played a role in transforming Alaska from "Seward's Folly" into an integral part of the American empire. Tourists cleared the way for future gold seekers, Campbell concluded. Muir served as an "agent of empire," and tourists represented the "reach of national power into the new territory."[7]

The first traders to set up a commercial enterprise on the Yukon River were partners Jack McQuesten, Arthur Harper, and Alfred Mayo, who established Fort Reliance on the Canadian Yukon in 1874. The three were prospectors at heart, but at first their success depended on the fur trade, supplying Indian trappers with modern goods in exchange for marten, wolf, beaver, and other valuable skins. Eventually, McQuesten, Harper, and Mayo branched out to operate independently, providing all trading as far downriver as Nulato until competitors moved in with the growing white population in the early 1890s. They, especially McQuesten, became well-known and popular figures in the Interior for the generous credit they extended to the growing numbers of prospectors who were scouring every tributary of the Yukon for signs of placer gold.

In 1883, sixteen years after the purchase, US Army Lieutenant Frederick Schwatka led a party to chart the Yukon River from its source to its mouth. Starting at the coast and packing their supplies over the Chilkoot Pass to Lake Lindemann, where they built rafts, Schwatka and his men pioneered a route that thousands of gold seekers would follow a dozen or so years later.[8]

Schwatka's exploration of the upper and middle Yukon River and published accounts aroused public awareness of a new frontier waiting to be opened and developed. His journey occurred at a time when Americans were beginning to sense the limits of frontier expansion. The West was largely settled, and railroad tracks laid from coast to coast had made transportation across the continent easy and affordable. Vast areas of land had been opened to agricultural and industrial development, yet Americans were not ready to stop there. Seward's vision at the time of the Alaska purchase was to broaden the country's influence in the Pacific, and settlement and occupation of Russian America was a vital part of that plan. The mood in the mid-1880s favored continued expansion, and the Schwatka party, as historian William R. Hunt remarked, "encountered a region poised on the threshold of the momentous changes that had occurred everywhere else in North America where white traders or trappers had been joined by miners and settlers."[9]

A strike on the Stewart River above Fort Reliance in 1885 prompted initial excitement, but prospectors who rushed to the area were mostly disappointed in the amount of gold it yielded. The next year, a much more promising and productive strike was made on a tributary of the Fortymile River, which has its headwaters on the American side of the border but enters the Yukon in Canada below Dawson. The town of Forty Mile was quickly established at the mouth of the Fortymile River as word reached eager gold seekers at Stewart River and other creeks in the Interior. It was the first mining town on the Yukon, and for a time it supported a seasonal population of up to one thousand miners.[10]

The first gold town on American soil got its start following a discovery on Birch Creek in 1892. Miners quickly staked claims on that river and found lucrative placer gold on Mastodon, Deadwood, and Mammoth Creeks as well. The town of Circle was founded on the left bank of the Yukon, and Jack McQuesten built a two-story log trading post to serve the miners and settlers. Circle became not only a supply center but a winter residence for miners as well. With a population of nearly seven hundred in 1896, it claimed to be the largest log cabin city in the world, with a dozen or so saloons and dance halls and the usual complement of gamblers and prostitutes.[11]

The year 1896 marked the beginning of events that changed everything on the Alaska-Yukon frontier. In August, George Carmack found gold in quantities never before seen in the North. Men who had toiled on their own for years with a pick and pan or had worked for wages of a dollar a day in the placer mines of Birch Creek or Mastodon Creek heard tales of prospectors panning out seventy-five dollars in four hours on Bonanza Creek and finding the occasional twelve-dollar nugget. Word that the gold was coarse, one prospector wrote later, "was enough to set the miners wild."[12]

The towns of Circle and Forty Mile emptied as prospectors stampeded to the Klondike to stake their claims. The strike on Bonanza and Eldorado Creeks was only the beginning. Word quickly spread Outside, and when the steamer *Portland* arrived in Seattle the next July carrying several lucky prospectors and "a ton of gold," the mad rush was on. The town of Dawson, established on the right bank of the Yukon at the mouth of the Klondike River, grew to a population of five thousand within a year. The winter of 1897–1898 marked the height of activity on the White Pass and the steeper but shorter Chilkoot Trail leading to the Klondike goldfields. Steamers arriving at the head of Lynn Canal disgorged gold seekers by the thousands at Skagway and Dyea, where they began the tortuous work of transporting themselves and the required year's supply of goods to their destination in Dawson. The typical miner's "outfit" comprised perhaps twelve hundred pounds of flour, bacon, beans, and canned goods along with the clothing and implements needed to survive in the North and the tools required for prospecting placer gold. All of it was ferried over the pass one load at a time on the miner's back.

As historian Melody Webb has pointed out, Alaska and the Yukon had been widely explored, surveyed, and mapped by the mid-1890s and thus were not "discovered" with the Klondike gold rush.[13] Though ignored by the American government for roughly seventeen years following the purchase, Alaska drew increased attention in the public eye as the century moved on and Americans still felt the itch to control and dominate the entire continent.

The Alaska-Yukon frontier opened new opportunities for a nation that was in the mood to explore and grow but for the first time faced a limit imposed by geography, as the westward movement at last reached the Pacific shore. The most influential American historian of that era, Frederick Jackson Turner, noted in 1893 that the US Superintendent of the Census had decided that as of 1890 the American frontier no longer existed. That is, a discernible line marking the advance of white settlement across the continent, "the meeting point between savagery and civilization" in Turner's words, had disappeared as the last large contiguous unsettled areas of the West had given way to farms, communities, and schools. Americans' three-century march from east to west had ended at the Pacific coast, marking, in Turner's view, "the closing of a great historic movement."

Turner, who presented his thesis, "The Significance of the Frontier in American History," at a meeting of the American Historical Association held in Chicago during the World's Columbian Exposition, saw the United States as a unique civilization molded as no other nation ever had been by its adaptation to a dynamic frontier. The steady movement westward provided continuous rebirth and opportunity. It was the dominating force that shaped the American character and social structure and fostered a love of democracy and individual liberty. The environment was too strong to overcome at first, and so the pioneer changed himself to fit the conditions. Over time, he transformed the landscape, and the outcome, Turner concluded, was "a new product that is American." Access to free land formed the basis of American democracy, and the westward advance of settlement furnished opportunity unequaled anywhere else in the world.

For Turner, the closing of the frontier marked the end of the first period of American history, but it did not, in his estimation, forecast any lessening of Americans' expansive character. The historian made no mention of Alaska, but by the time he had delivered his paper in Chicago, waves of prospectors and explorers were seeking new opportunities in the North. "The stubborn American environment is there with its imperious summons to accept its conditions," Turner declared. "And yet, in spite of environment, and in spite of custom, each frontier did indeed furnish a new field of opportunity, a gate of escape from the bondage of the past."[14]

The Alaska-Yukon frontier was poised to become the new field of opportunity that Americans craved. The challenges and excitement of the gold rush brought the region to the forefront of public attention and, in scholar Roxanne Willis's opinion, established Alaska as the "Last Frontier."[15] In short, it became a part of the broad historical sweep of the American West, as it was defined by Turner. It was the last chance on the continent for pioneering Americans to carve a living for themselves out of the wilderness, conquer the forces of nature, and build a civilized society where only savagery had existed before.

Author Susan Kollin credits John Muir for popularizing Alaska in the late-nineteenth-century American mind and debunking the "Seward's Folly" myth. Through Muir's writings, the North was reinvented as a destination of adventure and beauty, where the pioneering spirit could prevail and the United States could continue its natural course of expansion across the continent.[16]

The editor of the *Alaska-Yukon Magazine* surely agreed, and the Seattle-based periodical eagerly promoted Alaska as a new American frontier and the place where a pioneering spirit still lived. "There is not a great quantity of unoccupied land in the West," the writer observed fifteen years after Turner delivered his famous thesis. "Horace Greeley's sage advice to young men is not filled with the wonderful possibilities it had when uttered. There are greater possibilities in the paraphrase of this advice: 'Go north, young man, go north.' Today Alaska contains almost all the potentialities that the great West contained fifty years ago."[17]

One Fairbanks-based newspaper voiced the same enthusiasm in 1914. "All history shows that human progress is ever traveling westward," the editor wrote. "For more than 100 years the settlement and development of North America has been slowly working westward, and now the only remaining frontier is Alaska."[18]

This Turnerian view of the American West prevailed among the public. As historian Patricia Limerick explained it, European immigrants saw North America as an empty continent "where free land restored opportunity and offered a route to independence." It was an inevitable process through which civilization replaced savagery and a new nation was formed.[19] From the pioneers' perspective, the West was a process, not a place, where the action occurred at the moving edge of the frontier. Limerick asserts that these assumptions were fundamentally ethnocentric, with the focus concentrated on English-speaking white men and ignoring the lives of Native Americans, Hispanics, and women. She argues for a "rethinking" of the American West as a place of "complicated environments occupied by natives who considered their homeland to be the center, not the edge."[20]

Suddenly, within the context of Turner's frontier thesis, Alaska jumped from obscurity and neglect to a destination of wonder and possibility. It is impossible to overstate the excitement that was sparked nationwide and even around the world by tales of plentiful gold. And it was in the two decades following the gold rush that the foundation of modern-day Alaska was laid, when the region's two largest cities were settled with permanent populations, systems of transportation and commerce were established, and a structure of representative locally controlled government was erected. All these accomplishments occurred in Progressive-era America with its emphasis on federal regulation of business and its attention to government-mandated reform of outdated social systems. I do not contend that Alaska developed *because* of Progressive-era politics. The region would have grown and its resources would have been developed even without the benefit of Progressivism's considerable influence. It is my intention to present Progressivism as the context within which events came together at the beginning of the twentieth century to transform Alaska in time from the dark and frozen unknown into the modern state we have today.

Many factors contributed to the allure of the Alaska and Yukon goldfields. A severe depression known as the Panic of 1893 brought hard times to the working class nationwide, and certainly the numbers of gold seekers increased as men in every sector of the economy found themselves out of work. Farmers were especially hard-pressed to make ends meet, as prices for corn and cotton and other crops dropped drastically. Working men and women turned to prospects in the North as a solution to economic hard times.

Also in response to the economic depression of the 1890s, a strong populist movement focused on the plight of the farmer took hold. Populist Party candidates polled well in elections in the South and West. The party moved quickly to expand its reach to take on issues of fairness in labor practices and reform of the financial structure, including the eight-hour workday and public ownership of railroads. In 1896, William Jennings Bryan, the "Prairie Populist" of Nebraska, had risen to the top of the movement on the strength of his eloquent voice as the champion of the poor and underprivileged in their struggle against the power of the banks and railroads. Yet his message had broad appeal within the establishment party structure as well. That year Bryan won the nomination for president on both the Populist and the Democratic Party tickets.

Bryan's vision for economic and social justice focused on reform of the system that placed gold as the foundation of wealth. Gold was the most sought-after substance on earth. It was the heart of the US economy and the most valuable commodity in world trade. In 1890s America, it set men wild with excitement. It sparked a mass movement in which many thousands of people risked everything they had and endured unimaginable hardships in the unknown North on the slim hope of finding their fortune. Yet striking it rich was only part of the power of and fascination with gold in contemporary life. Gold became a primary issue in the politics of 1896 as well. Bryan despised the gold standard, which demanded that every dollar in circulation must be backed by an equal value of gold held by the US Treasury. His Republican opponent, William McKinley, embraced the gold standard and enjoyed the support of the wealthiest business leaders of the Gilded Age. The 1896 presidential election became a heated struggle between rich and poor, between the interests of corporate wealth and the concerns of the farmer and factory worker in a depressed economy. In the year of the Klondike discovery, the gold standard played a major role in the national debate over economic policy and reform. It thrust William Jennings Bryan onto the national stage after he made a thrilling speech at the Democratic National Convention in Chicago. Moreover, it helped to push the farm-based Populist movement into the Progressive era with its emphasis on returning government to the people and reining in the excesses of corporate tycoons.

Modern Alaska was born with the gold rush. The federal government took notice of the rapid increase in population at the turn of the century and responded by improving institutions of civil government and education and creating a workable judicial system to serve the entire territory. Alaska contained huge stores of mineral wealth, but it was gold—not copper or coal—that captured public imagination and commanded the attention of the public in late 1890s America. Those other resources became important elements of the territory's economy in the twentieth century, but their development depended on large corporate investment and employment of laborers working for wages. It was gold that drew prospectors by the tens of thousands to a new frontier, where riches lay waiting in creek bottoms for any prospector with a shovel, a pick, and a pan. They left the world they knew behind and came to the North with dreams of striking it rich on their own. As a Fairbanks editor commented in 1906, their previous trades and professions were only "makeshifts" which they used as a means to get a "grubstake for a prospecting trip." "They did not come to this country to reengage in their regular occupations," he added. "Owning and operating a mine for themselves is their mission and hope."[21]

When considering the factors that contributed to the rise of modern-day Alaska, foreign immigration must be seriously taken into account. Beginning in about 1880, the growth and changing character of immigration markedly transformed American cities. Prior to 1880, the traditional Nordic, Caucasian European immigrants had easily assimilated and had been rapidly accepted as Americans. In contrast, however, the new immigrants, who were predominantly Catholic and Jewish, began to vastly outnumber the mainly Anglo-Saxon and Protestant immigrants from northern and western Europe. Suddenly, people from Russia, Italy, Poland, Greece, Turkey, and the Balkan countries arrived in great numbers to escape poverty and overpopulation and to take advantage of the new industrial economy in urban America.[22] The new immigrants stuck closely to ethnic communities within urban areas and tried to maintain old-world cultural patterns. The "native Yankee" was not prepared for such a shift, and he found himself outnumbered and overwhelmed.[23] In a day when it appeared that the open spaces of the American West were retreating quickly with settlement, and the industrialized cities of the North and East were beginning to feel foreign and unbearably crowded, the Alaska-Yukon frontier appeared just in time.

This safety-valve view of the westward movement was integral to Turner's frontier thesis. When social and economic conditions weighed heavily upon the masses in the East, Turner wrote, "this gate of escape to the free conditions of the frontier" was always open. "This promised land of freedom and equality was theirs for the taking."[24] Poor and middle-class Americans saw the Klondike as not only a source of unimaginable riches but also an opportunity to create a new life. It provided hope for an escape from the despairing conditions of industrialized urban centers and the endless hard work of the farm during a time of depression.

The social and economic conditions of 1890s America supplied a perfect environment for the Progressive movement to take root and grow. Progressivism was a broad-based popular reaction to the excesses of Gilded Age industrialists, bankers, and railroad tycoons who had amassed fabulous fortunes by creating monopolies and operating virtually free of government regulation. The Alaska-Yukon frontier provided a natural breeding ground for Progressive ideas. The men and women who flooded into the northland were keenly aware of the class conflict created by the rise of the railroads and industrial giants. To them, the Alaska-Yukon frontier offered hope for relief from oppression. The vast majority of gold seekers either gave up on their dreams before even reaching the goldfields or, upon completing their journey, found that earlier stampeders had already staked every inch of every creek worth prospecting. But the few who stayed were eager to settle in a last frontier where open land was available to start new cities and build an economy based on mining and agriculture. Alaska pioneers expected government to clear the way for exploitation of resources and to assist them by ensuring that their individual efforts would not be restricted, and they were quick to complain about any actions by Congress or federal agencies to do otherwise. For example, in 1900, Territorial Governor John G. Brady protested bitterly when Congress explicitly stated that the general land laws of the United States would not be applied to Alaska.

"Why should there be a departure from the settled policy of granting 160 acres as a homestead?" he demanded. "Is it too much for the people of Alaska to ask that they be treated as well as have settlers in other frontiers?"[25]

A year later, Brady was still fuming. "We have had a long schooling in patience and have learned to wait for the second table," he charged. "The day is coming when we shall be grown folks and shall sit down with the company."[26]

During the first decade of the twentieth century, many Alaskans were willing to accept the role of an active federal government in securing certain measures. As the Progressive movement gained strength nationwide, reformers within government and muckraking journalists exposed the unfair, exploitative, and monopolistic practices of big business. The result was a series of conservation measures, antitrust regulations, fair labor laws, and, ultimately, voting rights for women.

Settlers in the new territory of Alaska demanded progress as well, and the society benefited richly. Advancements included the right of Alaskans to elect a delegate to Congress, establishment of the Alaska Road Commission, and creation of an elected territorial legislature. But the greatest victory of all was Wickersham's prized Alaska Railroad Bill, which President Wilson signed into law in 1914. It was

a Progressive-era coup for two reasons. First, it was a federal government response to an economic need in a developing frontier. Never
before in the history of the westward movement had Congress stepped
in to build and operate a transportation system where private enterprise could likely have provided comparable service. Through the
Alaska Railroad, the federal government would play a key role in developing new lands and making settlement possible for a new generation of pioneers. Second, it was a repudiation of the excessive power
of unregulated big business and an expression of the antitrust, antimonopoly mood that prevailed in early-twentieth-century America.
Wickersham framed the debate on the Alaska Railroad Bill in terms
of a battle fought by the huge and rapacious Morgan-Guggenheim syndicate against the interests of everyday Alaskans struggling to make
a living. Progressives favored public control of utilities and strict regulation of corporate affairs to limit profits and protect the consumer
from the greed and excesses that had been so apparent in the Gilded
Age economy. In short, Progressive reformers wished to bring big business to heel and send the message that government was in control.
Private-sector business leaders would play by the rules and regulations
established by Congress. "Which shall it be," Wickersham thundered
from the floor of the US House of Representatives, "shall the government or the Guggenheims control Alaska?"[27] Progressive leaders in
Congress and the White House gave him a clear answer: it would not
be the Guggenheims.

In the meantime, however, Alaskans complained bitterly about the
federal government's neglect. One crusty resident of Coldfoot on the
upper Koyukuk River told a Senate investigative subcommittee visiting the territory in 1903 that Congress's lack of attention to the needs
in Alaska was appalling. "Thus far we have been sadly and, may I say,
shamefully neglected. It seems strange that our government spends so
large sums of money in trying to civilize those foreign greasers, while
wide awake and intelligent American-born citizens here in Alaska can
barely receive any recognition whatever."[28]

At the same time, Alaskans chafed under the oppressive rules
and outright abuse they suffered because of interference in their
everyday lives. Journalists carried the theme regularly in newspapers
across the territory and as far south as Seattle. "Think of it!" a writer
in Skagway cried in 1906. "Here we are a people denied the right of

self-government, taxed without representation . . . all our money taken from us without our consent and expended under the direction of departments in Washington—a system compared with which the government of the American colonies under George III was broad and liberal."[29] Another editor denounced as "burdensome" the taxes and operating fees that roadhouse keepers were forced to pay. Alaska was a land of "liberty and lack of restraint," he wrote in 1908, and yet "our great and beneficent government was exacting a quadruple toll from a citizen for the privilege of conducting a wayside inn. . . . Any tax upon thrift, industry or enterprise does not seem right."[30] The outrage was expressed in contemporary fiction as well. In Rex Beach's novel *The Iron Trail,* set during construction of the Copper River and Northwestern Railroad, one leading character, an engineer eager to put his crews to work laying track but held up by the federal government's interference in access to much-needed coal resources, spat out his frustration. "We have been treated unfairly by the government," he said angrily. "We have been fooled, cheated, hounded as if we were a crowd of undesirable aliens and I'm heartily sick of the injustice."[31]

It is evident, then, that Alaskans have long exhibited a split personality in regard to their relationship with Washington, DC. They decry the neglect and oppressive ill treatment perceived on all levels, and they complain about a lack of federal assistance where they see a need. They eagerly seek and accept large federal subsidies for infrastructure, yet at the same time they want government out of their lives and off their backs, leaving them free to develop the land and exploit the resources without interference or excessive taxes and regulations.

Historians who have pondered the question of the federal government's role in Alaska tend to fall into two camps. William R. Hunt is an example of what he himself has labeled the "traditional neglect opinion," at least for the period from 1870 to 1914, citing as evidence the lack of law-and-order provisions made by the government for Alaska.[32] Ernest Gruening, who served as a territorial governor and as one of Alaska's first US senators, also espoused the traditional view. After he was replaced as governor in 1953, Gruening became one of the most prominent and effective advocates for Alaska statehood, and his highly opinionated history of Alaska painted a picture of continued federal neglect.[33] Similarly, Robert Atwood, in using the full power of his position as publisher of Alaska's largest newspaper, promoted the traditional view of history to advance the cause of statehood. "83 Years of Neglect," a headline screamed on the cover of an *Anchorage Times* special statehood edition.[34] Jeanette Paddock Nichols, who authored a classic political history of Alaska focusing on its struggle for home rule, portrays Congress's attitude toward the territory as "one of indifference, inaction, and fumbling." Continuing the theme of federal neglect, she concludes her 1924 work by saying that "departmental red tape has hindered and bound Alaska development."[35]

The opposite end of the spectrum is represented by historians William H. Wilson and Stephen Haycox. Wilson argued in several articles that Alaska had fared very well as a result of the actions of the federal government. He contends that, during the Progressive era, the prevailing belief in Congress was that government action could produce stable business competition and social benefits in Alaska. Congress felt an obligation toward the territory, he wrote, and passage of the Alaska Railroad Bill was the result of that feeling.[36] Similarly, Haycox recognizes the federal government's role during the Progressive era as one of persistent support for Alaska settlement and economic development. "The magnitude of the response disposes of the idea of federal neglect of Alaska," Haycox asserts,[37] and he goes on to cite a number of Progressive reforms that had immeasurable positive effects on the territory, culminating with the Alaska Railroad and construction of the town of Anchorage, which grew up around the railroad headquarters. Settlers who came to the new territory enjoyed an array of benefits provided by the federal government, including communications, public safety, health care, and education.[38] Historian Ross Coen expands on this range, writing that Washington has "determined our destiny in ways almost too numerous to list." Benefits include subsidized mail delivery, weather forecasting, military spending, the Homestead Act, the University of Alaska, fisheries protection, the Matanuska Colony, and others.[39]

The events recounted in this work have been detailed previously in the historical record. I do not claim to have uncovered any new facts or influences or any unknown sources. But history is interpretation. It is a process of examining the record, analyzing the past, and offering a fresh slant from a distant point of view. It has been said that newspapers serve as the first draft of history, and I believe that is so. The journalist and the historian are alike in that they strive above all for fairness and accuracy in reporting—even though ultimately, for both, objectivity is impossible to achieve. Journalists enjoy an awareness of context that lies beyond historians' grasp. They are immersed in the moment and write from within a framework that to them is natural and completely comprehensible but which for historians comprises only the impenetrable past. The challenge for journalists is to be as unbiased as possible in reporting the day's events; for historians, it is always to avoid value judging the last century's actions and opinions on the basis of today's knowledge and standards of conduct.

Alaska emerged from obscurity in the late 1890s, and the growth of its population and economy occurred during an era of Progressive change, when the centers of power were shifting from giant business conglomerates to government-mandated regulation and socio-economic reform. The territory benefited greatly, but progress arrived piecemeal over the course of decades. The pioneers were eager to see Alaska develop. They wanted systems of transportation, communication, and effective law, and they wanted them now. When Congress was slow to act, Alaskans responded with cries of neglect and abuse, and those complaints festered and persisted. Such feelings were not wrong or misplaced. Alaskans living in the moment had no way of peering into the future. But from today's perspective, we can see that over time Alaska as both a territory and a state has been enriched far more than neglected or abused by the United States government. The journalist and the historian view the same events through different colored glasses. Each writer brings a unique point of view, and it is these fresh interpretations that keep history alive and vital.

1

THE PROMINENCE OF GOLD
IN 1890S AMERICA

Gold! Gold! Gold! Gold!
Bright and yellow, hard and cold,
Molten, graven, hammered and rolled;
Heavy to get, and light to hold;
Hoarded, bartered, bought, and sold,
Stolen, borrowed, squandered, doled;
Spurned by the young, but hugged by the old
To the very verge of the church-yard mould;
Price of many a crime untold;
Gold! Gold! Gold! Gold!
Good or bad a thousand-fold!
"Miss Kilmansegg and Her Precious Leg"
Thomas Hood (1799–1845)

⸻

ON JULY 9, 1896, a little-known thirty-six-year-old former congressman from Nebraska stepped to the podium at the Democratic
National Convention in Chicago and delivered one of the most stunning speeches in American political history. The orator was William
Jennings Bryan, and the issue at hand was gold. Reporters covering
the convention for newspapers across the nation were effusive in the
words they chose to describe the event. He made an "impassioned
speech" and "stirred the convention to frenzy by his eloquence," the
Seattle Post-Intelligencer[1] reported. One day later, Bryan, the "boy orator of the Platte," whom the *New York Times*[2] dismissed simply as that

"gifted blatherskite," came from far back in the pack and claimed his party's nomination for the presidency of the United States.

That Bryan was able to arouse such passion was due not only to his abilities as a speaker but also to the prominence of gold in the mind of the public. Gold occupied a central place in the American economy of the 1890s, and with the nation mired in a deep and persistent depression, the Democrats and Republicans as well as the newly insurgent Populists made it the key piece of their party platforms in that election year. Gold was central also to the social, economic, and political future of Alaska. The events that unfolded at the national level would greatly impact America's developing northern possession, and gold production in Alaska would have its effect on the national economy as well.

Specifically, the 1896 presidential contest became a battle of the standards, with the Republican Party holding a firm line in favor of the gold standard. In the view of most Republicans, and in the view of the leading industrialists of the day, gold was the rock-solid foundation of every dollar in circulation. It represented stability and security. "Gold was the shield of a civilized life," historian Robert Wiebe explained. For many political and financial leaders, "it represented a fixed scheme of things in which all values, epitomized by the intrinsic worth of their dollars, would never change."[3]

The Republican Party, at its convention in St. Louis in June, had thrown the nomination to William McKinley of Ohio, a man whom delegates could trust to carry an unequivocal message of pure gold to the voting public and ensure that the gold standard remained in place. The Democrats, however, were led by a strong contingent from the agrarian West and South who formed an unwavering bloc of votes in favor of the free and unlimited coinage of silver. These "bimetallic" Democrats advocated the minting of both metals at a ratio of sixteen ounces of silver to one ounce of gold as a way of increasing the supply of money in a depressed economy. The issue split the party down the middle. Conservative eastern Democrats allied themselves with their party's leader, President Grover Cleveland, and stubbornly supported the gold standard.

The silver movement had its roots in the Populist Party, and it divided the country not only politically but also regionally between the urban East and the rural West and South. Times were extremely hard for farmers in the 1890s, as the prices they received for their pro-

William Jennings Bryan, the "prairie Populist," the "boy orator of the Platte," whom the *New York Times* dismissed as that "gifted blatherskite," was the Democratic Party candidate for president in 1896 and a fierce opponent of the gold standard (Library of Congress Prints and Photographs Division LCUSZ62-8425).

duce fell and railroad transportation rates rose uncontrollably. More importantly, farmers needed credit to purchase equipment, land, and supplies, and under the prevailing gold standard, the amount of money in circulation and available to the common man was severely limited. The government was allowed to circulate only as much money as its treasury possessed in gold. As prices for agricultural commodities declined, farmers found it increasingly difficult to repay existing loans or to borrow more money to continue operations. The gold standard, they believed, was responsible for the continued deflationary spiral because it could not provide the amount of money the country's economy needed in circulation. Continually falling prices meant that farmers were in effect required to repay more in commodities than they had borrowed in the beginning. They contended that the unlimited coinage of both gold and silver would put more dollars in their pockets and would have an inflationary effect that would bring back some form of stability.[4]

Republicans, backed by the financiers of the industrial North and East, saw the world differently. Sound money based on gold was at the heart of their platform. Gold was anti-inflation, and an inflationary trend was, after all, a burden on creditors. The Populist push for repeal of the gold standard represented to the world's bankers an attempt to force them to accept cheaper dollars in the form of silver in payment for money loaned.

This Populist agrarian revolt had a profound effect on Democratic Party politics, and it thrust William Jennings Bryan into the national spotlight. The battle over the nation's currency intensified after the Republican Party adopted the gold standard as the heart of its platform, and Bryan and the Democrats saw their opportunity. As he prepared himself to deliver his speech before the 20,000 delegates assembled in the Chicago Coliseum, Bryan based his message on the stark differences between the well-heeled financiers, bankers, and railroad tycoons of the Gilded Age and the struggling masses who toiled on the nation's farms and in its factories. It was the farmer whom the Nebraskan held up as the bedrock of society, and he promised that that portion of the population would not be allowed to suffer at the hands of the rich. His speech vilified the money lenders of the world and extolled the "toilers" as the foundation without which industry could not exist. The crowd, sensing a resounding ending of Bryan's remarks, was ready to erupt, and the orator did not disappoint. He concluded with a warning for the wealthy classes and his political foes: "We will answer their demand for a gold standard by saying to them, 'you shall not press down upon the brow of labor this crown of thorns; you shall not crucify mankind upon a cross of gold.'"

Author Sean Dennis Cashman has cited three specific elements at the root of the controversial gold standard debate in the 1890s: a drop in the worldwide production and supply of gold between 1865 and 1890, an increased supply of silver brought by mining in the West, and fluctuations in the amount of currency in circulation. The underlying need under such conditions was for a flexible currency that could grow with increasing population and an expanding economy.[5]

That flexible currency lay at the heart of the Populist movement. The prices farmers received for their products fell drastically at the end of the nineteenth century due to a combination of factors, including improved production methods, restrictive tariffs imposed by some foreign countries, and decreased demand for farm products in American urban centers. The emerging idea of Populists was that government had a role to play in the common welfare of the people and it ought to step in to help where it could to ensure that the farmer was treated fairly. In this case, the high cost of credit combined with the deflationary spiral made life on the farm practically unsustainable.

Still other factors added to the nation's economic woes. Giant corporations and railroads had overextended themselves through speculation and borrowing, and industrial overproduction was a cause of falling prices. Before the end of 1893, 15,000 businesses, including giant railroads such as the Reading Railroad and the Atchison, Topeka and Santa Fe, had failed, and as many as one in five industrial workers nationwide was out of a job. The Panic of 1893 quickly spread to rural America, where farmers had become highly dependent upon urban industrial markets as consumers of their products. The price of wheat grown in the West dropped from a high of $1.05 per bushel to 67 cents, while the cost of shipping a ton of produce by rail was more than three times higher for western farmers than it was for farmers east of Chicago.[6]

Workers toiling in the fields and factories saw the system as grossly unfair, and they blamed the financiers and those at the top of the corporate chain for the desperate conditions. Especially in the agrarian and mineral-rich West, Populist ideas gained favor, and there was an increased push for free coinage of silver and an end to the gold standard. It was not a new idea. In fact, from the founding days of the republic, currency in the United States was based on free coinage of both gold and silver. The term "free coinage" meant that the US mint would convert both metals into legal-tender currency at a specified ratio, effectively establishing the new nation on a bimetallic—that is, gold and silver—standard.[7] Both were part of the money supply. However, in the 1830s the price of silver relative to gold on the world market had risen to the point where silver miners realized a better profit by selling their product on the open market than by presenting it to the US mint. Silver coinage was drastically reduced, and gold reigned as the primary medium of exchange.

During the Civil War, paper money was introduced without the backing of gold or silver as a necessity for financing the war, and these "greenbacks" remained as the primary currency for several years, although gold was in circulation as well. In 1873, Congress was determined to return to a single currency based on a hard-money standard and do away with the paper dollar. This was accomplished with the Coinage Act of 1873, which called for the minting of gold coins and silver coins of small denominations but not the silver dollar. The loss of the silver dollar essentially ended the legal status of bimetallism, economist Milton Friedman explained, by establishing gold as the unit of value. Two years later, Congress followed up with the Resumption Act of 1875, which called for full convertibility of paper into gold[8] beginning in 1879. The result of placing the United States on a single gold standard was a deflationary trend that lasted until the end of the century and brought severe hardship to rural America. The demand for gold for monetary purposes increased while growth of the world supply of gold declined and production of industrial goods increased. "These forces put downward pressure on the price level," Friedman concluded. "With gold scarcer in relation to output in general, the price of gold in terms of goods went up and the nominal price level went down."[9]

Among proponents of silver, the Coinage Act became notorious, and for more than twenty years it was referred to as "the crime of 1873." Hardship on the family farm led to social unrest and invigorated the Granger movement, which gave rise to Populism, the strongest political movement of the late nineteenth century. The farmers and miners who formed the base of Populist support knew that the US Treasury held large supplies of silver while gold reserves had scarcely risen since the days of the California gold rush at midcentury. Unlimited coinage of silver became a rallying cry not only for Populists but also for reformist groups of Republicans and Democrats from the West and South who represented the majority of the nation's farmers. The silver movement received additional impetus when, in 1889 and 1890, six new western states with substantial silver production entered the union.[10] Free coinage of silver on an equal basis with gold would bring higher prices for the metal produced from western mines.

Farmers, miners, small businessmen, and labor pressed hard for an increase in the money supply. In response to mounting pressure to do something, Congress passed the Sherman Silver Purchase Act of 1890. The legislation was an effort by Republicans to appease silver advocates who wanted the US Treasury to purchase and coin the nation's entire silver output. As passed, the law required the government to purchase 4.5 million ounces of silver per month and issue silver certificates redeemable in either gold or silver. It was a compromise that left both sides bitterly disappointed and the public unsure of whether its money was backed by gold or by silver. Radical proponents of inflation felt that they had been forced to accept half a loaf because the law did not allow unlimited coinage of silver; at the same time, eastern conservatives feared that the measure would set in motion a dangerous trend toward the depreciation of US currency.[11]

Meanwhile, economic conditions only grew worse. Prices for agricultural commodities, particularly wheat and cotton, continued their downward slide, and losses of manufacturing jobs made life in the nation's urban centers increasingly difficult. Discontent with the two major political parties reached a high level, and in early 1892 farmers were ready to revolt. The first Populist Party convention met in Omaha, Nebraska, on July 4. The thirteen hundred delegates adopted a platform that blamed Democrats and Republicans equally for the intolerable social and economic conditions that had beset the country, and they called for a new third party—a party of the people—to instantly put a reform program into place. The preamble to the Populist Party platform of 1892, written by the tireless reformer Ignatius Donnelly of Minnesota, described "a nation brought to the verge of moral, political, and material ruin." It charged that the two traditional political parties wished to "drown the outcries of a plundered people . . . so that corporations, national banks, rings, trusts, watered stocks, the demonetization of silver, and the oppression of usurers may all be lost sight of."[12]

Specifically, the Populist platform called for free coinage of silver as a way to increase the money supply, which was restricted by the nation's adherence to the gold standard. Yet the party had far broader ambitions as well, including a graduated income tax, federal ownership of railroads and communications including telegraphs, and an eight-hour workday.[13] In the era Mark Twain aptly labeled the Gilded Age, Populists directly confronted the growing disparity they saw between the wealthy class of financiers and industrialists and the common man. Donnelly hammered home this theme in his eloquent preamble:

> The fruits of the toil of millions are boldly stolen to build up colossal fortunes for a few, unprecedented in the history of mankind, and the possessors of these in turn despise the Republic and endanger liberty. From the same prolific womb of governmental injustice we breed the two great classes—tramps and millionaires.

The disparity between rich and poor was the result of a monumental change in the entire face of the American landscape in the last four decades of the nineteenth century. Settlement of lands west of the Mississippi opened millions of acres to farming and mining, and railroads and telegraph lines vastly improved transportation and communications. At the same time, the industrial revolution transformed the nation's northern and eastern cities into centers of manufacturing and commerce. By the early 1890s, the promise of land and jobs in America had produced a wave of immigrants far greater than the economy could absorb, and masses of unemployed workers crowded the streets. This sudden transition from an almost exclusively agrarian economy to one built on industrial production and consumerism gave rise to large corporations unregulated by any effective government oversight.

At the heart of the Populist philosophy was the radical belief that a strong central government should bear some responsibility for ensuring the general welfare of the masses. The party's 1892 platform demanded federal support for policies that would limit the power and privilege of corporations while protecting the rights of the working class and posited that government should be the agent of reform. The Populist cause was only bolstered by the Democratic Party's nomination that year of Grover Cleveland as its candidate for president. In 1892, Democratic Party support had not yet swung to the Populist cause. Cleveland was hugely unpopular across rural America for his support of the gold standard and his opposition to any sort of change in the monetary system. To those who made up the rank and file of the new third party, the very survival of the nation's economic system was at stake, and the two major political parties had no interest in enacting the sort of reforms Populists believed were needed to curb the excesses of corporate monopolies. In short, it was time for the federal government to involve itself in reforms of the capitalist system in the interests of working citizens.[14]

The 1892 Populist Party ticket was headed by presidential candidate James B. Weaver of Iowa, who based his third-party campaign on an abiding disdain for the other two national political organizations. Both, he charged, supported an economic system in which the world's bankers and financiers conspired with one another to keep farmers and urban workers in a state of poverty. Weaver was aided in his message by other firebrand orators, notably the temperance crusader Mary Elizabeth Lease, who preached not only against the evils of alcohol but also against the corporate monopolies who were the owners and masters while the common people of the country remained enslaved. "What you farmers need to do," Lease shouted to cheering crowds, "is to raise less corn and more hell."[15] The 1892 Populist campaign suffered from a lack of funding, but Weaver still managed to poll more than one million votes, about 8.5 percent of the total cast in the presidential contest. The Democrat and staunch supporter of the gold standard Grover Cleveland won a second, nonconsecutive, term, but the Populist Party continued to be a force in national politics for the next four years as the gold standard and the coinage of silver shredded old alliances and tore both traditional parties down the middle.

As Cleveland took office in 1893, the economic panic was reaching a high pitch, and the president, along with other conservatives, viewed the Silver Purchase Act of 1890 as the source of the trouble. To make matters worse, America's reserves of gold were being depleted at an alarming rate as foreign creditors feared increasingly unstable conditions in the American economy. Continued pressure on behalf of silver caused a run on gold as European bankers demanded payment of outstanding loans in gold as a hedge against the inflation that would occur if the United States abandoned the gold standard.[16] The country was in the midst of a large trade deficit. Foreign investors viewed the rising popular demand for cheap money as a threat and began to sell off American securities and transfer the proceeds in gold to European banks. The US Treasury had traditionally considered $100 million to be the minimum acceptable level of reserves in gold coin and bullion in its possession. By late in 1893, those reserves had declined to $60 million and, with no income tax and no power to buy or borrow gold, the government was helpless to stop the free fall.[17] To make matters worse, the government was using Treasury notes to purchase silver, and those notes were then being redeemed in gold, pushing the gold reserve even farther below the $100 million level.[18] Five hundred banks across the nation failed for lack of currency, and a great number of farm mortgages were foreclosed.

Yet Cleveland's priorities lay with the interests of the bankers and industrialists who urged him to protect the gold standard. In his effort to repeal the Sherman Silver Purchase Act of 1890, he called on Congress to "put beyond all doubt or mistake the intention and ability of the government to fulfill its pecuniary obligations in money universally recognized by all civilized countries."[19] The conservative argument for repeal was based on the principles of sound money, confidence in the nation's currency, and resistance to any inflationary trend. Conservatives blamed the nation's farmers and Populists for causing the panic, which led to the most desperate economic crisis since the Civil War. What must be done, they maintained, was to end the government's purchase of silver, return to the gold standard, and thereby restore stability and confidence in the nation's monetary system.

Andrew Carnegie, the great finance capitalist of the American steel industry, made it known that the Silver Purchase Act was the "evil agent" directly responsible for the Panic of 1893. Foreign owners of American securities became alarmed at the government's required purchase of silver and the growing mass of silver bullion, he said. Those investors began to sell their holdings and demand redemption in gold. As a result, American reserves of gold were depleted, and to foreign investors the time seemed near when the nation would be unable to redeem the notes in gold on demand. "Fear took possession of the commercial public," Carnegie concluded. "Credit was paralyzed, and panic came."[20]

Opposition to repeal in the House of Representatives was led by two members of the president's own party, men who hailed from central interior agrarian states. Richard Bland of Missouri and William

Jennings Bryan of Nebraska framed the issue in terms of a class struggle between wealthy capitalists and the working populace. Bryan in particular used his considerable skills as an orator to speak on behalf of the "work-worn and dust-begrimed" masses who had scarce access to social justice and the halls of political power.[21] As a member of the American Bimetallic League, Bryan had honed his arguments at numerous conventions and rallies around the country. However, it was his three-hour speech on the House floor in August 1893 that caught the attention of the Democratic Party and led to his triumph at the national convention in Chicago three years later. The question of repeal fell not along political party lines but along lines defined by region and economic class. Members of both parties in both houses of Congress broke ranks and followed their loyalties for or against the gold standard. Democrats from the West and South revolted against their own party's administration, while Republicans who represented the "sound money" interests of the industrial Northeast were forced into the uncomfortable position of supporting the opposing party's president.[22]

In the end, the uncompromising President Cleveland won his repeal, but the result did nothing to diminish the resolve of Bryan, the bimetallic wing of the Democratic Party, and a cadre of Populists determined to make their cause the focus of national attention. It was a highly divisive issue, and the national press heaped on coverage from both sides of the debate. One of the most popular and effective single documents of the day was William Hope Harvey's *Coin's Financial School*. This small work of fiction, printed in Chicago and filled with clever cartoons, was circulated widely among the working classes nationwide. It was written in the form of six lectures given by an instructor named Coin to an audience populated by hardened conservative journalists and businessmen who entered the auditorium determined to trip up the young "expert" with their knowledge of the real world of finance. One by one, however, the detractors were won over by Coin's sound logic and vivid explanations of the social and economic damage wrought by the nation's adherence to a single gold standard. "The eyes of the people have been blinded with the gold craze," he told them. "In the midst of plenty we are in want. Helpless children and the best womanhood and manhood in America appeal to us for release from a bondage that is destructive of life and liberty."[23]

In the lecturer's view, the Coinage Act of 1873 was the great culprit. That law took the silver dollar out of circulation, replaced it with the gold dollar, and thus struck down one half of the currency in circulation, causing ruinous deflation and misery for the nation's working people. "It is commonly known as the 'crime of 1873,'" Coin told his students. "A crime because it has made millions of paupers. . . . A crime because it has brought tears to strong men's eyes and hunger and pinching want to widows and orphans."[24]

Coin's primary argument was based on his conclusion that all the combined reserves of gold in the world provided an amount that was insufficient for the population's money needs. Those reserves, he said, if consolidated into a single brick, would easily fit into one corner of the lecture hall where the audience was seated. It was absurd to suppose that all of the world's business could be transacted on such a small amount of money. This point was highly enlightening to the listeners and moved many to change their view of the monetary system. One businessman stood to announce his conversion. "I have been until today in favor of a single gold standard, but hard times and the fact that all the gold in the world available for money can be put in a space of twenty-two feet each way has knocked it out of me."[25]

Repeal of the Sherman Silver Purchase Act had little economic effect. The depression continued unabated, and, still worse, gold leaked from the US Treasury at an astonishing rate. Investors continued to sense instability, and holders of silver certificates demanded that their notes be redeemed in gold. Europeans remained fearful that the Populists might yet force the country off the gold standard, and compelling them to accept unwanted silver. Cleveland and his advisors feared that the day was near when the United States government would not be able to meet its financial obligations in gold. Attempts in 1894 to secure gold for the Treasury by public issue of government bonds proved to be of very little help because, as it turned out, a large percentage of people who purchased the bonds did so by redeeming legal-tender notes for gold with which to buy the bonds. Essentially, gold moved into and out of the Treasury at about an equal rate.[26]

In January 1895, with gold becoming increasingly scarce, Treasury reserves fell below $60 million, and default appeared to be a real possibility. *Scribner's Magazine* reported that at the beginning of February, reserves reached a low of $41,340,181, and foreign exchanges could demand payment in gold for their notes at any time they wished. "The government hoard was at their mercy," *Scribner's* observed. "None could tell when it would all be gone and the country forced to a silver basis."[27] It was at this point that J. Pierpont Morgan, the powerful head of the New York house of Morgan, stepped in and accomplished what one Morgan biographer called the "most dazzling feat" of the renowned financier's life.[28] Above all, Morgan wished to save the gold standard, for it was that security that assured European faith in American finance. He sought to build up European confidence in order to count on capital from those foreign money men for greater investments in American markets. It was Morgan's efforts in this regard that marked his emergence, one author noted, as "the symbol of the money power and plutocracy against which Bryanism and its successors thundered."[29]

President Cleveland was intent on a plan to sell government bonds for gold. To Morgan and others, however, it was clear that the crisis could not be averted solely through issuance of these bonds to American banks. Furthermore, Congress, seeing the poor results of recent bond offerings, was in no mood to give its approval of another such sale. In addition, silver advocates in Congress saw the move as nothing more than an effort to solidify the gold standard and an outright declaration of war against silver. Without congressional approval, the president needed the assistance of an independent international agency, one that had the ability to draw a large quantity of gold from European banks. J. P. Morgan was just the right man to organize such a syndicate. The financier met with Cleveland in a series of discussions in January and February and offered a plan to save the American financial system from disaster and at the same time preserve the gold standard. Morgan knew that he held all the winning cards and that Cleveland, facing imminent default and widespread financial panic, had little room to negotiate.

Morgan and his advisors uncovered an obscure Civil War statute passed in 1862 that allowed the government, without congressional approval, to buy gold from private sources in return for bonds. Under the authority of that act, Morgan promised to deliver 3.5 million ounces of gold—obtained largely from foreign sources—in exchange for $65 million in thirty-year US Treasury bonds. The deal would be done through a private contract with the United States government. Morgan negotiated an interest rate that was highly profitable for his banking syndicate, and he used his power to control the international exchange market to prevent gold exports from the United States.[30] As one observer remarked, "Wall Street, in the person of Mr. John Pierpont Morgan, dealt out the bonds and collected handsomely for its services."[31]

Cleveland accepted the deal, and as a result the market settled temporarily. However, the long-term political effect stemming from the secret negotiations and the harsh, even extortionate, terms was disastrous for the president. Cleveland sent a message to Congress announcing the terms of the deal and reporting that the amount of gold added to the Treasury would restore the reserve to more than $100 million. He scolded Congress for failing to approve a bond sale on its own and declared that as a result he was forced to "employ executive authority to reinforce and maintain an adequate and safe gold reserve." He continued, "At least one-half of the gold to be obtained is to be supplied from abroad, which is a very important and favorable feature of the transaction."[32]

Silver advocates in Congress responded with outrage. In essence, Morgan had wielded his power over a dependent federal government and had dictated terms of the deal to the president of the United States. Even more galling to some members of Congress, especially the president's fellow Democrats, was American dependence on British bankers. William Peffer of Kansas led the charge in the Senate. The president and the secretary of the Treasury, he thundered, had gone so far as to "confer privately with foreigners or with agents of foreign banking institutions, taking the credit of the people of the United States to our ancient enemy."[33]

In the House, Jeremiah Simpson traced the origin of the economic troubles to the law of 1873, which, he said, substituted a gold dollar for a silver dollar and established the country on a gold standard. Like Peffer, Simpson was a Kansan and a Populist. Both men had seen the ravaging effects of deflation and a short money supply on the lives of western farmers. "How are you going to remedy this evil?" Simpson demanded. "You are never going to remedy it until you restore silver to its proper place in the currency of the country, . . . until your Secretary of the Treasury obeys the law and redeems the outstanding obligations in silver as well as gold."[34]

Richard Bland of Missouri, a longtime fierce opponent of the gold standard, charged that nefarious characters from foreign countries were forcing the American people to act according to the dictates of Great Britain. "It is an indignity," he shouted. "It is an insult to our people. It is un-American."[35]

Bland and fellow westerner William Jennings Bryan formed the powerful core of resistance to their party's leader, Grover Cleveland. This was Bryan's chance to spell out in explicit terms the differences between the agrarian West and South and the industrial North and East, and it was gold that formed the basis of that separation. Cleveland's deal with the Morgan syndicate amounted to gross discrimination against silver, Bryan charged, and gave further impetus to the gold standard. The issue was not partisan; it was regional. Bryan warned in a speech on the House floor that if Democrats and Republicans of the East formed a united front to preserve the gold standard, the people of the rest of the country would rise up to fight such a plutocracy. "The time will come when the unjust demands and the oppressive extractions of our Eastern brethren will compel the South and West to unite in the restoration of an honest dollar . . . a dollar based upon two metals."

To Bryan, the battle of the standards was part of the epic war of the working poor against the "robber barons" of the industrial age. "We seek to protect the debtor from the greed of the creditor," he continued. "We seek to protect society from the avarice of the capitalist. We believe that in the restoration of bimetallism we shall secure the reestablishment of equity and restore prosperity to our country."[36]

In the East, however, the president's actions were seen as a necessary result of Congress's failure to act at a time when the nation's supply of gold was at a crisis level. According to the *New York Times*, Cleveland's deal with the Morgan syndicate was "the right thing at the right time." The country was on the verge of suspension of gold payments, and the only solution Congress was able to devise was the "insane proposition," as the *Times* editorial writer put it, of free coinage of silver, and that would have made that catastrophe inevitable. With such lack of congressional leadership, the *Times* concluded, it was obvious that the administrative branch of government was left to deal with the situation alone.[37]

President Cleveland continued to stand firmly behind the gold standard even in the midst of furious opposition in the months leading up to the election season of 1896. He represented his party's old guard and no longer saw eye to eye with either the working people who elected him or the congressmen who represented those restless and growing masses. William Jennings Bryan reached the end of his term in Congress in March 1895, one month after the conclusion of the president's deal with the Morgan syndicate, but even out of office he heightened his attacks on the gold contingent of his own political party. "The Democratic Party cannot serve God and Mammon," he declared in one published editorial. "It cannot serve plutocracy and at the same time defend the rights of the masses."[38]

THE 1896 REPUBLICAN NATIONAL CONVENTION

Gold was the defining issue of those middle years of the decade as the heated battle of the standards swept across the nation. Leaders of all three parties—Democrat, Republican, and Populist—anticipated the dominant role that the precious metal would play in selection of candidates and the formation of their platforms. At the 1896 Republican National Convention in St. Louis in June, regional differences within the party reached a breaking point with the dramatic "bolt" of twenty-one delegates, led by Senator Henry Teller of Colorado, in protest of the gold plank. Republicans had been wrangling for weeks over the monetary policy portion of the party platform, and master political strategist Mark Hanna was caught in the middle. A week before the convention opened, the *New York Times* reported that a strong gold plank was by no means a certainty, although it said "sound money is not in as much danger here in St. Louis and in the hands of the Republicans as it promises to be in Chicago."[39]

Hanna, as William McKinley's campaign manager, was determined to protect the interests of his fellow Ohioan's voter base, the finance capitalists of New York. Yet Hanna could not help but be aware of the "silver craze" that was increasing in national popularity, and he did not wish to alienate a huge bloc of voters by making too strong a statement in favor of gold. The dilemma was to write a monetary policy that would satisfy the gold states but not scare off the silver states. With McKinley's blessing, Hanna urged the party platform writers to "straddle" the issue by calling for a plan for maintaining the "existing standard," leaving out the volatile word "gold." The moneyed men of Wall Street immediately declared this "Ohio plank" unacceptable, and sound-money conservatives greeted it with "jeers of disapproval and derision."[40] To them, as one writer explained it, America's monetary policy "must be made not only 'as good as gold,' it must *be* gold."[41] Charles W. Fairbanks of Indiana (for whom the Alaska gold rush settlement on the Chena River was later named) offered still another alternative, which, though a bit stronger, still did not satisfy the conservative wing of the party. Fairbanks was a hearty McKinley supporter and wished to construct a compromise plan that would hold everybody in. His proposed plank clearly opposed any effort to depreciate the currency, including the free coinage of silver, but it did not explicitly champion the cause of the gold standard.

New York Times editorial writers excoriated Hanna and McKinley for their lack of conviction and devotion to principle. The paper wished to expose Hanna as the supreme party boss, the "puppeteer" who controlled all the strings and dictated the movements of the candidate. The Ohio compromise amounted to "contemptible evasions and cowardly paltering," the paper scolded. "The straightforward, courageous, manly course" would be to defy the silver states. However, four days before the convention was due to begin, it appeared to the *Times* that party leaders had chosen a different direction.[42]

J. P. Morgan and other financiers foresaw the political demise of the Cleveland administration, and they accurately predicted that the president would be replaced on the Democratic ticket either by the highly visible and influential Richard Bland or by another leading silver advocate. Morgan was determined to oppose any such candidate and to see to it that the next occupant of the White House, no matter which party he belonged to, would bring with him a stern and unequivocal commitment to the gold standard.[43] The message to Hanna and the presumptive Republican presidential candidate was clear, as Morgan personally had a hand in changing the words in the party platform from "existing standard" to "existing gold standard."[44] Such pressure was impossible for the advocates of compromise to resist. The final platform as presented to delegates for an up-or-down vote stated that the party was "opposed to the free coinage of silver" and that "the existing gold standard must be preserved."

Historians have pointed out that for McKinley, the currency issue was personally irritating. He did not consider it to be nearly as important as Bryan and the pro-silver Democrats did, and he wished to emphasize the more familiar and less controversial issue of tariff protection, for which he had taken a very well-known positive stand. McKinley was, in fact, on record as having previously taken a compromise bimetallic position for fear of alienating fellow Republicans from the West. In the end, however, he gave his agreement to the decision on the currency plank of the party platform.[45]

Hanna's fears of a regional split within the party were realized when silver Republicans from western states refused to go along with the unequivocal endorsement of gold. These delegates wished to remain loyal to their party, but the voters in the silver states of the West had told them in certain terms that their support at the polls was contingent upon a commitment to silver. Henry Teller, the leader of the pro-silver Republican group, seemed almost relieved when word came down. He told the press that the firm gold plank was, after all, the true expression of the will of the Republican Party, and the party would look better to the public in silver states by stating an honest representation of its position than if it tried to straddle the issue. He labeled Hanna's efforts to evade the truth as a "dishonorable and puerile attempt to deceive the country."[46] On the night the platform was adopted, everyone in the convention hall knew that a Teller-led bolt was sure to come. The Colorado senator certainly recognized the seriousness of his actions as he rose to address the delegates and spectators for a final time. The American people were in greater distress than at any time in their history, he said. The financial question facing the convention was a matter of principle. "It is not a mere idle thing, but one on which hangs the happiness, the prosperity, the morality, and the independence of American labor and American producers. . . . I believed that the Republican Party was good for the great masses of men, that its legislation was intended to lift up and elevate and hold up and sustain the unfortunate and the distressed and give all American citizens equal opportunities before the law. I do not believe it can be had with a gold standard."[47]

Teller's speech, one reporter wrote, "was made in broken tones and while the tears rolled from his eyes and streamed down his face."[48] He concluded with an expression of the political consequences of his opposition to his party's platform. "This gold plank means ultimate disaster and distress to my fellowman. I cannot subscribe to it, and if adopted I must, as an honest man, sever my connection with the political organization that makes that one of the main articles of its faith."[49]

The majority of delegates were unmoved. The chairman quickly called for a vote on the financial plank of the party platform, and it was adopted overwhelmingly. In a final dramatic moment, a pro-silver delegate from Utah, Senator Frank Cannon, announced his group's intentions. "We withdraw from this convention and return to our constituents the authority with which they invested us." He and his supporters chose to remain "unsullied," he added, rather than "give cowardly and insincere endorsement to the greatest wrong ever willfully attempted within the Republican Party, once the redeemer of the people but now about to become their oppressor unless providentially restrained." The masses of conventioneers had heard enough and interrupted the speaker with "an uproar of hisses." Cannon abruptly left the stage and, with Henry Teller and his fellow silver delegates, walked out of the arena to the wild derisive cheering of the crowd.[50] Hanna himself was reported to have joined in the shouting.[51]

Alaska's interests at the Republican National Convention were represented by four voting delegates, who cast their ballots unanimously in favor of a strong gold platform. Alaska was a gold-producing economy, and the delegates' interest in that emerging industry outweighed any alliance they might have had with Republicans from the silver-mining states of the West. The national party originally had allotted two convention delegates for Alaska, and the choice of only two had caused a chaotic scene at the Alaska Republican Party convention in Juneau on May 14, one month before the national meeting in St. Louis. The *Alaska Searchlight*, a Juneau paper, reported that "throughout the meeting of the Republican territorial delegates, unfriendly feeling was particularly manifested, bolting was in order, and pandemonium reigned supreme."[52]

The disruption was caused by an insurgent group of "Independent Republicans" who came from remote areas that had not received credentials from the party and thus were not recognized as voting delegates in Juneau. These independents attempted to take over the proceedings and elect their own delegates to the national convention. It was "a disgraceful scene," a correspondent for the Juneau-based

Alaska Mining Record wrote. A handful of "interlopers sought to carry through their pernicious designs by means and methods worthy of the lowest dregs of political organization." When the attempted insurrection was at last put down by the majority in the regular Republican Party, "a howl was raised worthy of savages fit for Bedlam."[53] In the end, the Alaska Republicans decided to send two delegates and two alternates on the chance that the national party would allow Alaska to seat four voting delegates, as the other US territories had been allotted. The question of two or four delegates for Alaska was not settled until the opening day of the national convention, when the Committee on Rules presented its report. Each state had a number of delegates equal to double the number of its senators and representatives in Congress. The territories of Arizona, Indian Territory, New Mexico, and Oklahoma had six delegates each. Alaska, which was a customs district and not yet officially a territory, and the District of Columbia had four delegates each.[54]

The pro-gold, staunchly Republican *Alaska Mining Record* was pleased with the nomination of William McKinley on the convention's first ballot, and it expressed "not the shadow of a doubt" that the former Ohio governor would be the next president of the United States.[55]

THE 1896 DEMOCRATIC NATIONAL CONVENTION

As Henry Teller and the silver Republicans bolted from the convention hall in St. Louis, they were met with wild enthusiasm across the West and South, and many Democrats and Populists openly courted the Colorado senator as their party's candidate for president. Although Teller had emerged as perhaps the most highly recognized silver proponent in the nation, other prominent men within the silver movement had much deeper roots in the Democratic Party. In the days leading up to the Chicago convention, the leaders in the race for the Democratic nomination were Richard Bland of Missouri and Iowa Governor Horace Boies. The name of William Jennings Bryan was rarely mentioned.[56]

There was no doubt that silver advocates were in the great majority in Chicago on the eve of the Democratic convention. Yet pro-gold Democrats, sensing defeat, nonetheless conferred on a strategy to make themselves heard and to prevent a strong party statement in favor of silver. The *New York Times* urged party leaders to listen to these business-men from New York, Philadelphia, Boston, and Baltimore and heed their advice against adopting "a course that would alienate old friends and menace business interests by inviting instability and promoting panic."[57] Senator George Gray of Delaware took charge as chair of the beleaguered group of gold-standard Democrats who met to devise some strategy to oppose the "silver craze." At this late date, the small caucus appeared to be at a loss. "None of us is clear as to a definite policy to be pursued," Gray confessed. "All we can do and all we are seeking to do is to hold an informal conference of those who recognize the impending danger, to take counsel with one another and act as wisely as we may under the circumstances."[58]

Gray and his cohorts were clearly outgunned by the likes of "Pitchfork" Ben Tillman, the colorful and bombastic senator from South Carolina, and John Altgeld, the master strategist and governor of Illinois. Tillman lived up to his nickname by handing out pitch-fork badges on which he had skewered President Grover Cleveland and other well-known "gold bugs."[59] He spoke for the masses who, he said, had suffered at the hands of a few wealthy financiers who had "stolen the fruits of the labor of millions." Tillman continued with a warning for those who held the reins of power. "The millions are not going to bear the oppression longer. Popular sentiment is now sweep-ing on with irresistible force. Silver is our salvation. It is to be the issue of the campaign." He predicted that the convention would nominate a "sound silver man on a sound silver platform."[60]

Altgeld, because of his influence on party policy and his dedication to the free silver cause, was relentlessly denounced by the eastern press. He espoused a fierce and uncompromising position, and he worked hard to ensure that the party platform articulated an anti-gold stance. Altgeld was one of the most visible and popular politicians in the ranks of the Democratic Party and could probably have won the nomination for president, but as a foreign-born American citizen he was ineligible for the office. In a fiery address to the full convention on the morning of the second day, he blistered the money lenders and the security-holding classes who hoarded gold because its scarcity preserved its high value. When silver was demonetized in 1873, he said, gold doubled in impor-tance. "Thereafter, the gold dollar bought twice as much labor, twice as much property, twice as much of the bread and sweat of mankind as it did before." The bankers of New York and London amounted to a powerful force, he continued, and the question before this convention was whether the Democratic Party would allow those forces to "make the great toilers and producers of this country mere vassals, mere tribute-paying serfs." Compromise was out of the question. "The hand of compromise never yet ran up the flag of freedom," he concluded. "No compromising army ever fought the battles of liberty."[61]

New York Times editorial writers greeted such rhetoric with scorn. The paper launched its attack against Altgeld even before the convention began. His actions were intended "only to stir the passions on which his crazy silver movement depends for its popularity," it said. "He does a mean thing—base, ignoble, treacherous. It is a pity he cannot be punished for it; if he could, no punishment would be too severe."[62] One day later, the *Times* charged that Altgeld's thinking was based on the assumption that those people who have less than they wish should be allowed to take from those who have more. "He is a genuine European Red.. . . His mind is saturated with the ideas of German Socialism of the type that would prostitute all government and authority to the advantage of the multitude."[63]

The Democratic Party platform took shape over the course of the convention's first two days. The pro-gold faction had its say in the process, but as the monetary plank was presented for adoption during the morning session of July 9, it was clear that the free-silver insurgents were in control. The platform named the act of 1873 as the culprit in the fall of commodity prices, the appreciation of gold, the burden on the working people, and the enrichment of the money-lending class. As a remedy, it demanded the "free and unlimited coinage of both silver and gold at the present ratio of 16 to 1."[64]

Yet those Democrats who clung to their belief in the policies of the Cleveland administration were still not finished. Sixteen minority members of the Resolutions Committee viewed the free-silver movement as extreme radicalism that differed fundamentally from "vital Democratic doctrine." Coinage of silver, the minority said, would "disturb business, diminish the purchasing power of wages and labor, and inflict irreparable evils upon our nation's commerce and industry." The group concluded with a statement of loyalty to the sitting president, saying, "We commend the honesty, economy, courage, and fidelity of the present Democratic National Administration."[65]

Such praise for the hated Cleveland brought "Pitchfork" Ben Tillman out of his seat and to the front of the assembly. To repudiate the president for his stand in favor of the gold standard and then to honor the very same president for his honesty and courage would be "to write ourselves down as asses and liars," he shouted. Tillman then delivered a fifty-minute oration, which concluded with a scorching indictment of the president's character, especially surrounding the "secret contract" he signed to sell government gold bonds to the banking syndicate headed by J. P. Morgan. "We denounce the administration of President Cleveland as undemocratic and tyrannical," he continued, "and as a departure from those principles which are cherished by all liberty-loving Americans."[66]

Historians analyzing the event have characterized the Democrats' thorough rejection of the sitting administration of their own party as extraordinary and an act of protest and transformation.[67] Tillman left the podium after giving a solid affirmation of the party platform and a pledge that any presidential candidate who was a true representative of that platform would receive the vote of every Democrat south of the Potomac.[68]

William Jennings Bryan's turn at the rostrum came later that evening. His speech was a triumphant climax to a day of heated rhetoric, and it alone was enough to propel him into contention for the presidential nomination. There was nothing new or surprising in the message he delivered to the convention. It was his grand style of oration and theatrics that brought the crowd to hysteria. He spoke of the plight of the nation's farmers and industrial workers whose lives were impoverished while the money lenders and financiers, the powerful robber barons of Wall Street, protected the gold standard. "We are fighting for our homes, our families and posterity," he intoned. "We have petitioned, and our petitions have been scorned. We have entreated, and our entreaties have been disregarded. We have begged, and they have mocked when our calamity came. We beg no longer; we entreat no more; we petition no more. We defy them."[69]

The crowd interrupted incessantly with wild cheering, and Bryan asked for quiet so he could finish in his allotted time. With his final defiant statement, "You shall not crucify mankind upon a cross of gold," the crowd erupted in a sustained frenzy that spilled out the doors of the Coliseum and onto the streets of Chicago. A *New York Times* correspondent described a scene of "tumult almost beyond the power of the chairman to restrain." There was a "dance of the standard bearers and after that a march around the section occupied by delegates with two bands playing furiously and helping on the babble of confusion."[70] The reaction to Bryan's speech was so strong that delegates immediately viewed him as a contender for the nomination. A reporter for the *Seattle Post-Intelligencer* wrote that if Bryan's name had been placed in nomination at that point, the voters would have stampeded to his side. "They turned to him with an impetuosity that nothing could balk. They wanted a tribune of the people. They felt that they had him in the eloquent young Nebraskan who set their imagination on fire."[71] The party's old guard could only stand by and observe as their months of planning and organizing were overwhelmed by the enthusiasm following the speech, and indeed on the following day Bryan outpolled Bland and Boies to win the nomination on the fifth ballot.

Alaska Democrats were represented at the national convention by six delegates who, following rules they had agreed to in advance, voted as a unit in all balloting. The Alaska Territorial Democrats had gotten together for their convention in Juneau on June 1 and had conducted their business in a short two-hour session that was remarkably free of contention and infighting, especially in comparison to the raucous meeting the Alaska Republican Party had conducted in May. The *Alaska Searchlight* described the atmosphere as a "singular unanimity of sentiment." Only one desire was expressed by the Democrats assembled, the paper said, and that was to elect delegates who would "conscientiously work for the good of the territory and their party." The party members then passed a resolution directing their delegates to the national convention to vote as a unit in accordance with the will of the majority of the six in all questions to come before the full body in Chicago.[72]

Once seated at the national convention, the Alaska delegation came down solidly on the pro-gold side. The young territory's culture and emerging economy were so closely tied to gold production that the delegation could hardly vote otherwise. The gold standard was good for Alaska miners. It assured that, so long as the nation's monetary system was dependent on the precious metal as the basis of its currency, both demand and value would remain high. One of the Alaskans,

Charles D. Rogers, secured a seat on the fifty-one-member Resolutions Committee, and he quickly joined fifteen others on that committee to form a minority faction. That was the group that unsuccessfully introduced a resolution not only condemning the pro-silver monetary plank of the platform but also heaping praise on Grover Cleveland for his handling of the economy. The six-member Alaska delegation supported Rogers and voted on the losing side, in favor of the resolution. In addition, Alaska gave its approval to David Hill, the pro-gold senator from New York, in the contest for temporary chairman of the convention. Later, when the time came to vote on adoption of the full platform, Alaska cast six "nay" votes, the only one of the territories to do so, no doubt in protest of the strong silver monetary plank. In voting for the presidential nomination, Alaska took a curious turn, joining the other western territories in support of the solidly pro-silver candidate, Richard Bland, on the first four ballots and then switching unanimously to the eventual winner, Bryan, on the fifth. Finally, in the contest for the nomination of the candidate for vice president, which was won by pro-silver businessman Arthur Sewall of Maine, the Alaska delegation declined to vote on all five ballots.[73]

Popular reaction in Alaska is difficult to gauge because news of the national convention was scarcely reported in the local press. However, it is clear that free silver had its proponents in the North. The *Alaska News*, based in Juneau, ran a front-page analysis on August 6, nearly a month after the Democrats finished their business in Chicago, sharply criticizing the delegation's voting record and charging that the delegates did not properly speak for the wishes of the people they were sent to represent. Even though Alaska was a gold-producing country, the paper said, there were many free-silver advocates, especially within the ranks of the Democratic Party, and their interests were completely ignored. The *Alaska News* scolded the delegation for its unanimous vote for "avowed gold man" David Hill for temporary chairman of the convention, for its failure to support Bryan even on the fifth ballot when his victory was assured, and for its repudiation of vice presidential nominee Arthur Sewall by choosing not to vote. "Their attitude appears to be one of combativeness to the nominee and platform of their party," the paper concluded. (It must be noted that in laying out its argument, the *Alaska News* reported one fact incorrectly. The

Alaska delegation did indeed cast its six votes for Bryan on the fifth ballot after voting unanimously for Bland on the previous four ballots.)

Prominent Juneau Democrats interviewed by the *Alaska News* expressed convictions on both sides of the battle of the standards. Attorney W. E. Crews was thrilled with the outcome even though in his view the Alaska delegation failed to represent the will of Alaska Democrats. Yet he was happy to see the defeat of the old party leaders. "I can hear the voice of the great common people saying 'give us Bryan for our nominee and we will give you victory in November.'" Crews was uncompromisingly pro-silver. "We are a Western people," he said, "and our interests are allied with the interests of the West. I honestly believe that three-fourths of the Democrats West of the Mississippi River are in favor of the free and unlimited coinage of silver."

The same opinion was expressed by other interviewees. John Y. Ostrander pronounced himself "in perfect accord" with his party's strong free-silver platform. He expressed admiration for Republican candidate McKinley but said that he could not support a man who advocated a single gold standard. "Mr. Bryan, more than any other man in the United States, has made it possible for the free silver people to elect a president," he said. Another Juneau Democrat expressed the regionalism that was inherent in the controversy. "I was born in the West," J. D. Matthus said, "have always lived in the West, and consider the remonetization of silver necessary for our welfare and prosperity."

Finally, however, Juneau merchant and banker B. M. Behrends, chairman of the Democratic Territorial Committee, stuck to the pro-gold side and refused to be moved from his strong gold standard position. "I consider myself a good Democrat," he said, "but I can't stand the platform the silver men have put up." Behrends held out hope that the pro-gold Democrats would convene again and advance a platform and a candidate whom he could endorse even though the effort would be futile. "I could scarcely expect such a ticket to win," he conceded, "but it would help defeat the free silver movement."

The *Alaska News* itself pronounced that it was satisfied with the choice of the presidential nominee, but it had nothing good to say about the national leaders of the silver movement who were clinging to Bryan's coattails. "In his train and among his foremost lieutenants," the editor screamed, "are some of the craziest wild-eyed, long-haired, and red-handed anarchists that ever went unhung." He named "Pitchfork" Ben Tillman, John Altgeld, and several others as "the toughest and most insane lot of thieving mendicants that ever cursed fair America."[74]

THE 1896 GENERAL ELECTION

From the moment the Democratic convention adjourned, it was clear how fiercely the battle for the November election would be fought, how firmly both sides of the monetary question were entrenched, and how deeply the issue had divided both major parties. The eastern press was relentless in its attacks. "The Populist scheme announced at Chicago is as complete in its wickedness as in its absurdity," the *New York Times* editorialized. Bryan was "an unknown man bound by no record . . . with revolutionists pressing at his heels, nothing could securely check him. He must be crushed."[75]

The *New York Daily Tribune* reported that eastern Democrats would overwhelmingly spurn the "anarchists." They would reject the Bryan nomination and jump to the McKinley side in order to "maintain the financial honor of the nation." The *Tribune* quoted one banker as saying that he had never in his life cast a vote for a Republican, and he was "grieved beyond measure" at the necessity of doing so in this election. "I cannot accept the anarchistic and revolutionary doctrines which have been proclaimed by the Chicago convention," he said. A *Tribune* writer added that bankers and brokers of both parties were united in their belief that the financial integrity of the nation depended on their support for McKinley to "put an end to the free silver craze."[76]

The Republican establishment, with master strategist Mark Hanna as McKinley's campaign manager and with the backing of hard-money financiers of Wall Street, put everything they had behind the effort to defeat the upstart Bryan. Hanna was a businessman from Cleveland who had made a fortune in oil and coal, and he sought to use the political system as a means of protecting his own interests and those of American capitalism.[77] The election offered two clear and opposing views of the world economy. For financial conservatives, McKinley and the gold standard represented economic stability and growth, and a vote in its favor was a vote to limit government control over the free market. For the other side, however, the gold standard stood in the way of needed reform. It was a severe hindrance to economic opportunity, and it killed the competition that was needed in a healthy free market.[78]

Bryan's surprising nomination and the intense focus on gold versus silver changed the entire political landscape in the four months leading up to the general election of 1896. Prominent Republicans, including the presidential nominee himself, had expected to achieve an easy victory by directing the public's attention to the relatively benign issue of tariff protection. Now, however, with the ouster of the pro-gold President Cleveland and a large voter base aroused by Bryan's populist rhetoric, conservatives knew they were in for a fight. Hanna was so concerned about the Democratic threat that he canceled his vacation plans and set up headquarters in both Chicago and New York to give his full attention to the campaign to elect McKinley.[79] With Bryan's nomination, one historian observed, Hanna saw the "raw emotional appeal both he and the free coinage of silver held for voters."[80] Republican leaders were stunned by the impact that the currency issue had on the populace during those times of severe economic hardship, and many feared that if the election were held in the first weeks after the Democratic convention, Bryan would be an overwhelming winner.[81] McKinley himself was preparing for battle. The Civil War, he said, was fought to preserve the union. The political war now at hand was a fight to preserve an established and sacred financial system. From that point on, he knew, gold versus silver would be the campaign's defining issue.[82]

Hanna conceived a strategy that would turn the Democratic contender's primary issue against him, and he embarked on a mission to raise funds from the wealthy business sector in order to mount a campaign of voter education. His efforts amassed at least $3.5 million to spend on printed literature, compared to a meager $300,000 by the Democrats for Bryan. The Republicans wished to portray Bryan as a revolutionary backed by wild-eyed enemies of sound money such as Altgeld of Illinois.[83] They believed that the public saw the gold standard as an oppressive force that was controlled by a small group of rich financiers and deprived them of opportunity and welfare. In order to dispel that image, they employed the widespread well-organized use of printed material dealing with the currency issue, and by the last weeks of the campaign it was apparent that the postconvention enthusiasm

for Bryan had begun to fade. "The hurrah for Bryan had been converted into a hurrah for McKinley," Hanna biographer Herbert Croly
wrote. "Enthusiasm could not be maintained at such a pitch."[84]

The *New York Times* had all along shrugged off the popular passion
for Bryan as the result of "demagogy in action." The Democratic candidate, the paper concluded, had "inspired [his followers] with the feeling of martyrs, crushed and torn but not degraded. He made them hold
up their heads and put off their shamefacedness. He made them feel
that they were fine specimens of American manhood who had been
under the heel of oppression."[85]

The crowning event of the campaign occurred on Wall Street in New
York on the Saturday before Election Day with a massive display that
the *Times* described as a "businessmen's parade in behalf of sound
money." The paper estimated that one hundred thousand marchers
and a quarter of a million spectators turned out to rally in support
of the Republican ticket, and the marchers represented every sector of
the economy from the wealthiest of financiers to the urban working
poor.[86]

McKinley's decisive general election win solidified the Republican
position and effectively ended any challenge to the gold standard.
Herbert Croly, who became a leading light in the Progressive movement of the early twentieth century, concluded in his 1912 biography of Hanna that, as a result of the election of 1896, the Republican
Party became the representative of American business. "Inevitably,
American businessmen came liberally to its support," he wrote. "These
leaders, irrespective of partisan ties, knew that the free coinage of silver would be disastrous to the credit and prosperity of the country."[87]

The *New York Times* expressed relief that the threat of a Bryan presidency had finally passed. "We have given three months to Bryan," the
editor sighed. "Capital has been frightened, enterprise benumbed,
industry paralyzed. Now that we have utterly annihilated Bryan and 16
to 1, let everybody pluck up courage and get to work."[88]

The election of 1896 had little immediate impact on the few residents
of remote Alaska. "We are in the attitude of an interested spectator
sitting on the fence calmly viewing the work of the 'great unwashed,'"
the editor of one Juneau newspaper observed when commenting on
the campaign.[89] Indeed, in its status as a customs district without representation in Congress and with no local legislative body, Alaska had

no electors in the Electoral College and therefore no voice in the process after the party conventions and no influence on the outcome in November. Still, the solidly pro-gold *Alaska Mining Record* expressed post-election satisfaction and predicted good economic times in the future. "Already," it said, "the effects of restored confidence are shown throughout the East in the resumption of business, the startup of mills and factories, and the immediate increase of home and foreign commerce so long suspended by the uncertainty of the future. The new era of prosperity has opened and the nation is in safe hands again."[90]

In the years soon to come, the politics of gold as it unfolded in the 1890s profoundly shaped the development of America's northern possession. No commodity in the world was more valued, more sought after, more lionized than gold. Gold ruled the economy and it drove the debate. It stirred otherwise sane men to frenzy at the prospect of finding it free for the taking in the gravel bottom of a creek on the last frontier, and it fired the passions of the most wealthy and powerful financiers and politicians of the Gilded Age. The battle of gold versus silver had given rise to the Populist movement, which greatly influenced Democratic Party policy and led to the complete and radical repudiation of a sitting president by the majority of his own party. The hard-money financial conservatives won decisively in 1896. Populism died out, and the free-silver movement never again played a significant role as a political force. But the era of great reform was yet to come as the more urban-based and widespread Progressive era took shape. Concurrent with this movement was the birth of modern-day Alaska.

2

THE BEGINNINGS OF
MODERN-DAY ALASKA

A ton of gold
Prosperity is here

～～

FIVE WEEKS after William Jennings Bryan's remarkable triumph in Chicago, a part-time prospector named George Carmack, working his way along a tributary of the Klondike River in the Canadian Yukon a few miles east of the Alaska border, discovered a vein of gold richer than anything his mind could imagine. Carmack was following a tip he had received from Robert Henderson, a serious and determined miner who had found promising ground a few miles upstream from the confluence with the Yukon. Henderson was willing to share the news, and he expected Carmack to return and inform him promptly if the prospect panned out. Carmack, however, had no such intentions. He was a man with an easygoing temperament who had lived in the north country for at least a dozen years and whose interests lay as much with living the lifestyle of the Native Tagish Indians as with striking it rich in the goldfields. Carmack had married a Tagish woman, and when Henderson encountered him on the Yukon River near the mouth of the Klondike in the summer of 1896, he and his two Tagish brothers-in-law, Skookum Jim and Tagish Charley, were busy catching and drying salmon. Henderson told Carmack that no claims had yet been staked and that there was room for him on the creeks—but, he added, his "Siwash" companions were not welcome. This bit of racial hatred apparently aroused such ire in Carmack that he determined to go with the two Indians into the hills and find a creek of their own.[1]

In early August, Carmack, Skookum Jim, and Tagish Charley left their fish camp and moved up the Klondike to Rabbit Creek, panning the gravel bed as they went. On the sixteenth of the month, the three men reached a point where a smaller stream jointed Rabbit Creek, and there, in a place where the bedrock reached the surface, they found a small nugget along with much more gold in the cracks of the rocks. Carmack knew immediately that it was a monumental strike, and the next day he staked his two allotted claims as discoverer, and his partners staked one claim each. They immediately renamed the creek Bonanza.[2] The men filled an empty shotgun shell with coarse gold and left immediately to file their claims, telling everyone they met along the way that they had struck it rich and showing the shotgun shell filled with gold as proof. Word spread quickly, and soon miners from the districts of Fortymile and Circle converged on the Klondike. Within a month, every inch of the creek had been staked. Discoveries on other nearby creeks yielded wealth in gold just as startling as Carmack's claim, and the ensuing mad rush to the Klondike brought stunning and irrevocable changes to the Alaska-Yukon frontier.

The incredible gold strikes of the late summer and fall of 1896 were not merely the product of blind luck. The upper Yukon River watershed had long been known to be prolific gold country, and prospectors who knew the geology of gold-bearing ground had been searching for years for the rich veins of the precious metal that they had no doubt were there. "Gold discoveries are rarely serendipitous," author Ken Coates wrote in his history of the Yukon. "People do not stumble over gold while out for a walk.... Gold was discovered in the Yukon because miners knew or had good reason to believe it was there and had spent years looking for it."[3]

The Juneau-based newspaper *Alaska Mining Record* had long been an enthusiastic booster of gold mining in the upper Yukon basin. One year and four months before Carmack's great discovery on that small tributary of the Klondike, the paper heartily endorsed the region's potential as a source of riches in gold:

There is scarcely a mining district . . . that is not sending a quota of long-range prospectors who expect to reap golden harvests . . . and their Mecca this year is the Yukon basin in Alaska, from whence come tales of rich fields, huge nuggets, and sudden wealth that rival the cave of Monte Carlo. Since the first Alaska steamer started north early in February, men have been swarming to the Yukon fields. The riches of the Yukon fields have not been exaggerated. Probably no section of country in the world has such uniformly rich claims, and in a more favored climate they would make the monometallic nations of the earth tremble for the stability of that metal.[4]

As word of the great strike brought miners rushing upriver from Fortymile and Circle, a settlement grew quickly where Joe Ladue laid out a site on the banks of the Yukon near the mouth of the Klondike. Ladue named the booming town after Canadian geologist George Dawson, and within months the population had swelled to nearly five thousand. Every inch of Bonanza Creek had been hurriedly staked, and miners there as well as on many nearby creeks were already producing gold in astonishing quantities. Yet news was slow to filter out of the remote and isolated region of the upper Yukon. From his office in Sitka, Governor James Sheakley reported to the secretary of the interior on October 1 that the region continued to attract a constant stream of miners and that one thousand men and forty women had traveled over the Chilkoot Pass on their way to the goldfields that year. However, he added, "no rich developments or discoveries have been reported from there at this writing."[5] Word of some increased activity reached a Douglas newspaper, which noted in late October the "fever of excitement over the recent discoveries in the Clondyke District."[6]

Miners worked their claims through that winter and spring, thawing ground and sinking shafts where gold-bearing bedrock lay as much as twenty feet below the surface. One miner described the exodus from Circle in a letter printed in the *San Francisco Chronicle*: "Circle City is just now deserted; everybody is up at Clondyke or preparing to go soon. . . . It is the richest district the world has ever known and will produce millions this year." The writer explained that he had staked a claim himself and had hurriedly returned to Circle for supplies and was headed back the next day. "The gravel runs in gold from $5 to $150 per pan," he said, "and a young fellow on a claim above me panned out $40,000 in two days. I was offered $25,000 cash for my claim. I still hold the ground and will be either a millionaire or a pauper by fall." He indicated, however, that a shortage of food for the burgeoning town of Dawson was a looming possibility. "The only phantom that stands in our way to the goal of the millionaire is Mr. Grub. I have provisions enough to last me until next June and I am as well fixed as any man in the country. If the boats do not get up the river until next July, we will be in rather hard times."[7]

The backbreaking work paid off for a few, and in the summer of 1897 several of those who had secured their wealth in Klondike gold loaded their fortunes on stern-wheelers headed downriver to St. Michael, and then boarded the first two steamers headed for West Coast ports. The *Excelsior* departed first, headed for San Francisco, followed by the *Portland,* destined for Seattle.

Newspapers in both cities greeted the fortunate miners with all the excitement and hype their writers could muster. Passengers aboard the *Excelsior* arrived at their destination on July 14 brimming with stories of goldfields "rivaling in intensity of interest those told of the fabulous wealth of Monte Cristo," the *San Francisco Chronicle* reported. "There was tangible evidence on the little steamer," the paper continued, "for in the cabins were scores of sacks filled to the very mouths with dust taken from the placers of the far North." The reporter estimated the total value of the gold at close to $750,000. On the front page, the *Chronicle* ran a letter from a local resident who wrote to his brother telling of the biggest placer discovery ever made in the world. "The excitement on the river is indescribable," the letter writer said, "and the output of the new Clondyke district almost beyond belief. Some of the stories are so fabulous that I am afraid to repeat them for fear of being suspected of the infection."[8]

But the fervor in San Francisco was mild compared to the hysteria whipped up in Seattle. The *Portland* was still three days out from its destination when the *Excelsior* docked in San Francisco, and the *Seattle Post-Intelligencer* printed wire service copy informing its readers of the tremendous fortune in gold that had arrived in that California city. The paper screamed with headlines. On its way to Seattle was "the Steamship *Portland* with 68 miners and a ton of gold," and the *P-I* did not waste a minute in reporting the news. It dispatched a reporter on a chartered tug at Port Townsend to meet the incoming boat at Port Angeles at three a.m. on July 17. A special edition hit the streets at nine that morning, blaring the news that "hardly a man [on board] has less than $7,000 and one or two have more than $100,000 in yellow nuggets" ranging in size "from a pea to a guinea egg." More than five thousand people rushed to the docks to meet the miners as they disembarked with their fortunes loaded in boxes and suitcases. The newspaper assumed the role not only of provider of the latest news but also of unabashed promoter of commerce for Seattle as an outfitter for the Yukon trade. "There is plenty of gold," the *P-I* announced at the head of its page-one news columns, "but only the hardy and provident can secure it. No man without a suitable outfit should tempt fortune in that remote region. There will no doubt be a great rush for the new discoveries, and the majority will outfit in and leave from Seattle."[9]

The arrival of the *Portland* was sudden and welcome news to a city that had been hit hard by the Panic of 1893 and was still suffering its effects. Unemployment was rampant, and money was scarce as banks had foreclosed on mortgages and many went out of business when depositors closed their accounts. Lending was impossible, construction projects ceased, and businesses failed for lack of trade.[10] For the masses of men and women struggling for a few dollars a day on farms and in factories, the Klondike was the opportunity of a lifetime and they seized it with startling impetuousness. The professional and white-collar sectors of the workforce joined in as well. Policemen, firefighters, politicians, medical students, salesmen, and clerks bolted from their jobs in astonishing numbers, spent their savings on tools, canned food, and rugged clothing, and secured transportation on the first boats bound for the unknown Yukon. Seattle, one historian concluded, was "demented."[11]

For at least six years before the big discovery, Seattle businesses had conducted a steady trade in supplies for prospectors headed for the Alaska-Yukon goldfields, and the city considered itself to be the natural jumping-off point for any northbound traveler. For example, Cooper & Levy promoted itself as the place to secure all the necessary provisions a miner would need to tackle the challenges of the Yukon, and dry goods stores such as Fraser & Wilson advertised clothing fit for the Klondike. With the image of the "ton of gold" fresh in the eyes of the public, Seattle instantly became the center of the Alaska-Yukon trade and transportation network. Only three days after the *Portland* arrived in port, another steamer, the *Al-Ki,* was fully loaded and headed to sea with one hundred men eager to try their luck in the goldfields. Already the *Post-Intelligencer* sounded a new note of optimism, announcing that the city was "on the threshold of an era of great prosperity."[12] The *Portland* itself was in port for barely a week before it sailed northward once again, "heavily freighted with seekers after gold."[13]

"Prosperity is here," the *P-I* shouted in a front-page headline a week after the news of the Klondike bonanza first appeared in the paper, and a subhead read, "No longer any doubt that the tide has turned." The demand for supplies to outfit prospectors headed for the Klondike had boosted commerce in all sectors of the economy, and business had also increased noticeably in the Pacific coast cities of Tacoma, Portland, and San Francisco. Historian Pierre Berton estimated that by the first of September, nine thousand people and thirty-six thousand tons of freight had left the port of Seattle and that over the winter of 1897–1898 at least one hundred thousand people had set out for the Klondike.[14] Few had any idea of the hardship and suffering that lay before them.

Seattle faced fierce competition from other cities that wished to be recognized as the point of entry to the Alaska-Yukon mining frontier. The Seattle newspapers were joined by the Chamber of Commerce in promoting the city over the efforts of Tacoma, Portland, and San Francisco. Long before the stampede began, Juneau had been making its case as the logical place for intrepid prospectors to outfit themselves for the journey to the Yukon goldfields. In that small city on the Gastineau Channel, entrepreneurs such as B. M. Behrends and Decker Brothers advertised "Yukon outfits" and a full line of goods "especially suited for the Yukon trade." The *Alaska Mining Record* did its best to convince the public that only Juneau merchants were familiar with the conditions that miners would face in the North and only they could supply the quality of goods that would be required on the trail. The paper charged that journalists at the *Seattle Post-Intelligencer* "have seen little and know less of what they are writing about," and it happily took on the job of correcting the *P-I* upon certain facts with which it was "struggling so wide at sea."[15]

There were two primary routes to the Yukon goldfields. The first was to board a steamer in Seattle or another West Coast port destined for St. Michael in western Alaska at the mouth of the Yukon, then book passage on a riverboat headed upriver to Dawson. This was by far the easiest route, but its cost was beyond the reach of most travelers, and tickets were almost impossible to obtain.[16] Much more commonly, the gold seekers chose to journey to the head of Lynn Canal in southeastern Alaska, where the supplies for which they had spent their life's savings were deposited on the beach at one of two boomtowns—Skagway and Dyea—that had sprouted up as staging areas. From there, the travelers chose either the White Pass from Skagway or the Chilkoot Pass from Dyea as their passageway to Lake Lindman, the headwaters of the Yukon River, a little over thirty miles inland. Historians have estimated that as many as thirty thousand to forty thousand attempted one of those two trails in 1897–1898. Most chose the slightly shorter but steeper Chilkoot.[17]

The Chilkoot was a well-known route to the Interior. Since long before the great strike of August 1896 generated mass hysteria, the Juneau-based *Alaska Mining Record* had been running a standing column entitled "Over the Pass," touting the Chilkoot as "The shortest, quickest, and cheapest way to the Yukon." The column was part information and part promotion for the local advertisers who specialized in mining supplies, clothing, and food provisions. "Long experience" had taught these Juneau outfitters the exact needs of those seeking gold in the Yukon basin. Yet the paper included blunt warnings of harsh conditions and slight chances of immediate success. "The road is long, supplies are costly, seasons are short, and Fortune fickle. Failure to find gold the first season entails suffering upon those whose funds are insufficient to carry them through the long winter when absolutely nothing can be done. Not one in a hundred makes a strike the first season. Inexperienced persons . . . should stay away."[18]

Scarcely any of the thousands who rushed headlong into the mountains that year paid any heed to such warnings. The Chilkoot and the White Pass trails quickly became scenes of indescribable hardship and suffering. Both started in Alaska but soon crossed into a corner of British Columbia before continuing for 600 miles to Dawson City in the Yukon Territory. The Chilkoot Trail rises to 3,500 feet in altitude, the last portion of which is at a nearly 40 percent grade. At the summit, the Royal Canadian Mounted Police operated a scale to weigh the travelers' goods to ensure that they possessed enough to sustain themselves for at least six months. Many of the miners carried up to two thousand pounds, all of which had to be transported over the treacherous pass on their backs one load of perhaps one hundred pounds at a time.[19] Many of the prospectors turned back immediately upon realization of the difficulties of the trail. Others who succeeded in transporting their outfits over the pass spent the remainder of the winter in crude cabins or canvas shelters at Lake Lindman, where they built boats out of whipsawed lumber and waited for the spring thaw. Those who reached Dawson by the summer of 1898 found that already by then every possible gold-bearing creek had been staked by prospectors who were old hands in the North and had reached the Klondike a year ahead of them.

By far, most residents of the booming city of Dawson were Americans, and in fact the American public paid little attention to the fact that the Klondike was on the Canadian side of the international boundary line. In the public mind, "Alaska-Yukon" was a single frontier. The rush northward was an American movement, a resumption of the great expansion westward that had seemed to end at the Pacific coast with the settlement of the American West in the early 1890s. The American frontier had always offered unique opportunities, and its availability played a major role in shaping the character of the new nation. But in the 1890s, the freedom and open land associated with the frontier appeared to be a phenomenon of the past. A depressed economy had brought widespread suffering and despair in both the urban industrial and the rural agricultural areas of the country, and people who had felt the urge to go west found themselves stuck at the poverty line and limited by circumstances. America had reached the limits of its great westward expansion. The image of a closing frontier had effectively ended most thoughts of the freedom associated with open land.

The Klondike changed things overnight. Alaska-Yukon was a beacon of hope and opportunity in a new land waiting to be developed and settled. It was an escape from the dreary realities of the Gilded Age economy in which rich industrialists enjoyed the benefits of their investments in railroads and factories while the working masses only grew poorer. Suddenly, with the strike in the Klondike working people in all areas of society saw a chance to establish equity and make some gains where economic forces had been stacked against them. Significantly, it was gold itself that sparked a level of excitement that no other commodity in the world could have raised. The presidential election of 1896 had brought gold to the center stage of American politics, and the election of William McKinley had settled the question of the gold standard versus free silver. Yet the national debate that raged around that issue was still fresh in the public mind, and gold continued to arouse deeply held passions. Adding to the mystique and allure of gold was its scarcity. Under the gold standard, the nation's currency depended on an adequate supply of the precious metal to back up every dollar in circulation. Production, however, had not kept pace with the need for ever-increasing monetary circulation in a growing economy. Scarcity creates value, and the suddenness of the Klondike discovery added the element of excitement to the economic value of gold. The result was a rush northward that was far out of proportion to the true nature and size of the resource. It was three concurrent factors—the scarcity of gold, the opportunity to escape poverty and hard times, and the status of gold in the world economy—that worked together to ignite the Klondike gold rush. Many miners found a fortune in gold, but thousands more returned home disappointed and penniless.

The gold rush was Alaska's watershed event. Up to that time, settler life in America's northern possession was centered in the southeastern Panhandle with the capital city of Sitka and the larger, more vibrant, and economically diverse community of Juneau. In the thirty-year period following the 1867 purchase, while the nation was preoccupied with the westward movement and settlement of the Great Plains and the Pacific coast, Alaska was, as historian Ted Hinckley has pointed out, simply irrelevant.[20] Gold production and the salmon canning industry provided a few jobs and offered some possibilities for economic development, but farming and ranching, which drew settlers in great numbers to the American West, did not appear to be workable in the North. Then, beginning in 1897, the uncounted thousands who rushed to the Klondike forced irrevocable changes in Alaska's social, economic, and political life. The burgeoning population spurred the beginnings of modern systems of government and business in areas of the territory beyond the confines of the Panhandle. In that year, Hinckley concluded, "the Great Land's frontiers lay northward and westward."[21]

The prominence of gold and the search for it influenced every aspect of life in Alaska and the Yukon in the 1890s. At the same time, to the few thousand residents of the northern frontier, the American political arena was a far distant scene. As the editor of the *Douglas Miner* observed in October 1896, "It is decidedly within the realm of possibility that all Alaska will sleep as peacefully upon the eve of the coming great political battle as will the most unaffected or distant country upon the globe."[22] Even so, it was a miner prospecting in the Susitna Valley that same year who, in the midst of the political battle for the presidency, named North America's highest peak for William McKinley because of the Republican nominee's position on the central political issue of the day, the gold standard. William A. Dickey and a partner had spent the summer in the vicinity of the mountain, and they were excited when the news of McKinley's run against Bryan reached them. "That fact was the first news we received on our way out of that wonderful wilderness," Dickey wrote in an article that appeared in the *New York Sun* the next January.[23] Years later, Dickey related more details to mountaineer and author Belmore Browne. Browne wrote that during their explorations in Alaska, Dickey and his partner had spent some time with two prospectors who were on the opposite side of the political fence, and Dickey's decision to name the mountain in honor of the Ohio Republican was a response to the other two men's views on the economy. "While they were in the wilderness," Browne wrote, "[Dickey] and his partner fell in with two prospectors who were rabid champions of free silver, and after listening to their arguments for many days, he retaliated by naming the mountain after the champion of the gold standard."[24]

THE ROOTS OF THE PROGRESSIVE MOVEMENT

McKinley's election was a decisive win for the wealthy class of financiers and industrialists over the populists and insurgents of both major political parties, but it did nothing to diminish the cries for reform that were heard throughout the 1890s from the farming and laboring classes and those who represented them. However, in the last years of the decade, the reform movement began to shape a new identity that, while sticking to basic principles, took on a broader and more urban-centered character. It reflected a major demographic shift that had been in process since the end of the Civil War. The growth of the industrial sector of the economy brought large numbers of people off the farms and into the cities. At the same time, immigration swelled the population of northern urban centers, where unskilled laborers were able to find work in the mills and factories that were working to keep up with the demand for steel and manufactured goods in a new and growing consumer economy. The nation was in the midst of a transition from an agrarian past to a modern market economy, and changes demanded reform of systems of labor relations and social welfare. The activities of big business were largely unregulated, and the time had come, many believed, to institute laws guaranteeing fairness and controls over avaricious and monopolistic business practices. Railroads expanded at an astonishing rate, and a few corporations controlled production and distribution in most major industries.[25]

Meanwhile, the disparity between rich and poor grew wider than ever as the corporation displaced the family farmer as the central component of the means of production. For the industrial workforce, wages increased steadily but not nearly enough to help workers rise from extremely impoverished conditions of the cities. For those remaining on the farm, economic conditions began to improve markedly in the last years of the 1890s, leading to what one noted historian has labeled the "golden age of American agriculture."[26]

Alaska-Klondike gold made at least a partial contribution to this new era of prosperity on the farm. The sudden influx of gold sharply increased the Treasury reserves, put more money into circulation, and initiated the monetary inflation that Populists had tried to achieve through free coinage of silver. Prices for wheat, corn, and other produce rose steadily and stayed high from the late 1890s to the end of World War I.[27] At the same time, the burgeoning urban population created a huge market and a limitless demand for farm products. McKinley's win was a victory for the gold standard and a resounding defeat for free silver. Yet the Populists realized their goal of inflation when gold from the creeks of the North began to pour into the nation's Treasury and increase the supply of currency.[28]

The last years of the nineteenth century were a turning point in the nation's history. It was a time in which the general public became increasingly discontent and aware of the need for the kinds of reform that radicals and Populists had been shouting for. Even as McKinley and the Republican Party gained political strength, a significant movement progressed toward changes in the business practices of the robber baron owners of the railroads and other corporations.[29] The era of Progressivism took shape and grew during a time of unprecedented economic growth while the urban working classes suffered under conditions of exploitation and poverty. The two major political parties were bitterly divided, with Republicans defending unfettered free-market capitalism and Democrats calling for limitations and federal regulations. It was in this "time of great social transformation and economic dislocation," as one historian termed it, that Progressivism was born.[30] Progressive members of both parties sought to use the powers of government to effect sweeping changes in a nation suddenly transformed by the growth of corporations and the growing population of immigrants.[31]

Increasing industrial production, employment, and prosperity in the agricultural sector brought the country out of depression in the late 1890s, and with these advancements came a concern for social reform that crossed political lines and spread equally through urban and rural America. In Chicago, for example, Jane Addams operated the highly renowned Hull House as a center of respite and education for the city's poor and immigrant populations. By 1890, Chicago had surpassed the one million mark in population, becoming the nation's second largest city. Addams was an influential voice for reform for many years after the turn of the century. Also in Illinois, the liberal activist for social justice John Altgeld served one term as governor, beginning in 1892, and continued thereafter to speak out on behalf of the poor and oppressed. He was a strong advocate of organized labor and public education.[32]

Progressive political action took root as well in neighboring Wisconsin, where Robert La Follette earned a reputation as a fighter in the populist agrarian tradition. La Follette achieved great success in promoting Progressive ideas and enacting sweeping reforms. The core of Progressive doctrine lay in the belief in a strong national government, with ultimate power over that government held by "an informed and active citizenry."[33] La Follette began his career in public service as a district attorney. He served three terms in Congress as a representative of Wisconsin, beginning in 1884. During his time in Congress, he was an advocate for the Interstate Commerce Act and the Sherman Anti-Trust Act, both of which became law.[34] In 1900, he was elected governor of Wisconsin, and from there he went on to the US Senate. Always he remained faithful to the basic tenets of Progressivism, focusing particularly on regulation of the railroads and corporate monopolies. In his autobiography, La Follette explained that Progressivism began in Wisconsin when farmers rose up in revolt over the "arrogance of the railroads and the waste and robbery of the public lands." The farmers saw the railroads as only another form of highway, he said, and therefore they should be the ones to grant the right-of-way through their property and have the right to control the use of the highway.[35] La Follette never strayed from what he called the "one great struggle"—his dedication to social and economic justice for the working people, urban and rural alike. "The supreme issue involving all others," he wrote, "is the encroachment of the powerful few on the rights of the many. This mighty power has come between the people and their government."[36]

The direct primary issue became the perfect fit for La Follette's insurgent Progressive politics. To him, the party system was rife with corruption and overwhelming influence from railroads and other corporations in the party caucus system. Beginning in 1897, he campaigned throughout Wisconsin on the premise that if voters held direct control of the election process, corporations would not be able to exercise such great influence over local and state politics.[37] The message was received well by the crowds that gathered to hear his impassioned speeches. The rise of large corporations, particularly the railroads, brought with it a system in which those business entities dominated party politics and the choice of candidates for offices at all levels of government. The direct primary, he said, would restore representative government and place ultimate control of the election process with the people, where it properly belonged. Within a year, La Follette's Progressive ideas had come to dominate the Republican Party in Wisconsin, and the insurgent wing had incorporated many reform policies into the party platform, including direct primary elections and increased taxes on railroads and other corporations.[38] La Follette's Progressive reform movement, known as the "Wisconsin Idea," became a model for change nationwide.

REVISED CIVIL AND CRIMINAL CODES FOR ALASKA

The late 1890s saw the beginnings of significant change in Alaska as well, although the impetus was not so much progressive reform as it was a need recognized by Congress to implement a system of functional civil government and a criminal code in response to a growing population. As early as 1896, Governor James Sheakley had complained to the secretary of the interior that the federal government had done nothing to administer justice and order in the region of the upper Yukon. The laws and regulations under which Alaska had been governed since passage of the Organic Act of 1884 were grossly inadequate a decade later. Sheakley recommended that a commission be formed immediately to draft a code of civil and criminal laws for the government of the territory.[39] The Alaska Chamber of Commerce, based in Juneau, added its voice with letters sent to both houses of Congress requesting immediate action, especially expansion of the court system. The backlog of criminal cases made it impossible for civil business to be heard, the chamber wrote. "It is imperative that Congress take action."[40]

Such pleas reached the top levels of government. President McKinley, in his formal message to the Fifty-Fifth Congress in December 1897, told legislators that conditions in that "vast, remote, and yet promising portion of our country" required their prompt and early attention. The great influx of population in the past summer and fall, and the prospect of even greater numbers in the coming spring, demanded the presence of civil authority and "establishment of a more thorough government," he said. McKinley followed with a statement of his belief in the government's responsibility to "encourage the development and settlement of the country and its duty to follow up its citizens there with the benefits of legal machinery." He urged Congress to pass legislation that would provide a civil and criminal structure adequate for the future needs of the Alaska territory.[41]

The cause was taken up by Thomas H. Carter, a Republican senator from Montana, who introduced a bill in the US Senate in February 1898 intended to address those concerns. Carter informed his fellow senators that Alaska, as a customs district, had only a governor and one judge, both based in Sitka, to see to the judicial needs of the entire region. "The result," he said, "has been a very feeble and unsatisfactory administration of justice in the country."[42] Carter spoke of the sudden rush of people into the district during the past two years following the discovery of gold in paying quantities, and he predicted that one hundred thousand more adventurers would "invade that country for legitimate purposes during the next year." He described conditions of lawlessness and near anarchy along the length of the Yukon River between Dawson City and St. Michael, where there was no government authority of any kind and no means of settling disputes. "There are no jails," he continued, "no means of punishing offenders except by hanging them by the neck or ordering them out of the country."[43]

Carter recognized that, because of the scattered nature of settlement in Alaska, plans to seat a locally elected legislative body were premature. "The attempt to hold an election in Alaska during the gold excitement," he said, "would be something like holding a general election at a circus." Instead, he called for the establishment of three judicial districts, with a judge, a clerk, and a US attorney for each district. Judges would be given authority to appoint commissioners as needed to enforce the laws in new settlements as they arose. Carter found it impossible to predict how many new communities would spring up and where they would be located in interior Alaska, and therefore he expected district judges to respond to the demands for justice by hiring commissioners. The bill also allowed the US Army, then increasing its presence in Alaska, to act as a posse and administer justice as needed. "It will be difficult to maintain courts to enforce the rights of property and to protect persons in the country unless some force exists behind the courts," Carter concluded.[44]

The Senate approved the bill on March 30, and from there it moved to the House of Representatives for its approval. The House adjourned for the year before taking any action, and in January 1899, the third session of the Fifty-Fifth Congress took up the revisions to Alaska's civil and criminal codes in separate pieces of legislation. The criminal code aroused a fierce debate when advocates of strict prohibition laws objected to a provision to grant legal licenses for the sale of liquor in Alaska. Under the criminal code of 1884, the importation and sale of alcohol was expressly outlawed in Alaska except for very specific and limited purposes. Permits for the use of alcohol for medicinal, mechanical, and scientific purposes were issued by the collector of customs in Sitka. However, it was widely recognized that the restrictions were blatantly violated as well as universally unenforce-able, and saloons were operating across the territory in open defiance of the law.

Indeed, as historian Mary Ehrlander pointed out in her study of alcohol abuse in territorial Alaska, alcohol was a valued commodity among the prospectors who came flooding into the North following the Klondike discovery. "Many miners valued the bottle in their sup-plies as much or more than the pick and shovel," she concluded.[45]

It was a "vexed question" according to the Juneau-based *Alaska Mining Record*. Prohibition in the territory violated the personal lib-erties of Alaskans and made them "criminals in the commission of acts perfectly legal, legitimate, and honorable elsewhere the world over." The law was humiliating and onerous, the paper shouted in its editorial columns, and it must not be tolerated in a country where the government derives its power from the will of the people. The present law was "an outrage upon American citizenship which must no lon-ger be tolerated without sharp and vigorous protest," it concluded.[46] The *Seattle Post-Intelligencer* agreed, editorializing that no law can be enforced without the support of the people governed. The prohibition law in Alaska, the *P-I* editor wrote, had worked to "cripple efforts to put Alaska upon the same basis as other communities inhabited by white men." It was harmful to the Indians because they could not afford to buy smuggled whiskey and instead manufactured a form of rum, com-pared to which "all known intoxicants are as simple and innocent as milk; it would put the blush to the most crimson redeye." The paper charged that conditions in Alaska were inexcusable, and Congress should accommodate the reasonable request to legalize and license the liquor trade.[47]

Representative Vespasian Warner of Illinois sought to end the sham and at the same time raise some revenue to support the administra-tion of federal programs. He offered an amendment that would charge a license fee of $1000 to liquor establishments and a bond of $3000 for each establishment for the protection of anyone injured by the sale of liquor. "It is a notorious fact in Alaska that the liquor law is absolutely a dead letter," Warner stated in defense of his amendment. "Liquor is sold there free and without question." He cited reports claiming that there were 162 places in the territory where intoxicating liquor was sold, and, he added, "their location is so certain and plain that even a blind man could find any of them." The amendment would put a stop to the illegal trafficking in liquor, he said, and would raise $162,000, which could be used for educational purposes.[48]

Warner found guarded support among other members of the House who agreed with the merits of his amendment but wished to make certain that their views on the temperance issue remained clear. Representative Alston Gordon Dayton of West Virginia declared himself to be "an honest believer in prohibition in the true sense," but experience had proved that the liquor traffic could not be controlled in Alaska and the public did not support the restrictive laws. Under the "peculiar conditions now existing in that territory," Dayton stated, the license law would produce better results than absolute prohibition.[49] The majority of the House agreed, and the amended bill passed. It was returned to the Senate on January 16 and referred to the Committee on Territories.

On the day the legislation was reported out of that committee for debate on the floor, hard-line prohibition senators, led by Jacob Gallinger of New Hampshire, were ready to do all they could to defeat the liquor licensing amendment. "I am quite unwilling to admit that this great government of ours is so weak and so impotent that it cannot enforce the laws of its own making," Gallinger charged. The only advantage gained by this legislation, in his view, was the increased revenue from the sale of licenses, but even that was overshadowed by the evils of profiting from the whiskey trade. "We will legalize an immoral traffic and claim that because we get some revenue out of it we are legislating wisely and well," he concluded before offering his own amendment striking the licensing of liquor from the Alaska criminal code.[50]

Other senators were sympathetic to the argument for prohibition but were not moved to support Gallinger's efforts. George Perkins of California spoke of the impossibility of enforcing the ban, saying it would take an army as large as the one the country then had stationed in Cuba to prevent smugglers from transporting illegal liquor to Alaska. Perkins quoted a customs collector in Juneau who was ordered by an assistant secretary of the treasury to enforce the law and close the saloons. "Mr. Secretary," the collector replied to the bureaucrat, "detail every Marine from your revenue cutter and I will endeavor to carry out your orders." According to Perkins, the man from Washington soon changed his opinion about the federal government's ability to stop the flow of whiskey in Alaska. Perkins contended that the majority of saloon owners in Alaska supported the licensing plan as a way of legitimizing their business, but the more sordid of them—"the dance hall element and keepers of houses of ill-repute in Juneau, Skagway, Dyea, and Douglas"—were sending money in support of the prohibitionist party's efforts to defeat it.[51]

George Vest of Missouri declared his undying wish to destroy the last drop of alcohol on the face of the earth, but he gave up in despair at the notion of stopping the desperate residents of Alaska from indulging in intoxicating drink. "Intemperance is the greatest evil that ever afflicted the human race," he said. "But you cannot eradicate the appetite, especially in a climate like Alaska. The man who goes to Alaska, under perpetual fog and without seeing the sun more than once in six weeks, who is a strict teetotaler, is a marvel and very rarely to be found. The climate is such as to induce an appetite for stimulants." Vest concluded that any attempt by Congress to pass laws prohibiting those passions and desires would only make matters worse in Alaska. "It cannot be done."[52]

Gallinger's amendment received only eleven yea votes in the Senate. The revised criminal code for Alaska passed on March 2, 1899, with the liquor license provision intact, and President McKinley signed it into law the next day. "Some teetotalers in Congress" opposed the act, the *Alaska Mining Record* had noted in January. "But great Alaska is on the eve of recognition, and the evils with which she has been afflicted will soon be eradicated."[53]

Meanwhile, the revised civil code was moving through Congress at a slower pace. The House Committee on Territories issued a report on January 23 spelling out the need for an expanded court system to meet the growing demands in interior Alaska, and accordingly the bill before Congress established three judicial districts and provided allowances for the courts to construct jails and courthouses in new settlements. The proposed salary of $6000 per year for judges was considered quite high, but the committee approved it on grounds that "the harshness of the climate, the onerous character of the duties to be performed, and the very great responsibility cast upon the judges will demand the services of vigorous lawyers of unusual discretion and unquestionable ability."[54]

Congress failed to pass the civil code before the end of the session in March, and any action on it had to wait until the next year, much to the lament of Alaska Governor John G. Brady. The bill "would have afforded us very great relief," Brady noted in his report to the secretary of the interior in October. "The consequence is that the people up and down the Yukon valley, along the entire western coast of Alaska, are left helpless . . . and millions of dollars invested in steamships, canneries, and mercantile enterprises are left without any adequate protection." The governor hailed the presence of the army in new installations along the river, but he added that in the absence of courts, prosecuting attorneys, and judges, the military officers' effectiveness was limited.[55]

By January 1900, Brady was prepared to do all he could to see to the passage of such needed legislation, and with a contingent of civic leaders from Juneau he traveled to the nation's capital to mount a concerted lobbying effort. Thomas Carter of Montana again led the charge in the Senate, introducing his bill on March 1. He relied on two major themes: the record of continued federal neglect of Alaska since the purchase from Russia in 1867 and the new need for a modern code of laws with the sudden growth of population following the gold rush in the upper Yukon region and, more recently, at Cape Nome. As evidence of the need for a revised civil code, Carter relied on the testimony of Alaskans who had witnessed the effects of the lack of order that prevailed. He quoted a letter from Major P. H. Ray, commanding officer of the army in northern Alaska, who reported that the single district court based in Sitka left the remainder of the nation's northern possession essentially ungoverned. The lack of jurisdiction was especially acute in cases of disputed mining claims, where the length of time required to file a complaint in Sitka and wait for a judgment allowed either party enough opportunity to extract the valuable minerals from the ground before title was determined by the court. Carter told his fellow senators that failure to pass his bill would "invite anarchy and confusion, which will be distressing to the unfortunate people there and a disgrace to the Congress of the United States."[56]

The Seattle Chamber of Commerce, which had a vested interest in maintaining a positive environment for business and trade in Alaska, chimed in with a letter addressed to both the Senate and the House Committees on the Territories and read on the Senate floor. Failure to pass a bill establishing additional courts and a revised civil code would be unfair to the army in Alaska, the chamber said, compelling the military to act in a judicial capacity and involve itself in property issues and titles to mining claims.[57]

What many saw as a relatively quick and easy solution to the settlement of such disputes soon became snarled in a complicated argument involving the rights of nonresident alien miners to stake and file claims. The heart of the controversy lay with the gold discovery made in the early fall of 1898 by "three lucky Swedes" on Anvil Creek at the tip of the Seward Peninsula, which juts out into the Bering Sea in far western Alaska. Word of the strike brought a stampede of prospectors from the length of the Yukon River and its tributaries and provided a new destination for gold seekers embarking from Seattle and other West Coast ports. The boom town of Nome grew to two thousand by the next summer, and by the middle of 1900 some estimates placed the population at twenty thousand.[58] To many it appeared that Senator Carter's predictions of a surging population could be accurate and his urgent pleas for congressional action could be worthy. Strongly prejudiced feelings against foreign immigrant miners ran rampant in the new mining camp, and many American prospectors, angry at having to take second place to foreigners who had beaten them to the most promising pay streaks, felt free to jump those claims. With practically no law enforcement present in Nome, claim jumping was a common practice, and many miners learned that they were able to hold their ground only at gunpoint.

In the Senate, Carter and his ally, Senator Henry C. Hansbrough of North Dakota, supported an amendment to the Alaska civil code expressly prohibiting noncitizens from staking mining claims. Hansbrough charged that the situation in Nome demanded such a restriction. He cited one case in which six foreign miners organized their own mining district, made their own laws, and declared the size of the district to be twenty-five square miles. Their purpose, he contended, was to take all the claims they could within that area and shut out everyone else. "In my judgment," he continued, "an alien has no rights whatever upon the public domain. . . . He is a mere trespasser."[59]

Arguments against Hansbrough's amendment were led by Senator William M. Stewart of Nevada, a leading expert in American mining law and a participant in passing major mining legislation in 1866 and 1872. Stewart urged the Senate to leave American mining law unchanged for Alaska. The miners know better than anyone else how to make regulations governing locations and recording and possession of claims, he said. "If we have no mining law for Alaska except that which the miners make, you will see it is all right. . . . The general public sentiment where all are interested in having good laws and in enforcing them is so strong that no wrongdoer can withstand it. . . . I tell you the miners are a pretty good set of men." He opposed any law restricting access to mining claims filed by noncitizens.[60]

In reality, Carter and Hansbrough were participants in a grand scheme involving a corporation set up to buy and sell mining claims in Nome, and they were attempting to manipulate federal civil code legislation to favor their own particular interests. Hansbrough took to the floor of the Senate to warn of a "monster conspiracy afoot to grab the richest gold region on the face of the earth" by an East Coast syndicate that was hurrying to work those claims held by foreign stakeholders before Congress could pass any laws to stop it. This syndicate was actually a rival of the corporation in which Hansbrough had a personal financial interest. He rose to speak on behalf of those who worked to make a living digging gold from the gravel and muck, "the man with the pick, the man with the pan, the American miner, the man behind the rocker in the gulches, on the creeks, and in the sea sands, instead of the insatiable millionaire."[61] Hansbrough's efforts aroused such tension within the Senate that it soon became apparent that some members were willing to debate the bill to death rather than see it passed with the restriction against noncitizen mining claims attached. In the end, Carter saw the political reality of the situation and agreed to a compromise. "We are in the middle of a dilemma," he announced on May 1. "This amendment must be abandoned or the bill must be abandoned." Hansbrough withdrew his amendment, and the bill passed the Senate without further delay.[62]

In the House of Representatives, the civil code bill faced fierce partisan debate surrounding two key issues: a provision for an Alaska representative in Congress and the need for three, rather than two, judicial districts in the territory. The bill on the floor did not include a congressional delegate for Alaska, and Democrats demanded to know why their rival party members were ignoring a plank in the 1896 Republican platform calling for one. Indeed, four years earlier, both parties in their national conventions adopted formal statements of support for that very thing.[63] William E. Williams of Illinois led the effort in the House, asking his Republican colleagues why, after such a pledge was made, they were not insisting on its inclusion in the present legislation. "At Circle City and at Eagle City and at St. Michael and at Cape Nome there are permanent residents who are more capable of legislating for themselves than we are of legislating for them," Williams shouted. "You say in your platform declaration that these people are entitled to their independence and yet you refuse and deny it to them."[64]

Williams was onto a hot-button issue in Alaska, and Governor John G. Brady stood in the middle of it. Brady was one of those whom Williams and many others, including the editors of a number of newspapers, vilified on grounds that they were outsiders and political cronies of the McKinley administration. "We oppose sending these men to govern Alaska," Williams declared to his Republican rivals. "You send carpetbaggers there." In his view, the appointed governor was merely a figurehead who held very little power or responsibility and, with a $5000 yearly salary designated for him in the current bill, was grossly overpaid.[65]

While Brady had his legions of detractors, even within the Republican Party, the "carpetbagger" label was undeserved and misplaced. He had arrived in Sitka in 1878 as a missionary working with fellow Presbyterian Sheldon Jackson in his efforts to educate and Christianize the Native populations of southeastern Alaska. Both men received federal administrative appointments, with Jackson being named general agent for education and Brady becoming a commissioner in charge of minor criminal and civil matters when the district court was established in Sitka in 1884. Jackson's political stature grew steadily, and in 1897 he used the power of his influence to secure Brady's appointment as Alaska governor.

The two men were of like minds on most issues, but the governor parted ways with his mentor on one significant question when in 1899 he saw the reality of the liquor problem in Alaska and supported the licensing system that was written in to the revised criminal code. For that Brady was generally applauded in the territory, but the praise ended one year later with his action to block the movement to authorize a congressional delegate for Alaska. The editor of the *Skaguay News* was furious, accusing the governor of using his position to advance his own personal interests by advocating a bill that would designate the governor as the congressional delegate. "The people who labor under the impression that Gov. Brady's chief aim and mission is in elevating the meek and lowly Alaska Indians are somewhat mistaken. The governor has loftier motives; he has congressional ambitions." The paper acknowledged that as a longtime resident of Alaska, Brady "has the best interests of the district at heart." But, it added, those interests come into play only "insofar as they do not conflict with the interests of John G. Brady." After noting that Brady and Jackson had been "running things" for a long time, the editor concluded his piece with the hope that "the national interest in Alaska which has been awakened during the past year will lead to the appointment of better officials as well as the enactment of better laws."[66]

Brady was at odds as well with two lobbyists who had been sent to Washington by the Juneau Chamber of Commerce to advocate on behalf of their community during debate on the revised civil code bill. The two lobbyists were active in pushing not only for the congressional delegate but also for another provision that Brady abhorred, moving the capital from Sitka to Juneau. It became obvious early in the process that the capital move would not be possible until the Juneau community was able to make a significant contribution of land and facilities. R. F. Lewis, one of the Juneau advocates in Washington, wrote in a letter published in the *Alaska Record-Miner* (Juneau) on March 24, 1900, "We will be lucky if we get the capital at all, and unless a good place for building is offered at a low figure, I am afraid we will fail." Lewis concluded that the best strategy would be to allow the civil code revision bill to pass without the capital move provision and then rely on the US attorney general to order the move when a site was prepared.

On the congressional delegate issue, however, the Juneau Chamber of Commerce found more significant reasons to part ways with Governor Brady. Juneau lobbyist John G. Price clearly regretted the fact that such differences with the governor existed, and for the public he chose to soften their impact. "The governor and I have been getting along as well as could be desired," Price wrote from his Washington office on March 3, "and in all matters excepting the delegate and capital questions the governor has been in accord with the general movement and been doing some good work." Price continued as though he felt the need to justify his disagreement with Brady. "I cannot explain to myself why he as governor should oppose the will of the people," he said, adding that it was only through a sense of obligation to Alaskans that he chose to advise them of the places where he was meeting with opposition. He continued, "I do not feel that I have done the governor any injustice for the reasons I assume he, like all other men, are willing and prepared to back up any public position they take."[67]

Just two months later, however, that conciliatory tone disappeared. At its territorial convention in Juneau on May 15 and 16, the Alaska Republican Party voted 32–13 in favor of a strongly worded resolution condemning Governor Brady's actions and declaring him unfit for office. The statement was introduced by the Committee on Platform and Resolutions, of which John G. Price was the chair. The *Seattle Post-Intelligencer* reported that opposition to Brady had begun when the governor refused to "work in harmony" with Price in Washington on the Alaska bill before Congress, and that now Republicans in Alaska were rallying around Price in nearly unanimous opposition to Brady. The party stated its strong support for an elected delegate to Congress and the capital move from Sitka to Juneau. Brady has "forfeited the confidence of the people, deceived the government, and is no longer worthy to be governor of Alaska," a spokesman said.[68] The Alaska Republicans voiced their support for William McKinley in the presidential election of 1900, and they passed along their condemnation of Brady to McKinley in hopes that the president would appoint a new territorial governor who would be closely aligned with the party platform.

In Washington, the Alaska bill moved through Congress with the help of key supporters such as Representative Francis W. Cushman of Washington, who stated that the close commercial relations between his state and the district of Alaska gave him reason to have a direct interest in the welfare of his northern neighbors. Cushman argued effectively for establishing three judicial districts rather than two, as some congressmen wanted, and he explained the need for increased spending in a district that had long suffered from the effects of federal neglect. "God knows that the magnitude of the amount that the U.S. government has spent in Alaska ought not to keep anybody awake," he pronounced, "for if there was ever in our history any portion of the country neglected so shamefully as Alaska, I do not know where it lies."[69]

The revised civil code as passed by Congress and signed into law by the president established three judicial districts and directed that the capital would move to Juneau when suitable facilities became available, but it did not provide for an Alaska delegate to Congress. Significantly, the law allowed for the incorporation of towns, which could elect a local council and mayor to effect a measure of self-government with the powers needed to run police and fire departments and a school system.[70]

Yet the new law left some close observers unsatisfied. The *Seattle Post-Intelligencer* lamented that the Constitution still had not been extended to Alaska, and even with the provision for the incorporation of towns, the level of self-government was limited. The paper had pushed for official designation as a "territory," giving the people an elected legislative body and some say in their own affairs rather than remaining under the direct authority of Congress. "The legislation for Alaska is based distinctly upon the theory that Congress has absolute power to govern that district precisely as it chooses," the paper said in a summary editorial. It was a law that could never have been passed if the people of Alaska had had any representation in the lawmaking body. It gave Alaska residents no voice in the administration of public affairs or in the selection of the officials sent to govern them.[71]

The *Skaguay News* sounded a more encouraging note. Clearly anticipating defeat of the provision for incorporation of towns, the paper declared the outcome "better than was expected."[72] And the *Skaguay News*'s local rival, the *Daily Alaskan*, hailed the good news that "Skagway is in a fair way to become a municipality before the summer is over."[73]

The legislation enacted in 1900 reflected a new national awareness of the existence of Alaska and the urgent special needs of the people living and working in that northern frontier. It was the beginning of a modern system of government and a legal structure that would accommodate social, political, and economic growth in the new century. The gold rush brought Alaska to the forefront and awakened Congress to its potential and to the need to pay attention to the development of a valuable possession. In other action, Congress passed the Homestead Act of 1898, giving settlers access to title to land, and it funded agricultural experiment stations in Alaska. The army established Fort Gibbon on the middle Yukon River and Fort Egbert near Eagle for the purpose of building telegraph lines to provide a much-needed communication system. These were significant actions, but strong advocates of home rule, including a territorial legislature and a delegate to Congress, considered them inadequate. The *Seattle Post-Intelligencer* concluded with the hope that such defects would be "remedied as the needs of Alaska become better understood and the country is settled with a population that is permanent."[74] Alaska stood ready to make its giant leap into the twentieth century with remarkable advances in communication, transportation, agriculture, and mining, all within the context of Progressive-age politics in America.

3

THE ROOTS OF PROGRESSIVISM

The country is new and the prospectors are poor and need help

~~~

THE PROGRESSIVE ERA had its beginnings at the turn of the twentieth century, formed out of the social and economic turmoil of the 1890s. It was a movement of people who represented the full spectrum of class and politics but were united by a few core convictions: that large corporations had grown to such size and strength that the government of the people had no mechanism in place to regulate them; that wealth had become too narrowly concentrated in the hands of a cluster of robber barons of industry; that the masses of workers in the fields and factories endured miserable conditions and possessed little or no opportunity to prosper; and that big-business interests controlled the workings of government at all levels. Even as Americans reelected the unwavering conservative William McKinley to a second term in 1900, reformers from both major political parties moved to correct social injustice and restrain the avarice of corporate monopolies under a system of direct regulation. And strong central government was seen as the agent of change. Progressivism was a product of the labor strife and depressed economic conditions that prevailed at the end of the nineteenth century. In its ranks were devout Democrats, who were joined by former Populists in support of the persuasive liberal leadership of William Jennings Bryan. Republicans came on board in response to leaders of their party, such as the newly elected Wisconsin governor, Robert La Follette, who exposed the corrupt influence of corporate power brokers at the state and municipal levels. Across the board, Progressives feared that large corporate trusts, particularly the railroads, had the power to monopolize sections of the economy, thwart competition, and dictate consumer prices. Only a strong federal government had the authority to enforce regulations that would protect the free and open marketplace. Many believed that American democracy itself depended on it.[1]

In Alaska, the new century brought with it revised civil and criminal codes and three distinct judicial districts with courts and judges to enforce the law. The long arm of the federal government was reaching into the last frontier with a new interest in the lives and welfare of the territory's growing resident population. As one early-twentieth-century historian of Alaska politics observed, "Alaska had secured federal recognition as a pressing problem and Congress had ventured a temporary solution."[2] The handful of towns in existence had in 1900 only just been granted the right to incorporate through federal legislation passed that year. The territory had no railroads and, indeed, no major system of transportation or communication of any kind. By 1900, however, the War Department had taken steps to address that problem and had placed the army at Fort Davis in Nome, Fort Gibbon at the confluence of the Yukon and Tanana Rivers, Fort Egbert at Eagle, Fort Liscum at Valdez, and Fort Seward near Haines. Immediately the signal corps began construction of a system of telegraph lines to connect those outposts with one another and with the outside world. Those lines were completed in 1903.[3] Additionally, the federal government took an interest in promoting food production in the North and established agricultural experiment stations in Sitka, Kenai, Copper Center, Kodiak, and Rampart.[4]

Among those living in the nation's far north possession, Progressive reform as it was taking shape in the large population centers of the United States had little direct application. Except for the powerful salmon canning interests, there was no presence of the giant corporations that the Progressive reformers had pledged to fight. Yet in the presidential election year of 1900, Alaska Democrats showed a full understanding of the basic issue behind the growing national reform movement. The party wrote a strong Progressive-minded statement into its election year platform. "We view with alarm the growth of monopolistic trusts," the Alaska Democrats declared at their party convention, adding that those who controlled such trusts had "secured an unfair share of the wealth of the nation" and they wielded "dangerous power" as well. "We favor legislation that will destroy the trusts and restore to the people their industrial liberty and a fair return for their labor and its products."[5]

Progressivism as it evolved in Alaska took on a distinct personality, formed in equal parts by a hatred of corporate monopoly and a spirit of rugged frontier individualism. Alaska was an extension of the American westward movement, but its unique characteristics set its residents apart in fundamental ways that influenced their relationship with Washington, DC, and conditioned their view of self-government. Progressivism in the United States developed during a time of diminishing opportunities on the western frontier after the nation's wild lands had been settled from coast to coast and the last of the Indian tribes had been defeated by the 1890s. There was a rapid rise in industrialization in the northern and eastern cities, and a shift in the focus of the national economy since the Civil War from mostly agrarian to mostly industrial in nature. Therefore, Progressivism's focus was urbancentric, concerned with factory conditions, wages, and the ways in which multilayered corporate trusts exploited workers, controlled prices, and stifled competition. At the same time, the Alaska frontier appeared open and limitless. Because of its small population and great distance to major US markets, Alaska never developed an economy based on manufacturing, finance, or transportation. Its economy was dependent exclusively on resource extraction. The salmon canning industry and corporate mines in the Juneau area provided a significant number of jobs at the turn of the century, but otherwise the territory was populated largely by men and women who rushed north with the notion that their individual hard work would earn them prosperity. They were inspired by the prospect of digging their own fortune from the creeks while at the same time escaping a dreary future of working for starvation-level wages in the nation's mills and factories.

Freedom and opportunity were elements of Progressivism both nationwide and in Alaska. Unregulated corporate trusts eroded those elements and thus posed a threat to the very idea of American democracy. As one of the era's leading journalists, Henry Demarest Lloyd, stated it, "Liberty and monopoly cannot live together."[6] The movement's second major emphasis was a reliance on the federal government as the agent of regulation and the protector of individual rights and freedoms.[7] Here is where Alaskans put their own distinctive stamp on the Progressive movement. With no representation in Congress, no locally elected legislative body, and no say in the selection of their own governing leaders, Alaskans harbored little faith in Washington's willingness or ability to see to their best interests. Even the civil and criminal code revisions and the Homestead Act were seen as weak-kneed temporary measures enacted after a generation of near-total neglect. Alaskans desired more than anything to be given the breathing space to develop the territory as they saw fit, and only self-government would afford them that freedom.[8] In June 1900, President McKinley reappointed as territorial governor the hated John G. Brady, whom members of the president's own party had blamed for killing the measure providing for an Alaska congressional delegate. Brady had also stood in the way of another initiative popular with residents of southeastern Alaska, that of moving the capital from Sitka to Juneau. The Skagway *Daily Alaskan* bristled at the idea of another four years of the Brady administration. "The hope was indulged that the president would take advantage of the opportunity which legislated our moss-backed governor out of office to remove this barnacle," the editor wrote. "Alaska must progress in spite of the governor."[9]

For Alaskans, then, the government's role was that of enabler, ensuring access to the land, guaranteeing basic needs, and protecting individual rights. They wanted government to open the door to the resource-rich northern frontier and then get out of the way and allow the miner, farmer, or small businessman to do his work. Self-reliance was highly prized, and Alaskans did not embrace the Progressives' view of government as an active regulator and agent of reform. This function was of value in the cities but unwelcome in the North, where the pioneering settlers believed themselves to be much better equipped than Congress was to attend to their particular needs. Alaskans could be heard to complain loudly about government neglect and with equal force about excessive government intrusion. Progressivism Alaska style meant that the people wanted the government's help but only on terms as defined by them. With Brady reappointed to another term, it was apparent to many people that it would not be possible to rely on the government to meet their needs and that they would have to fight for their own interests. "In all probability, he has now been fastened upon us for another four years," the *Daily Alaskan* lamented in reference to the governor, and that realization "intensifies the necessity for a unanimous demand for a delegate in Congress."[10]

Where Alaskans aligned themselves with the national Progressives was in their contempt for corporate monopoly, and that scorn was a second major driver behind the movement for self-government. The powerful consolidated salmon canning interests used their political influence to block government regulation and taxation. They opposed home rule for Alaska because they feared increased layers of government would bring regulation and taxation that would be harmful to their business operations. As Alaskans became more aware of the power of the salmon canning interests to control the market and dictate operating conditions, the more they intensified their push for the elements of home rule.[11]

Later in that summer of 1900, a man who perfectly understood Alaska's complex relationship with the federal government arrived in the territory and began his long career as its leading Progressive politician. James Wickersham, a Tacoma lawyer and politician, was appointed by McKinley as judge in the newly created third judicial district based in Eagle on the upper Yukon River. Wickersham, as historian Stephen Haycox described him, "articulated the understanding that Alaskans must look after their own interests, whatever they might be, and that they could not rely on the federal government or the absentee investors to do so."[12] From his first days in Alaska, Wickersham was an advocate for a representative voice in Congress, and, although at first he opposed it, he later became one of the fiercest activists in favor of an elected territorial legislature. By the time of his death in 1939, Wickersham had become, according to historian Terrence Cole, "the father of Alaska's most vital and enduring public institutions and the champion of territorial self-government and statehood."[13] At age forty-two, he set up his court in Eagle and began to travel the vast expanse of his judicial district to become familiar with the territory and dispense justice in a variety of civil and criminal cases. From the moment he stepped off the boat, his enthusiasm for frontier life impressed his fellow Alaskans. Fairbanks attorney Abraham Spring, who came to know Wickersham over the course of the following three years, praised his ability to learn the "needs and wants" of the territory and his willingness to endure the hardships of the North. "In plain words," Spring said, "he has become one of us. He is as much at home in the miner's cabin as he is on the bench. For him to travel 500 or 600 miles in the middle of winter, with two or three dogs, to a district where the miners need him to settle some litigation seems to be an easy matter."[14]

Coincidentally, in that summer of 1900, a group of men searching for minerals in the Wrangell Mountains near the Chitina River in south-central Alaska discovered a copper deposit so rich in value that it would, over the course of the early years of the century, significantly affect not only the life and career of James Wickersham but also the settlement and growth of the entire territory. The copper ore deposit located near the confluence of the Copper and Chitina Rivers would earn a fortune in profits for some of the wealthiest financiers in the world and spark political battles that had implications at the highest levels of national politics. Prospectors Jack Smith and Clarence Warner were members of a team of eleven miners led by R. F. McClellan, who traveled inland from Valdez that summer. On the basis of information given to them by the local Ahtna Athabascans, Smith and Warner located one of the richest copper ore deposits in the world. Immediately recognizing the size and value of the resource, they hurried back to Valdez to file claims in the names of all eleven prospectors. Also in Valdez at the time was the mining engineer and speculator Stephen Birch, who happened to be accompanying a US military expedition that was exploring and mapping the Copper River valley. With the backing of two New York moneymen, H. O. Havermeyer and Norman Schultz, Birch purchased the claims, amounting to about three thousand acres, from the eleven men for $25,000 each. Over time, that purchase grew into an amalgamation of companies headed by the renowned New York capitalist J. P. Morgan and the worldwide mining and smelting concern known as the Guggenheims.[15]

ROOSEVELT

The Morgan-Guggenheim trust did not fully take shape until 1906, but in the meantime the public grew increasingly intolerant of the large corporate monopolies. Antitrust sentiment heightened further when the reform-minded former New York police commissioner and governor Theodore Roosevelt stepped into his new role as president of the United States following the death of William McKinley, who was shot in the chest in Buffalo, New York, on September 6, 1901, and died eight days later. As vice president, Roosevelt had stuck closely to McKinley's conservative pro-business policies, and immediately upon taking the oath of office on September 14, he promised the public that he would continue along the same lines. Within a matter of weeks, however, it became clear that he intended to make major changes in the way government dealt with large corporations. Antitrust policies and federal supervision were to become central parts of his legislative program.[16]

The strongest hints at future significant reform measures came in the new president's first message to Congress, delivered in a lengthy presentation on December 3. In it, Roosevelt praised the "captains of industry" who in the generation following the Civil War had constructed a railway system across the continent and built an industrial economy that had made possible a new era of material prosperity. He warned against excessive interference in the delicate mechanism of modern business, and he seemed to lecture those who denounced the corporate trusts simply out of hatred and fear. What was needed instead, when dealing with the great industrial combinations, was "cool and steady judgment . . . undertaken after calm inquiry and with sober self-restraint."[17] The message was delivered not by Roosevelt himself but by reading clerks separately in the Senate and in the House. The antitrust section of the speech had been toned down considerably after the president's first draft was circulated to his fellow Republicans. In particular, Senator Mark Hanna of Ohio objected to words he considered to be too harsh and offensive to the magnates of Wall Street.[18]

However, even after considerable cutting, a formidable business reform message remained. Industrial development and the growth of the cities occurred so rapidly in the last decades of the nineteenth century that the nation found itself, in Roosevelt's words, "face-to-face at the beginning of the twentieth with very serious social problems." The old laws which worked in the past to "regulate the accumulation and distribution of wealth" were no longer sufficient, he wrote, and it was time for government to restore supervision through regulations and taxes, especially where monopolistic practices existed. In an earlier day, the states were able to act effectively in overseeing commerce, but in the new economy corporations regularly conducted business across state lines and there was no uniformity of laws governing their activity. "The conditions are now wholly different," Roosevelt stated, "and wholly different action is called for." He advocated new laws that would enable the federal government to regulate interstate commerce and exercise control over the large corporate trusts doing business in all phases of the economy under the authority of a new cabinet-level secretary of commerce. The "upbuilding of the great industrial centers has meant a startling increase not merely in the aggregate of wealth but in the number of very large individual and especially very large corporate fortunes," he noted, adding that "the process has aroused much antagonism." The goal of all government action, he concluded, was to secure a safe environment in which big business could operate profitably while also protecting the rights of the nation's workers and private citizens "so as to acquire equity between man and man in this Republic."[19]

It is possible that Roosevelt's tone had been sharpened by recent events in the world of finance. Just the previous month, three of the nation's wealthiest railroad tycoons—J. P. Morgan, James J. Hill, and E. H. Harriman—had announced the amalgamation of their separate empires into one giant holding company. These were men who, in the words of historian Edmund Morris, "had enriched themselves beyond imagination by anonymous deals in railroad stocks." The newly formed Northern Securities Company combined Morgan's Northern Pacific, Hill's Great Northern, and Harriman's Union Pacific into one of the largest corporate entities in the world, and the monopolistic threats it posed to the national transportation system were frightening.[20]

Mergers of large corporations had become increasingly common starting in the 1890s. The practice of consolidation proved especially beneficial in railroading, where large trusts were able to dictate freight rates to shippers and smaller companies and to control the costs and conditions of labor. In the first years of the twentieth century, there were hundreds of railroads operating nationwide, but only four groups of capitalists controlled 85 percent of the total enterprise. No one prospered more handsomely from this arrangement than the head of the New York House of Morgan, J. P. Morgan. In addition to his railroad empire, he controlled several banks as well as the nation's three largest insurance companies. In one historian's estimation, Morgan represented the sudden shift in economic power from the manufacturers of goods to the bankers who supplied money and financial services. He was uniquely skilled in organizing businesses into giant trusts and retaining financial control.[21]

Roosevelt, at forty-three, was an example of the new generation of Progressive reformers who came of age in the early years of the century. As historian George Mowry described them, they were educated, economically middle and upper class, and urban. They took on many of the old Populist causes, but their movement was defined by one central factor: it occurred during a time of relative prosperity in the industrial North and East rather than rising out of the desperate conditions that prevailed in the rural West and South of the late 1800s. Populist reforms were "belly reforms" led by angry men and women, Mowry observed, while Progressivism was "more the results of the head and the heart than of the stomach." And always the reformers held to a belief in the power of government to serve as a vehicle for advancement. Government, according to Roosevelt, was "the process of giving justice from above."[22]

The passion for reform was motivated by the new industrial economy with the building of a nationwide system of railroads and factories. The modern corporations had created a class of super-rich tycoons whose wealth, power, and prestige far exceeded anything that had been seen before in American history. Suddenly the professional class of small manufacturers and entrepreneurs—the "old gentry"—was overtaken by the newly rich heads of massive corporations, whom they believed to be corrupt and unregulated. Members of this economic class did not feel that their opportunities and fortunes were diminished, but, as historian Richard Hofstadter explained it, their position in the world seemed small in comparison with "the new eminences of wealth and power." Next to men such as the master financier J. P. Morgan, "they were less important and they knew it."[23] Many of the Progressives held tight to their conservative Republican loyalties. They were not antibusiness, but they were fiercely antimonopoly and eager to prove to the robber barons of industry that the federal government held the power to regulate predatory business practices and end corruption. A number of the reforms they promoted were the same as those that had been raised by Bryan Democrats in the 1890s.

FAIRBANKS

It was within the context of this Progressive awareness that modern-day Alaska took shape. A large body of federal legislation enacted in that political environment over the course of the first two decades of the century had profound impacts on the territory. Alaska was becoming increasingly prominent in the eyes of the American public, and the growing population in the North commanded continued interest in the halls of Congress. The rush to Nome had drawn attention away from the Klondike and to the shores of the Bering Sea in the far western edge of the territory. Then, in August 1901, a meeting of two men—one a weary but determined Italian-American prospector and the other a fast-dealing operator eager to find a location from which to sell his boatload of trade goods—led to the settlement of what would become the largest city and the center for commerce and the justice system in the Interior.

Felice Pedroni, who took the American name Felix Pedro, grew up in a coal mining family and as a young man came to the United States and worked in mines across the country, finally making his way to Washington in the Pacific Northwest. From there he heard of gold prospects in British Columbia, and eventually, in the mid-1890s, he followed the rush to the Forty Mile country on the Yukon River. While the Klondike stampede was in full swing, Pedro headed into the hills from Circle and found color in a number of unnamed creeks. One discovery on a tributary of the middle Tanana River was so promising that he carefully marked the location before being forced to return to Circle for supplies. To his dismay, he was never able to locate that creek bed again, but knowing of its existence had only heightened his belief in the mineral wealth hidden in the hills above the Tanana Valley. With his prospecting partner, Tom Gilmore, Pedro doggedly searched until his supplies were exhausted once again. He was just about to march back to the stores in Circle when he spotted smoke from a steamer moving slowly upstream on a tributary of the Tanana River. Pedro and Gilmore hurried to investigate, and on a high bank on the north side of the Chena River they met E. T. Barnette, Barnette's wife, Isabelle, and a handful of others whose provisions and trade goods were being offloaded on the opposite bank on orders from the boat captain.

E. T. Barnette was clearly disgruntled and Isabelle practically out of her mind at the thought of facing winter in the trackless wilderness. Pedro and Gilmore purchased supplies from Barnette, and as the two prospectors made their way back into the hills to the north, the small party huddled on the banks of the Chena set to work cutting logs and constructing a dwelling and a trading post. The riverboat captain was eager to be on his way in the late summer, and as soon he felt Barnette was settled well enough, he turned his vessel downstream and departed, leaving behind the first inhabitants of what would soon become the city of Fairbanks. Barnette established his post five miles up the Chena River from its confluence with the much larger Tanana. The location was not ideal, as the meandering Chena was often difficult for large stern-wheelers to navigate. However, it was close to the promising placer deposits that an increasing number of prospectors were uncovering in the creeks to the north. In the summer of 1902, Pedro and other miners filed discovery claims on Pedro, Gilmore, and Cleary Creeks, and in September the miners held a meeting and elected Barnette recorder of the district.[24] Word of the miners' success in the hills and creeks north of the Tanana reached Dawson in December and immediately set off a rush of several hundred men to the new district.

At Judge Wickersham's request, Barnette had named the growing settlement on the banks of the Chena in honor of Charles W. Fairbanks, a Republican Senator from Indiana and aspiring presidential candidate. Wickersham had promised his support to Barnette in developing the outpost, and historians have speculated that both men believed that adding the name of a prominent politician would work to the advantage of their venture.[25] Men poured into the new town not only from Dawson but from Rampart and Circle as well, eager to stake lots, which in those first days could be had for nothing more than a small recording fee.

Meanwhile, in Nome, scandal and corruption had grown to the breaking point, and when the inept judge Arthur Noyes left town in August 1901, Wickersham was sent by the US attorney general to take charge of the court. Violence and claim jumping were regular occurrences on the creeks outside of Nome, and the court was backlogged with hundreds of disputes that Noyes had failed to deal with. In addition, corruption was rampant among law enforcement officers and a variety of government officials who had defrauded the federal government through padded and falsified expense accounts. Noyes himself was a crony of Alexander McKenzie, who claimed much of the richest mining ground in Nome. In fact, Noyes had appointed McKenzie as an officer assigned to administer disputed mining claims. McKenzie had gone all out in an effort to work the claims while they were still in litigation, and Noyes, using his position as district court judge, had backed him up. Wickersham worked tirelessly for nearly a year to clean up the corruption and conspiracy that were evident in Nome, before being replaced in July 1902 by a newly appointed judge. Wickersham's work in Nome earned him a reputation for honesty and fairness, but it also resulted in a long list of enemies among those who came out on the losing side of his decisions.[26]

Back in Eagle after a year's absence, the judge was kept busy with a heavy case load, but it was during that winter that word of paying placer gold deposits in the Tanana country and the growth of a new town as a supply center had stirred excitement along the upper Yukon. By the early spring of 1903, Wickersham was eager to investigate and possibly, as district court judge, deal with increasing reports of lawlessness in the new camp. After an arduous journey downriver from Eagle and then overland from Circle, he arrived at an unappealing cluster of log structures and canvas tents on the banks of the Chena. "A disreputable pig sty," he wrote in his diary that day. "That was Fairbanks as I first saw it on April 9, 1903." Yet over the course of the next year, he proceeded to make good on the promise he had given to Barnette to promote the town as the metropolis of the booming Interior. He bought a residential lot two blocks off the south bank of the river and started building a house. The recording office of the Fairbanks Mining District was established, and soon Wickersham oversaw construction of a jail and a courthouse. Most significantly, however, the judge officially moved the seat of the Third Judicial District from Eagle to Fairbanks, making the new town the center of law and justice in addition to the center of population, commerce, and trade. In August 1904, Wickersham remarked that the town's growth was "remarkable," and he estimated its population at two thousand.[27]

FEDERAL ACTION

Activities and events in Alaska continued to draw the attention of prominent members of US Congress, who recognized the need to provide basic government services to the small number of US citizens who occupied this immense and remote northern possession. But Congress was at a loss to understand actual conditions on the ground and how best to serve the needs of Alaskans. In the Senate, the problem fell under the purview of the Committee on Territories, chaired by Albert J. Beveridge, a Republican from Indiana and an emerging leader in the growing Progressive movement. Beveridge shared a practically identical political philosophy with his fellow Indiana senator, Charles W. Fairbanks. They had like opinions on nearly all the major issues of the day, and both had a strong desire to ably serve the people of their state. However, the two men also shared a burning ambition that turned them into bitter rivals: both wished to occupy the office then held by Theodore Roosevelt. Fairbanks was wealthy and well connected in business circles and with the railroads, and he owned a controlling interest in Indiana's largest newspaper. The younger Beveridge gained strength and influence through his association with Roosevelt, and he worked constantly to undermine Fairbanks and secure the incumbent president's nomination over Fairbanks and Senator Mark Hanna of Ohio in 1904.[28]

Like Roosevelt, Beveridge was alarmed at the power wielded by big business trusts and the defiance of government regulation shown by many of the biggest tycoons of industry. As the Progressive movement grew, he became increasingly convinced of the necessary role of government in ensuring a level playing field and opportunities for the working class. Such a need was plainly evident in Alaska, where systems of transportation and communication were grossly inadequate for the new population of miners and farmers, and the federal government's presence had been spotty at best. In March 1903, Beveridge persuaded Congress to pass a resolution calling for his Senate Committee on Territories to form a subcommittee of four senators whose task was to travel to the last frontier, assess conditions and resources, and report back with recommendations for any needed federal legislation.

As the senators prepared to embark on their fact-finding trip, Roosevelt set out on a tour of his own by rail across the western states.

Since his younger days, the president had held a special affinity for the American West, a love of the outdoors, and an intense appreciation for the natural world. Now, twenty months into his presidency, he was acting on what would become the signature issue of his public life: conservation. The Great Loop tour began on April 1, leaving Washington, DC, with Roosevelt intent on drawing public attention to the nation's wild resources and the need for federal action to protect and conserve wildlife and forest lands. He stayed two weeks in Yellowstone National Park. Later in the tour, at the rim of the Grand Canyon in Arizona, he vowed to place this natural wonder under federal protection against the efforts of large corporations to extract minerals and other resources.[29]

In California, he met the renowned conservationist and founder of the Sierra Club John Muir, and the two of them hiked and camped for three days and nights in the Yosemite Valley. Muir found an ally in Roosevelt, who promised to seek congressional protection of the area's forests and wildlife.

In city after city, the president aroused wildly cheering crowds, and Seattle was no exception. His youth, vigor, and enthusiasm for the outdoors had made him a popular figure in the West, and those features along with his message of America's greatness added to his appeal. "He was greeted like an American immortal, never to be laid low," historian Douglas Brinkley noted. "No American president had ever expressed America's identity in such a flamboyant, kinetic way."[30] Seattle, in the years since the great rush to the Klondike, had established itself as the gateway to Alaska, and the people of the city welcomed Roosevelt's words when he declared that the northern frontier was the natural extension of the nation's pioneering westward expansion. Roosevelt "represents all that is most virile and enterprising in the American character," the city's leading newspaper reported. He appeared "with the good-humored laugh of a strong man confident in himself and in the destiny of a great nation."[31] Before an audience at an Alaska reception at Seattle's Grand Opera House, Roosevelt's message fell on a crowd eager to hear about Alaska's future as an economic power and its role in contributing to America's dominance in the Pacific.

He spoke of "the greatness of triumph, the greatness of conquest, the greatness of acquisition," and he predicted a future in which Alaska would take its place as "one of the rich, mighty, and populous states of the union." But even as he lauded the pioneering spirit of those who had done so much to develop Alaska's resources, the greatest applause came with his promise of Alaska's role in America's place as a world power. "We shall make our Atlantic and Pacific coasts in effect continuous," he proclaimed to shouts of approval, "so the possession and peopling of the Alaska seacoast puts us in a position of dominance as regards the Pacific which no other nation shares or can share."

A consummate politician, Roosevelt knew his audience perfectly, and he knew what they wanted to hear. To the Alaskans present, he pledged his help in enacting legislation that would help them prosper in mining, agriculture, and fisheries. And, significantly, his pledge was given in Progressive terms to the individual pioneer, not to large corporate trusts. Laws, he said, would be framed "not in the interest of those who wish to skin the country and then leave it, but in the interest of those who intend to go there and stay there and make it in very fact as well as in name an integral part of this republic." To cheers and applause, the president expressed his hope that Congress would soon pass legislation providing for a territorial delegate from Alaska so that the people would have a formal advocate for their needs in the national legislature.[32]

Of course, Roosevelt's conservation message was not greeted with universal approval across the political spectrum. His efforts drew bitter opposition from business interests and the less progressive wing of the Republican Party. "It is better for the government to help a poor man to make a living for his family than to help a rich man make more profit for his company," Roosevelt penned in his autobiography. And when these words were translated into deeds, "many rich men were stirred to hostility."[33] A considerable number of those men were members of Roosevelt's own political party, and among the most vocal was Mark Hanna, the Ohio senator who was widely recognized as the national leader of the Republican Party and the man who had done so much to help William McKinley win two consecutive elections. Hanna had been wary of Roosevelt since Roosevelt's nomination as McKinley's running mate in 1900, and those worries nagged him throughout the first months after the election. He feared that Roosevelt's reform-minded leanings would be harmful to corporate fortunes, especially if tragedy struck and the young man were suddenly thrust into the presidency. With McKinley's death, Hanna's nightmare was realized. "That damned cowboy is president," he is said to have remarked.[34]

Enmity was directed as well at Roosevelt's handpicked head of forestry, the Yale-educated crusading conservationist Gifford Pinchot. As a friend and cohort of John Muir, Pinchot had long advocated setting aside some of the nation's prime forestlands and protecting them in perpetuity from exploitation by corporate logging and mining interests. He was a pioneer in a brand-new field, and he quickly built a reputation for himself as the country's leading expert forester. In Roosevelt, Pinchot found a president who was eager to impress upon the railroads and other industrial giants that their actions would now be subject to federal oversight and regulation. Together, the forester and the president advanced the revolutionary idea that "the forest reserves should be set apart forever for the use and benefit of our people as a whole and not sacrificed to the shortsighted greed of a few." To railroad tycoons Morgan, Hill, and Harriman, and to the lumber giant Frederick Weyerhaeuser, all of whom were accustomed to operating free from any regulatory interference, such a notion was preposterous.[35]

One month after Roosevelt's triumphant appearance in Seattle, the four members of the Senate Subcommittee of the Committee on Territories arrived in the city on their way to Alaska. William Dillingham of Vermont, Henry Burnham of New Hampshire, Knute Nelson of Minnesota, and Thomas Patterson of Colorado boarded the steamship *Dolphin* on June 28 to begin a two-month investigation that took them through the Inside Passage to Skagway, over the White Pass, and down the length of the Yukon River to St. Michael. From there, the US Revenue Cutter *McCulloch* took them to Nome, Dutch Harbor, and Kodiak before returning to Seattle. Along the way, the senators took testimony from dozens of Alaskans who expressed the need to address problems that were like those that had been encountered in the American West but were complicated by the sheer size of the Alaska territory and distances between centers of population. Committee members marveled at the fact that in total they traveled 6,600 miles, all but 111 of which were on water.[36]

The senators found that the predominant issue on the minds of Alaskans was self-government, and immediately upon entering Alaska waters they heard frustration and impatience in people's voices over

Four United States senators, members of the Senate Subcommittee of the Committee on Territories, visiting Alaska in the summer of 1903 (Alaska State Library ASL-P487-57).

and over again. On board the *Dolphin* near Ketchikan, A. P. Swineford, who had served as territorial governor for four years starting in 1885, said that Alaskans should demand the right to govern and control their own affairs. "There is no reason why we should be treated by Congress any differently than any other fragment of American territory and fraction of American people have been treated heretofore" he insisted. "That is to say, give us a government of our own." In Swineford's view, that meant not only a delegate to Congress but a territorial legislature as well. He concluded his testimony by observing that the only opponents to local self-government for Alaska were large corporations operating in their own selfish interests. Those opponents, he said, "were properly named by the president in his speech to Alaskans in Seattle—those who came here to 'skin the country' and then get out of it."[37]

However, it became apparent that opinions on the question of what form that self-government should take were quite varied. Juneau lawyer and former territorial judge Arthur K. Delaney said that the great distance and difficulty of travel between southeastern Alaska and the

Yukon River rendered territorial government for the entirety of Alaska impractical, even though according to his estimation 70 percent of Alaskans favored it. He believed that the people should have a delegate to Congress, but because of the complexity of holding an election and counting ballots cast by voters across such a vast area, the delegate should be appointed by the president.[38] Alaskans were united in their call for a delegate to Congress, but when asked whether the delegate should be elected or appointed and if they believed a territorial legislature should be established, they expressed far less unity.

By July 20, the senators and their entourage, which included stenographers, the Senate sergeant at arms, and two journalists, had reached Rampart on the middle Yukon River. Over the course of the next three days, they took testimony from five Alaskans, including district judge James Wickersham, who spoke firmly in support of the need for a delegate but stated serious concerns surrounding an election. "Points where elections would be held are so far distant from one another, and the means of communication are so slow, and the means of determining who are and are not voters are so crude, that the election can hardly be satisfactory." He concluded, however, that even under such circumstances, election was better than appointment of a delegate.[39] Wickersham also reiterated a concern that the committee heard from one end of Alaska to the other: the need for the federal government to build roads in order to "open up a larger and better country." The Canadian government, he said, had done far more to provide transportation to aid the mining economy in the Klondike than the United States had accomplished in Alaska. As a result, Dawson merchants had a great advantage over their American competitors.[40]

The Senate subcommittee listened well, and its response was a detailed thirty-two-page report that focused on a theme of federal neglect as the source of economic difficulties in Alaska. "The inaction of our government is manifest," it charged. Food goods, tools, and supplies of every description destined for the Interior had to be brought in by boat during the short season of open water, making prices exceedingly high. "[The government] has done nothing to relieve this condition," the report continued. "It has neither built roads nor provided other means of transportation, and the hardy and adventurous citizens who have sought the wealth hidden in the valley of the Yukon, the Koyukuk, and the Seward Peninsula have done so amidst difficulties that can only be understood by those who have made a study of the situation."[41]

Presented to the full Senate by Albert Beveridge in January 1904, the report laid the obligation for road construction squarely on the federal government. Development of promising discoveries of mineral resources depended upon moving heavy modern machinery, and areas such as the new settlement of Fairbanks in the Tanana Valley were ripe for growth and agriculture. "The advantages which would accrue to the vast territory which would be opened by a system of wagon roads and trails cannot be overestimated," the report said. "Vast enterprises would be established, immigration would be induced, and a permanent population wedded to the soil might result."[42] The report strongly endorsed the sentiment it found nearly universal in Alaska: that the district should have a delegate to Congress. However, on the question of whether the delegate should be elected by the people or appointed, it took no stand, saying only that, if appointed, the appointment should come from the president. Finally, the committee reported that Alaska was not yet ready for a territorial legislature. The population was too small and too scattered, systems of transportation and communication were undeveloped, and there were as yet too few permanent homes. "The time has not yet come," the report concluded. "Until it is demonstrated that agriculture can be made profitable and the population thus made permanent by fixing it to the soil, the homemaker will seek other fields."[43]

As the Senate received the subcommittee's report, the House Committee on Territories was considering Alaska affairs as well. In February, James Wickersham was in Washington after attending his son's graduation from the Naval Academy. It was an opportune time for Alaskans in the nation's capital, as the need for legislation to aid the growth of the new territory had grabbed Congress's attention. Testifying before the House committee chaired by Edward L. Hamilton of Michigan, Wickersham touted the potential of Alaska and prodded Congress to provide support to enable and stimulate development. Fairbanks had grown to "quite a city" in a year's time, he said, and he promised that within ten years the mines of the area would yield ten times as much as they did in 1903. In addition, the future of agriculture was strong enough to support a population of miners and their families with garden produce, flour, milk, and butter. The Tanana and Yukon valleys had soil that could raise gardens as fine as any to be found in the city of Washington, he boasted.[44] "The value of Alaska is so apparent that Congress ought to take notice of its importance . . . and aid in its development with kindly and considerable and needful legislation."[45]

Two items at the top of Wickersham's list were an Alaska delegate to Congress and money for roads. The delegate should be elected, not appointed, he added, saying that the people would not be satisfied unless they were given the right to choose for themselves. "Certainly they are more competent to elect their own representative than any other man or set of men is to appoint him," he asserted.[46] Finally, he told the House committee that Congress should appropriate $200,000 to build a road from Valdez to the Interior, a road that would, in his words, "do as much to open up Alaska as the old Cumberland road did to open up Ohio." The judge was asked why private capital, specifically the mining industry, should not be responsible for road construction. "The country is new and the prospectors are poor and need help," he answered. "The pioneer prospectors who braved the dangers and deserve the success will not live to secure it without help from Congress."[47]

That spring, more than one hundred bills related to Alaska were introduced in Congress, including one by Representative Francis W. Cushman of Washington to create an Alaska delegate. In presenting his bill to the House Committee on Territories, Cushman acknowledged the problems associated with a general election but stressed his opinion that an appointed unelected representative "would not in any true sense represent all of the people of Alaska." Later, in debate on the House floor, Cushman, who had recently made two trips of his own to Alaska, reiterated his argument in even stronger words. If Congress makes the delegate an appointive office, he warned, "we would be contaminating the representative character of this great body by injecting an appointive agent into the belly of an elective body."[48] Cushman's legislation specified that Alaska's congressional delegate would have the same rights and privileges as the delegates from the other US territories, and every incorporated town in Alaska would be made a voting precinct.

The Alaska measures most dear to Theodore Roosevelt's heart were those that sought to manage and protect wildlife, forests, and natural resources. Others called for improvements to infrastructure for transportation, education, and the court system and for changes to the criminal code. The president urged Congress to pass the full package. "Is it not possible to give the Alaskans a show?" he asked House Speaker Joseph Gurney Cannon. "It would be a first-class thing if we could put them all through."[49] In Congress, Roosevelt found an ally in fellow conservationist John Lacey of Iowa, and he depended on him to help get the Alaska legislation passed. He knew he could count on Beveridge, Nelson, and Dillingham in the Senate, but he needed a strong advocate in the House. "Cannot we get that Alaska legislation through?" he asked Lacey. "It does seem to me to be very important that this republican Congress should show its genuine care for the welfare of Alaska."[50]

Yet very little was done before the close of the session in April. Cushman's delegate bill passed the House, but it died in the Senate despite impassioned arguments by Beveridge and Nelson. The fiercest opposition came from Senator Orville H. Platt of Connecticut, who feared that any form of self-government might eventually lead to statehood. Platt was adamant in his belief that no US holdings outside of what he called "our home territory," meaning the boundaries of the contiguous states, should be granted statehood. He made his position clear in a letter to Dillingham of the Committee on Territories. "Whatever territory comes in outside of that should be governed by us," he declared, "and not by the people therein in the capacity of states admitted upon equal footing with the present states."[51] Ernest Gruening suggested in his comprehensive history of Alaska that Platt's true motivation was his protection of business interests in the territory from increased taxation.[52] Alaskans were deeply disappointed, especially in light of such strong support following the subcommittee hearings in Alaska and its endorsement of the need for Alaska representation in Congress. In historian Jeanette Nichols's summation, the lack of action indicated to Alaskans how little the territory could expect from Congress, and thus they felt that "they were thrown back upon their own resources."[53] But the advocates of Progressive reform and improvement of conditions in America's far north possession were far from finished. The needs were not going away, and if the Fifty-Eighth Congress failed to address them, they would be brought forward with renewed urgency in the Fifty-Ninth.

4

CONGRESS CONSIDERS
THE NEEDS OF ALASKA

*The time seems now propitious for Alaskans to press
their claims for some attention by government*

～⁓～

SOMETIME IN THE early morning of April 10, 1904, on a bank above
the Chatanika River, James Wickersham threw back his blanket and
rolled out of the tent he had hastily pitched in the snow at eleven
o'clock the night before. He dressed himself in clothes still wet from
wading for most of a day in water flowing over the top of the river ice,
knowing that in the miles ahead he would face more of the same.

Wickersham was on the final leg of his journey from the nation's
capital to Fairbanks. He had left Circle six days earlier, riding in a cutter behind a double-ender sled pulled by a single horse. The driver was
E. T. Barnette. They were accompanied by a merchant from Dawson,
who was driving a rig pulled by a horse and carrying a load of trade
goods to the new camp. In pioneer days, before roads were constructed,
April was a difficult time of year to travel in interior Alaska. It is the
month of breakup, when daytime temperatures typically rise into the
forties and hard and fast winter trails turn to slush. Still, these travelers found conditions favorable in the first days out from the Yukon
River village of Circle. On the fourth day, they crossed Twelvemile
Summit with Wickersham walking behind the sled over glacial ice.
The route then followed the Chatanika roughly along today's Steese

Highway to Cleary Creek before dropping into the Tanana Valley for the last twenty miles to Fairbanks.

A series of roadhouses awaited those on the trail, offering meals, a bed, and stables for horses and dogs. Some accommodations were better than others. At the Miller roadhouse on the second night out of Circle, Wickersham enjoyed the "glorious sunshine" with good food and a comfortable bed, and he wondered, "What more can a man—miner—want in Alaska?" But the next night, at the Twelvemile roadhouse, the district judge, the man who was inarguably the most powerful and influential federal official in all of interior Alaska,* bunked with ten other men in a fourteen-by-sixteen cabin. "Hard bed—oh yes they were hard," he wrote the next day. "My sides ache." After descending from Twelvemile Summit, the travelers found solid ice and good footing on the Chatanika, but when they reached the confluence with Faith Creek, they learned that the warnings they had been given about thin ice and deep overflow were all true. The horses' hooves broke through, and there was no choice but to lead the animals on foot. The next day, April 11, Wickersham walked eighteen miles in knee-deep water running on top of the ice until conditions improved just before reaching Cleary Creek. From there he rode by dogsled over a good trail all the way to Fairbanks. "Am now going to bed tired and sleepy," he wrote that night after a bath and dinner at the home of his brother Edgar. It was "a long hard trip of 400 miles [from Dawson], mostly afoot."[1]

Wickersham was a man perfectly fit for the rigors of Alaska life in the first decade of the twentieth century. His writing reflected the harsh and primitive conditions he found on the trails and in the mining camps and frontier towns, but it is in a tone of adventure and hardship

---

* Two months earlier, on February 8, 1904, while testifying on Alaska matters before the House Committee on Territories in Washington, Wickersham asserted that he, as federal district judge, was in essence the governor in interior Alaska. "It is a judge-governed country," he told the committee. "I am the real governor in the third district and have more executive duties to perform than Governor Brady" (House Committee on Territories 1904, p. 512). This was not mere boastfulness; it was an accurate summation of federal administration in the territory. Besides issuing decisions on all civil and criminal cases before the court, the district judge was responsible for establishing municipal limits and controlling the organization of new cities. He oversaw all liquor and business licensing and controlled the funds derived from those licenses.

without complaint, challenge without despair. He was excited by the prospect of being in on the beginnings of something that was new and growing and that, because of the hard work and spirit of the pioneers he saw around him, held great promise for the future. As he passed Cleary Creek on his final run into Fairbanks on that spring day in 1904, he noted his surprise and pleasure at the mining activity in evidence there. Where one year previously had been only a single cabin and a few prospect holes, he now saw homes and stores and "a small army of busy miners" at work in the diggings.[2]

In Fairbanks, Wickersham set out immediately to aid in the growth of the new town. He rented office space and secured a lot in a central location to begin construction of a courthouse and jail. Personally, he owned commercial property in what would become the business district, and soon he bought a lot two blocks to the east, on the corner of First and Noble, as a site for his home. Before the end of May, he was pleased with progress on his residence, and he noted construction of homes and business in all directions, including a hospital funded by the Episcopal Church. Even more encouraging was the sight of new settlers choosing Fairbanks over the rival town of Chena at the confluence of the Tanana and Chena Rivers. Low water following breakup had made riverboat navigation difficult, and Fairbanks boosters, including Wickersham, feared that the Chena town site would be more attractive to those looking for a place to settle. But, he exclaimed, "to my surprise they are coming to this town!"[3] The Northern Commercial Company had established itself on First Avenue facing the Chena, adjacent to the site of Barnette's original cache, and Sargent and Pinska also opened for business to provide goods for the working man. "Town of Fairbanks is booming," Wickersham gleefully wrote.[4]

The less respectable element of frontier boomtown life was present as well. Along with mercantile and judicial buildings, a row of dance halls, saloons, and gambling houses sprouted along the muddy street facing the river. Soon a cadre of missionaries—Catholic, Presbyterian, and, most notably, Episcopalian—began their work in earnest to offer an alternative to a life of sin and vice to lonely miners who found themselves separated from their families. In late August, Wickersham was a passenger on the stern-wheeler *Koyukuk* leaving Fairbanks and headed down the Tanana when it passed another boat plowing its way in the opposite direction laden with men and supplies. Among those onboard the incoming vessel was the Episcopal priest Hudson Stuck, who was arriving for the first time in his newly assigned mission field. The boat swung from the muddy Tanana into the clear water of the Chena River and churned nine miles upstream, where, on the evening of September 1, Stuck caught his first view of Fairbanks.

At age forty, Stuck had earlier that year been named Archdeacon of the Yukon and Tanana Valleys, and he was eager to begin his career traveling throughout the area, building churches, and seeing to the spiritual, social, and educational needs of miners, settlers, and particularly the indigenous Native population. In ten years as a parish priest in Dallas, Texas, Stuck had earned a reputation as an extremely passionate reformer who was dedicated to the conviction that the church had a role not only in saving souls but also in speaking out as an advocate for justice and improving the lives of the people in the community it served. Three years earlier, Stuck had met Alaska Bishop Peter Trimble Rowe at a general convention of the Episcopal Church in San Francisco, and he was enthralled by Rowe's tales of his travels in the north country since 1896 by dogsled and boat. Rowe was equally impressed with the ambitious and physically vigorous younger man, and he offered to make him archdeacon of a territory that included "a thousand miles of the Yukon, nine hundred of the Tanana, the Koyukuk and Porcupine, and all the camps and settlements northward to the Arctic Ocean." Eager for a chance to make a midcareer change, Stuck jumped at it.[5]

Landing in Fairbanks, Stuck found his way to the Episcopal hospital and dashed off a note to catch the outgoing mail scheduled to leave on the same boat at eight the next morning. To a correspondent in the New York office of the Missionary Society of the Episcopal Church, Stuck expressed a grim assessment of the work completed by church workers so far but eagerness to plunge into the job that lay ahead. "The 'hospital' is a bare barn," he wrote that night, "unfinished and scarce habitable even for those here now. Of course the first thing is to finish the hospital and I shall set about it at once."[6]

Stuck's letters written in his first few weeks in Fairbanks chronicled the frenzied activity occurring to supply and house the camp. The Northern Commercial Company, he reported, was "straining every nerve" to bring in enough stock to feed the four thousand people who were expected to winter there. "And I am just as anxious," he added, "to get the hospital in shape to look after the four thousand bodies and the church to look after the four thousand souls."[7]

Stuck shared Wickersham's optimism about the prospects of the Tanana goldfields and the future of Fairbanks as a residential and commercial center. All evidence showed that the mineral was there in good quantities, he said, but so far the want of provisions and machinery had limited the miners' success. "Everybody here is living and trading on hope and expectation," he observed.[8] However, the archdeacon held a much dimmer view of the Christian values exhibited by the residents and the nightly activities taking place in the center of town. "The rascality of Alaska has flocked here," he complained in an early letter. "The whole of Front Street is given over to saloons."[9] To another correspondent Stuck reported, "This is really a very rough place, and vice and dissipation of all sorts are rampant." He related the story told about the city attorney who met incoming boats and asked every woman who stepped off, "Are you a lady or a whore? If you are a lady, pass on. If you are a whore, seventeen dollars and a half." This was only a joke, he admitted, but it had an element of truth because the city drew its income from taxes on liquor, prostitution, and gambling.[10]

Spending money out of his own pocket, Stuck hurried to buy logs before freeze-up and had them rafted down to a lot the church had purchased along the river three blocks west of the center of town. There he oversaw construction of a forty-by-twenty-four-foot structure, and by the middle of October Stuck was able to report triumphantly that the Episcopalians had a sanctuary of their own rather than being forced to share space in the courthouse on Sunday mornings with the Catholics and Presbyterians. The new St. Matthew's was, he boasted, "a little gem of a church" and "the only church of any kind in more than twenty thousand square miles." Soon the building served Fairbanks not only as a place of worship but also as a public reading room stocked with books mostly from Stuck's personal collection.[11]

In the fall of 1904, the future prosperity of Fairbanks was not a sure thing. However, construction of buildings for institutions of government, for trade and commerce, and for worship gave signs of permanence. The Northern Commercial Company put up two warehouses and an electric power plant. A public school opened for the few families with children, and with the arrival of the first printing press the town had its daily newspaper. Transportation infrastructure remained the greatest need, with passengers and freight moving to the Interior by sternwheeler for four months of the year and essentially shutting down for the remaining eight. In January 1905, however, Senator Knute Nelson's dogged efforts to improve conditions in Alaska produced results when the president signed a significant piece of legislation. The law, known as the Nelson Act, went a long way toward dragging the nation's forlorn northern possession into the twentieth century. It directed that annual taxes and fees collected from businesses and licenses in the territory be used to fund schools and an adequate system of public education for non-Native children and children of mixed blood. (Education of Native children in Alaska was provided by the federal Bureau of Indian Affairs.) Further, the Nelson Act mandated that funds from those sources also be used for sorely needed construction of roads and trails. It established the Alaska Road Commission to oversee such construction, and President Roosevelt quickly appointed army Major Wilds P. Richardson as its director. At forty-four, Richardson was a West Point graduate who had been assigned to Alaska in 1897. With headquarters in Circle, he oversaw the building of army installations in Rampart, Eagle, Nome, and Haines. Now, as director of the ARC, Richardson would have access to funds to build roads, bridges, and other transportation facilities essential to the growth of population centers and access to natural resources.

Transportation in the Interior took another step forward in July 1905, when the Tanana Valley Railroad began service from the town of Chena, at the confluence of the Chena and Tanana Rivers. The line's builder, Falcon Joslin, saw the need for rail passenger and freight service to the mines as well as to the growing Fairbanks community. Joslin was a Tennessee attorney who came to Dawson with the great rush in 1898 and built a twelve-mile railroad to the coal mines there. After he moved to Fairbanks, he immediately began construction of a rail line to replace the teams of horses that were carrying loads over rough trails to the mines. He recognized that the great cost of moving freight by horse from landings on navigable rivers was "the main obstacle to the growth and development of the district."[12] The golden spike commemorating completion of the first twenty-five miles of the line was driven on July 17 by Isabelle Barnette, wife of Fairbanks founder E. T. Barnette. James Wickersham, delivering the keynote address at the ceremony, praised Mrs. Barnette as "the highest type of that noble class of frontierswoman who have dared to risk their lives to assist in establishing the foundations of American states." He noted that she had seen "the rude trading post expand under the magic touch of the miner, the merchant, the railroad builder in the City of Fairbanks."[13]

The Tanana Valley Railroad brought transportation costs down immediately. Within three years the narrow-gauge line extended forty-five miles to the mining community at Chatanika, and it carried 54,000 passengers and nearly 15,000 tons of freight annually. Joslin reported that shipping rates from the Tanana River to the mines dropped from three dollars per ton mile to fifty-eight cents.[14]

Joslin was a visionary and a man of action, and Wickersham praised him for financing his railroad entirely with private funds. But as a developer Joslin had higher aspirations for Alaska, and he believed that the future depended on an active role played by a progressive federal government. "If you lay down railroads," he urged, "the people will come." He boldly predicted that the construction of two thousand miles of track would multiply the population many times over and increase gold production to $100 million a year. "The entire nation would feel the stimulus and be profited," he argued, and government should provide the subsidy to make it possible. Private capital could not do the job alone. "The time seems now propitious," he wrote, for Alaskans to press "their claims for some attention by government."[15]

PROGRESSIVE-ERA JOURNALISM

Perhaps no political movement in American history has been more closely linked with a group of journalists and a particular style of reporting than early-twentieth-century Progressivism is with the writers and editors who came to be known as muckrakers. Progressivism and muckraking molded a mutually beneficial relationship, as reform-minded politicians were aided in their efforts by reporters who dug into conditions of political corruption, corporate monopoly, and labor injustice with an intensity rarely matched in American journalism, and Alaska provided a fertile field for these investigations. Publications emerged to accommodate these lengthy and detailed investigative pieces, which did not easily fit into the established format of the daily newspaper. Muckraking magazines included *McClure's*, *Collier's*, *Hampton's*, and others, in which a new cadre of writers became nationally known to readers who provided a limitless demand for reporting on issues of corruption, excess, and exploitation in both the public and private sectors. *McClure's* is generally credited with the beginning of the muckraking style when the magazine hit the newsstands in January 1903 featuring an article by Lincoln Steffens on local government corruption in Minneapolis, the third installment of a history of the Standard Oil Company by Ida Tarbell, and a piece on working conditions for coal miners by Ray Stannard Baker. Editor Samuel S. McClure penned an introduction that tied all three together into a single theme, summarizing them as "an arraignment of American character as should make every one of us stop and think." The articles exposed, in McClure's words, "contempt of law," "capitalists conspiring among themselves," and "the trusts' unlawful acts."[16]

Ray Stannard Baker remarked in his autobiography that the public response to this groundbreaking issue of *McClure's* was "astonishing" and "overwhelming." He gave partial credit to "a new technique of reporting which demanded thoroughness of preparation and sincerity of purpose and gave the writer the time and the freedom to cultivate those virtues." Yet Baker concluded that the true basis of its popularity was that the reading public was hungry for such news after years of hearing "soap-box orators" and politicians decrying the corruption and privilege in American life. The people on the nation's farms and in the cities believed in the truth of these charges, but the facts had remained unsubstantiated until these writers exposed them. What the muckrakers did, Baker said, "was to look at their world, *really* look at it. They reported honestly, fully, and above all interestingly what they found. And the public, now anxious and indignant, eagerly read the long and sometimes complicated and serious articles we wrote. Month after month they would swallow dissertations of ten or twelve thousand words without even blinking and ask for more."[17] One historian has calculated that over the course of nine years, starting with the appearance of the January 1903 edition of *McClure's*, muckraking reporters were responsible for more than two thousand articles published in the nation's magazines.[18]

Like the Progressive politicians who grew in prominence after 1900, the muckrakers were born out of the Populism of the Gilded Age. An older generation of journalists, including Henry Demarest Lloyd of Chicago and Elizabeth Cochrane, who became known to her readers as Nellie Bly, took on issues of government corruption and corporate exploitation of workers and consumers. Lloyd's investigations into the social effects of the industrial age on the working masses earned him a reputation as a determined journalist and reformer. Working for the *Chicago Tribune*, he wrote extensive, thoroughly researched, accurate articles on the railroad trusts, and he penned editorials attacking railroad tycoons. Lloyd gained national attention with his 1894 book *Wealth Against Commonwealth*, which exposed the workings of the mammoth Standard Oil Company and its founder, John D. Rockefeller. In the same manner of employing the craft of journalism to advance a social agenda, Nellie Bly, reporting for the *New York World*, went undercover to research inhumane conditions in the city's insane asylums and prisons and deplorable working conditions in its factories. Her carefully documented first-person articles shocked the reading public and helped set the standard for a generation of investigative reporters who came to exemplify the muckraking tradition.[19]

Ida Tarbell's style of reporting was a perfect fit for the kind of journalism McClure had set out to achieve. He had established his magazine in 1893, running fiction and entertainment but also including lengthy pieces documenting the need for progressive reform. Tarbell joined McClure in the 1890s, writing pieces on corporate greed during the pro-business years of the administration of President William McKinley and leading to her extensive work on Standard Oil. Tarbell biographer Steve Weinberg commented that she wrote about what she saw, and "she saw greed; she saw indifference to the plight of the common worker." To her, "the fallout from the big trusts such as Standard Oil seemed antithetical to democracy." McClure, Tarbell, and the entire magazine staff were "on a journalistic mission" in their efforts to expose corruption.[20]

What separated the muckrakers from the investigative reporters who preceded them was the extent to which they reached a broad national audience. The country was fractured between the haves and the have-nots, and the greed and avarice of the corporate trusts was ever more in evidence. As president, Theodore Roosevelt and his Progressive antitrust leanings brought the issue into focus nationwide, and the muckrakers' skills as expert researchers and authoritative writers provided the means for communicating it to a massive readership.[21] Furthermore, the muckraking reports illustrated to the public that corruption and lawlessness were not confined to New York but were rampant as well in cities across the Midwest and West, and these reporters and editors paid the same attention to those places as they did to conditions on the East Coast or anywhere else.[22]

The swelling populations of the nation's urban centers also contributed to the rise of muckraking journalism. Single-copy prices averaging ten or fifteen cents allowed these journals to easily reach the masses of readers. Circulation figures ran into the hundreds of thousands, and the masses eagerly consumed fact-based stories about the graft, corruption, and excesses of corporate trusts that they saw around them every day.[23] Nowhere was the public interest more excited than in the question of federal regulation of railroads. The need for reform lay principally with the weakness of the Interstate Commerce Commission and its inability to enact and enforce effective rules of conduct for the industry and to ensure a fair and competitive rate structure. This led many shippers of manufactured and agricultural goods as well as consumer groups to plead with Congress to increase the ICC's powers.[24] At the end of 1905, Roosevelt identified reform of the railroad industry as a priority of his administration, and he enlisted the help of key congressmen to accomplish it. As Congress convened in January 1906, Senator William Hepburn of Iowa filled a leadership role, introducing a bill backed by the executive branch giving the ICC authority to determine fair and reasonable railroad rates. The Hepburn Act was contested by conservative members of the president's own Republican Party, who vehemently defended the right of private enterprise to set its own rates based on market forces, not government meddling. But in June the bill passed overwhelmingly, with support from a broad coalition of Progressives from both parties. The new law placed the railroads under federal control and gave the ICC new powers to regulate the industry and control rates.[25]

Throughout this political battle, the influence of investigative journalism was significant. In particular, Ray Stannard Baker wrote a series of articles for *McClure's* detailing the effects of railroad monopolies. As the large railroads consolidated into gigantic trusts, a small group of owners was able to charge unfair rates unhindered by threat of competition. As congressional debate on the Hepburn Act heated up that spring, Baker reported on various methods the railroads were using to defeat the bill, including propaganda, threats, and intimidation. Historians and journalists broadly concur that it was because of the work of Baker and other writers that Roosevelt succeeded with his legislative package. The combined efforts of these reporters, historian Doris Kearns Goodwin concluded, "generated a widespread demand for reform."[26]

Roosevelt, meanwhile, continued a love-hate relationship with the press. It was he who, in the midst of the battle over the Hepburn Act in 1906, first applied the term "muckrakers," and it was not intended as a positive or complimentary appellation. For years Roosevelt had railed against newspapers that aimed to boost sales in mass markets by printing unjust and unsubstantiated criticism of public officials and exploiting crime and corruption merely to attract readers. His seething disdain of this type of journalism went back to his days as New York City police commissioner, when he accused publishers such as William Randolph Hearst of using "gross exaggeration and misstatement" to vilify the law enforcement methods used by police on the streets. In a piece published in the *Atlantic* in 1897, Roosevelt charged that "the sensational press" stood as the greatest force for evil in the city. "It is difficult to realize the reckless indifference to truth and decency displayed by papers such as the two that have the largest circulation in New York City," he complained. "Scandal forms the breath of the nostrils of such papers, and they are quite as ready to create as to describe it." With that article, the metaphor that later stuck indelibly to an era in the history of American journalism was conceived in Roosevelt's mind. "If the editor will stoop, and make his subordinates stoop, to raking the gutters of human depravity, to upholding the wrongdoer and assailing what is upright and honest, he can make money," he wrote.[27]

In March 1906 the president reached the limit of his patience when *Cosmopolitan*, a publication owned by Hearst, printed a series of articles under the heading "The Treason of the Senate," which in Roosevelt's view viciously and unfairly attacked leading members of his political party. Speaking at a meeting of the Gridiron Club in Washington, he invoked John Bunyan's *Pilgrim's Progress* with a reference to "the man with the muck-rake, the man who could look no way but downward." Journalists across the board felt that Roosevelt's indictment was aimed at them, and those who prided themselves on their record of solid, accurate, fact-based reporting were stunned when the president made no distinction between them and the sensationalist press. Ray Stannard Baker urged Roosevelt to clarify his remarks so the public would understand that he was not applying his "muckraker" label to competent, responsible members of the press corps. A month later, however, Roosevelt reiterated his remarks in a prepared speech given at the laying of the cornerstone of the new US House of Representatives office building. He focused his criticism on those who concentrated only on the ills and scandals of society while ignoring all that was good.

"He had attached a name of odium to all the writers engaged in exposing corruption regardless of whether they deserved it or not," Baker fumed years later in his autobiography. "It was difficult for me to understand this attack, considering all that had recently happened, all that the President owed to the investigations and reports." Baker was particularly incensed because he knew that the work done by investigative reporters had aroused widespread public opinion in support of the president's efforts to pass regulatory reform of the railroads. "He did not think it worthwhile to acknowledge the service of those men who had been striving to tell the truth honestly and completely, whose work he had repeatedly approved, and for whose help he had again and again expressed his appreciation."[28]

In Alaska, at least one journalist concurred with Baker's view. The editor of the brand-new *Fairbanks Daily Times* contended that the man with the muckrake had accomplished much good in the past few years, and that Roosevelt himself had benefited from newspaper exposure of corruption. It was such investigation of criminal activity by New York politicians that "first brought Roosevelt into prominence as the head of the police department," readers in Fairbanks learned. "No man in the country owes so much to exposure as Roosevelt." Investigative reporters incited the public against large trusts and were "responsible for the large plurality he received when he was elected president."[29]

There is little doubt, writer Mark Neuzil has concluded, that foremost in Roosevelt's mind at the time of the muckrake speech was his political foe, William Randolph Hearst, even though he did not mention him by name. In addition to controlling a vast print media empire, Hearst held a seat in Congress and in the 1904 election year had desired nothing more than to unseat Roosevelt and claim the presidency for himself. Even though Roosevelt easily won reelection that year, the comments of 1906 were clearly intended to discredit the publisher and dampen any further political aspirations he might have had.[30]

In time, however, many of the best writers and editors of the day came to embrace the "muckraker" label, and the "name of odium" became synonymous with excellence in journalism. As historian Doris Kearns Goodwin articulates in her comprehensive work on the Progressive era, leaders of the reform movement mounted "an impassioned defense of the magazine crusaders," and the public showed its appreciation for their work.[31]

Over the course of the next several years, Alaska proved to be a gold mine for muckraking reporters, who dug into issues of conspiracy and corruption reaching to the highest levels of industry and government.

ALASKA 1906

In the history of modern-day Alaska, 1906 stands out as a significantly eventful year. A newly appointed territorial governor replaced an incumbent widely scorned for his ineffectiveness and his weakness in support of popular Alaska issues; the people of the last frontier elected a delegate to represent them in the US House of Representatives; a business syndicate organized by the largest mineral extraction company in the world, in tandem with one of the most powerful financiers in New York, set up operations in the territory; and President Roosevelt withdrew from access vast tracts of land rich with deposits of coal regarded as vital to development of the northern economy. Each of these events exacted its influence, and men named Hoggatt, Richardson, Jarvis, Birch, and, of course, Wickersham played prominent roles as the Progressive era unfolded over the course of the next ten years.

Territorial Governor

On March 10, 1906, Roosevelt named Wilford B. Hoggatt to fill the office of Alaska territorial governor. Hoggatt replaced John Brady, who had become increasingly unpopular since his appointment in 1897 by William McKinley. Although Brady had supported the movement to send an Alaska delegate to Congress, he refused to get behind efforts to establish self-government through a territorial legislature.

Moreover, he had dragged his feet in carrying out Congress's directive, in 1900, to move the capital from Sitka to Juneau. A former Presbyterian missionary, Brady was hated by some but viewed by the majority of the public as basically a good man who was unfit for the duties and expectations of the office. He made "many mistakes of the head but none of the heart," the *Fairbanks Sunday Times* concluded, adding that he was "a conscientious and strictly honest man [but] he has never at any time shown himself to be a man capable."[32] James Wickersham concurred. "Brady is a good honest man," the judge noted in his diary, "but he is hopelessly incompetent and lacks executive ability."[33] However, those issues, while bothersome, were not enough to force the governor from office. His ruin came as a result of his association with the Reynolds-Alaska Development Company, in which he was a trustee and investor. It was revealed that, while in office, he had produced promotional material for Reynolds-Alaska and that the firm had fraudulently reported its assets.[34]

Roosevelt accepted Brady's resignation, and, after being urged by Wickersham, offered the governorship to David Henry Jarvis, a distinguished former officer in the US Revenue Marine Service patrolling Alaska waters on the cutter *Bear*. Jarvis and Wickersham had formed a close friendship and each did much to support and advance the other's career. By the time of Brady's resignation, however, Jarvis had left government service and had taken a position as general manager of a company that owned several salmon canneries in Alaska. He turned down the presidential appointment, citing his desire to take advantage of business opportunities.[35] Roosevelt then turned to Hoggatt. The forty-one-year-old former navy officer and lawyer, who, beginning in 1898, had prospered through ownership of mining claims in southeastern Alaska, including one at Berners Bay near Juneau, accepted immediately. The Juneau press greeted Hoggatt warmly even amid concerns that he had displayed little enthusiasm for a territorial legislature, and in June residents cheered the new governor's actions when he approved funds to rent office space and living quarters in their city. Hoggatt officially moved the seat of government to Juneau on September 8, 1906.

In his first summer in office, Hoggatt embarked on a tour to investigate conditions across the territory. After stops throughout southeastern Alaska, he traveled from Skagway to Dawson and then boarded the *Lavelle Young* for the trip down the Yukon and up the Tanana, the first territorial governor to venture so deep into the Interior. The governor transferred to the smaller *Tanana* at Chena for the short leg up the Chena River and arrived at Fairbanks on July 17, accompanied by Alaska Road Commission director Major Wilds P. Richardson. The two were greeted by residents who were excited about the prospects that the future held for their booming community and eager to welcome representatives of a government that had pledged to help them prosper. A reporter for the *Fairbanks Daily Times* was clearly impressed with the governor, describing him as "a man of pleasing appearance and of magnetic personality." And Hoggatt easily won the affection of every element of Fairbanks society when he spoke at a public reception the next night. "The crowd was a motley one," a journalist observed. "Husky sons of toil, with the mud of the creeks still on their brogans, rubbed elbows with the business and professional men of the town," and the audience included "a number of ladies, the wives, mothers and daughters of Fairbanks' best homes."[36] Hoggatt fit right in as, in the words of a prominent local attorney, "an old resident of the territory" and "a practical miner." His message was a mixture of complimentary words for the people and promises of support for development of the area's resources. "I am impressed with the sturdy character of the Tanana men," he said, "and it is my hope that in some modest way I may be a means of assistance to them in advancing the interests of this section. It will be my great pleasure to do anything I can for you."[37]

Foremost on the minds of Fairbanksans was transportation, and to address that issue Hoggatt introduced Major Richardson as the man who promised to get things done. Richardson told the crowd that federal money was available to make improvements immediately. In a tongue-in-cheek reference, he said that he had once traveled the "roads" between Fairbanks and Cleary, and "the trip engendered a feeling of hope that before the winter sets in I may be in a position to make roads of them in fact as well as in name."[38]

The next day both Hoggatt and Richardson followed up with excursions north of town to see conditions for themselves. The governor spent one night at Cleary and concluded that the rich placer deposits guaranteed a future that fully justified the use of public funds to improve road access. His knowledge of the industry immediately bolstered his credibility among miners. "Governor Hoggatt knows the men of whom he spoke," the *Daily Times* intoned. "He has been in intimate touch with the genus prospector during the twelve years he has lived in the country and knows their character and capabilities." Richardson, meanwhile, directed road commission crews to complete a number of roads in the Fairbanks area, including Cleary and Fox. The move was cheered by the *Daily Times*, which expressed relief that the burden of construction would be shifted from local people to the territorial government, paid for with funds derived from taxation.[39]

Yet notwithstanding the popular support the governor enjoyed while in Fairbanks, there remained an element of uncertainty about his support for the issue most Alaskans held dear: self-government with an elected territorial legislature. Just days after Hoggatt departed Fairbanks and set off downriver on the next leg of his journey, the *Daily Times* reprinted as its lead editorial an opinion from the *Yukon World* stating explicitly that "the governor is against representative government for Alaska."[40] It was a position that, before it was resolved, would create a political rift, with Hoggatt and Richardson on one side and Alaska's congressional delegate on the other.

Alaska Delegate

On May 7, 1906, President Roosevelt signed a bill that provided, at long last, for an elected Alaska delegate to the House of Representatives. The death of Senator Orville H. Platt of Connecticut in April 1905 removed the measure's strongest opponent in Congress, and it moved quickly to the president's desk. The delegate bill was a victory for politicians such as Minnesota Senator Knute Nelson and Washington Representative Francis Cushman, both of whom had worked for six years to secure a voice for Alaskans in Washington. The *Tacoma News* gave Cushman the majority of the credit, claiming that he would forever be known as the "father of the Alaska delegate bill."[41] The law directed that a territorywide election be held on the second Tuesday of August 1906. Two terms were to be filled: the first for the remaining session of the Fifty-Ninth Congress and the second for the full Sixtieth Congress. Immediately, the defining concern in newspapers across the territory became the relative strength of each candidate's support for a bona-fide territorial form of government, including an elected legislature. "The issue in Alaska is self-government," the Skagway *Daily*

Alaskan explained. "The surest way to get this kind of government is to send as our first delegate to Congress a man who will ask for it as the paramount question."[42]

With only three months' time between enactment of the law and Election Day, political parties in Alaska were forced to move quickly. Conventions in July put forth three sets of candidates. Republicans meeting in Juneau on July 14 nominated C. D. Murane of Nome for both terms; Democrats in Juneau on July 16 named H. W. Mellen for the long term and former territorial governor A. P. Swineford for the short term; and in Nome an independent coalition representing the miners of the Seward Peninsula and of the Tanana region nominated Frank Waskey for the short term and Thomas Cale for the long term.

Press coverage and endorsements generally reflected regional familiarity with the candidates. In Skagway, Swineford stood out because of his long-standing unequivocal advocacy of home rule. "He stands for the government of Alaska by Alaskans," the Skagway *Daily Alaskan* wrote, adding a biting criticism of the opposing party's platform statement on the issue. Indeed, at their territorial convention, Republicans had called for appointment or election of a citizens' group, which would study the issue and then propose any necessary legislation. To the editor of the *Daily Alaskan*, this amounted to "a law-making bastard commission," which would be "selected in a manner and by an authority to be designated by a paternalistic congress."[43]

Both the Democratic Party and the coalition of Nome and Fairbanks miners agreed with this strident assessment of the Republican position. The Democratic platform stated that local self-government is "one of the cardinal principles of democracy" and should be granted to Alaska immediately. The party declared itself to be "unalterably opposed to any commission . . . such as proposed by the Republican platform," calling such a thing "un-American" because it denied the right of US citizens to make their own laws.[44] Likewise, the miners—self-described as "the intelligent and sturdy argonauts and pioneers resident in this productive commonwealth"—proclaimed home rule as their "God-given heritage." The first plank of their platform called for establishment of a territorial form of government at the earliest possible date.[45]

Observers in southeastern Alaska recognized the strength of the independent miners' coalition and knew that the combination of Waskey for the short term and Cale for the long term would be difficult to beat. The Skagway *Daily Alaskan* endorsed Cale and continued its support for Swineford. Meanwhile, its rival paper in Juneau, the *Daily Alaska Dispatch*, mocked Swineford as "a lightweight in the political game"[46] and refused to give him even the slightest chance of winning election over Waskey for the short term. For the long term, the *Dispatch* threw its support to local mining lawyer H. W. Mellen on the contention that southeastern, because of its long status as the center of population and government in Alaska, deserved the right to choose one of its own residents as the first delegate. "This section feels that its age as a settled district entitles it to the first delegate for the long term," the editor wrote.[47] As for Cale, a Fairbanks miner, the Juneau paper was dismissive of his qualifications for office and based its disapproval not on his politics but on his lack of success in finding gold. "He cannot be called a miner except that he has devoted considerable time to seeking paydirt in the placer region of the Tanana. In this his success has been so slight that he has to devote his time to wood chopping for a living."[48]

Election results produced a landslide win for Waskey and Cale. In the weeks leading up to the election, the *Fairbanks Daily Times* had spilled a barrel of ink across its pages in urging the miners to come out and cast their ballots in favor of sending their two cohorts to Congress, and the men working the creeks of the Interior and the Seward Peninsula and those living in the new communities of Fairbanks and Nome responded in surprising numbers to do just that. In the race for the short term, Waskey polled 4,849 votes to Swineford's 1,572 and Murane's 2,252; for the long term, Cale took 5,819 votes to Mellen's 1,093 and Murane's 2,324.

Two days after Election Day, the *Daily Alaska Dispatch* acknowledged that the people of southeastern Alaska had been deluding themselves into believing that they held the balance of political power in their hands. There was a slight suspicion that such was not the case, the editor said, but this election proved otherwise. "We have received a severe jolt," he said, noting that in the Tanana and Yukon River districts more votes were cast for Cale alone than the total number of votes cast for all candidates in the southeast. "The awakening is rude," the writer despaired, concluding that by all appearances, "Southeastern Alaska is a nonentity in territorial politics."[49]

Waskey and Cale had based their campaigns on unequivocal advocacy of territorial self-government in Alaska, and that is the issue that made it possible for an overwhelming majority of voters to support them.

The Alaska Syndicate

Stephen Birch was equal parts mining engineer and aggressive business speculator. He was not a man who was averse to risk. In 1900, when he saw the great potential of the copper deposits discovered in the Wrangell Mountains, he jumped immediately to acquire those claims, and even while his ownership and right to work the land were being disputed in court, he invested $400,000 in development. He knew that the claims held world-class quantities of high-grade copper ore, but the cost of accessing and extracting the mineral and transporting it to market was far out of his reach. In fact, the operation would require expertise that only the world's best mining corporations possessed and an investment that only the wealthiest of New York financiers could afford.

The lawsuit contesting Birch's ownership of the claims was settled in a decision rendered by Judge Wickersham after hearing arguments in the case in Valdez in 1903. As Wickersham explained the complicated matter in his memoir *Old Yukon*, the rich copper deposit was found in 1900 by Jack Smith and Clarence Warner, who were part of a group of miners, led by R. F. McClellan, working for an entity known as the Chittyna Exploration Company. That summer, while McClellan and the rest of the company were doing work in the area, Smith and Warner ventured out on their own and made the discovery. They immediately registered claims in the names of eleven members of the McClellan party, and it was these claims that Stephen Birch purchased from the individual titleholders at very reasonable prices. Soon, however, the Chittyna Exploration Company cried foul, contending that Smith, Warner, and all the members of the McClellan party were in their employ at the time of the discovery, and therefore the company was the true owner of the mines. In the end, Wickersham did not see it the company's way. He concluded that Smith and Warner were independent prospectors and were neither agents nor employees of the company, and he ruled in favor of the defendants.[50] With the judge's decision, Birch's title to the mines was uncontested, and the way was clear for him to seek the backing he needed.

Soon the Guggenheim family, which in the last half of the nineteenth century had amassed a fortune in large-scale industrial mining of lead, silver, copper, and other minerals across the American West, got word of the rich deposits and sent an assayer to Alaska to investigate. The man returned and reported millions of tons of 70 to 75 percent pure copper, making it possibly the richest copper deposit in the world.[51] Birch's efforts to persuade the Guggenheims to buy in clearly impressed the corporate leaders. On April 3, 1906, company president Daniel Guggenheim told the *New York Times* that he believed Alaska would soon become the greatest mineral-producing region of the United States. He added, however, that the days were past when an individual prospector could find his fortune with a pick and a pan. A huge investment in transportation and other infrastructure would be required for development in the far northern frontier. "We want to go into the territory and build railroads and smelters and mining towns and bring men there and populate the country where it is habitable and do for it what the early figures in American railroad building did for sections of the Great West," he said.[52]

In the summer of 1906, Guggenheim decided to inspect conditions in Alaska for himself. He left New York on July 21 and returned six weeks later to tell the *Times* that nothing he saw disappointed him and that his company was moving ahead with designs for large-scale operations. He said that the days of success for the individual prospector were over, but the future was bright for those with money to invest in roads and "great dredging machines and other modern devices for laying open the earth" and for those men who were willing to work at mining for wages.[53]

The *Times* itself noted in an editorial that Guggenheim's plans for Alaska brought to mind "the wonders of Aladdin's lamp." Yet the paper concluded that "success is a question of time, of capital, of intelligent business and technical administration, and of reasonable territorial government."[54]

For the capital part of that equation, Daniel Guggenheim turned to the greatest business mind and one of the wealthiest men of the era, J. P. Morgan. In a meeting arranged with the great financier of Wall

Street, Guggenheim gave an effusive description of Alaska's mineral potential, at the conclusion of which Morgan was convinced. "I am ready for action," Morgan said,[55] and by November the business alliance that formed the Alaska Syndicate had come into existence. Guggenheim provided about one-third of the money and would run the mining and administrative side of the deal; Morgan and a third investor, Jacob Schiff, guaranteed the remainder of the capital.[56] The Alaska Syndicate then moved swiftly to acquire interest in companies that would make it possible to develop the vast copper resources and transport and process the ore. The most significant of those business entities were the Copper River and Northwestern Railway, which when built would provide transportation from the mines to tidewater, and the Northwestern Commercial Company, which would operate steamships to move the ore to the Guggenheim smelter in Tacoma.

Stephen Birch and David Jarvis retained active roles in the newly formed multifaceted syndicate. Birch, whose focus remained exclusively on developing the mine, became one of three managing directors based in New York. Meanwhile, Jarvis, who had been general manager of a salmon canning subsidiary of the Northwestern Commercial Company, became one of three West Coast managers of the Morgan-Guggenheim operation. Jarvis's particular expertise was in steamships, and that, along with his executive abilities, made him a trusted member of the syndicate team.[57]

Coal Land Withdrawals

The key element of the Alaska Syndicate's plans for mining copper was undoubtedly the railroad. Without it, transportation of workers, building materials, tools, and supplies of every description needed to sustain the operation was impossible, and, of course, movement of copper ore from the mines to tidewater for shipment to the Guggenheim smelter was impossible as well. In order to run the trains, a reliable and economical source of coal was of paramount importance. The syndicate believed it had found that source in the Bering River coalfields not far from the mouth of the Copper River.

At the time of the formation of the Morgan-Guggenheim partnership, the best route for the railway two hundred miles inland to the copper mine site at Kennecott remained undecided. Geographically,

Valdez was the closest harbor, and townspeople there, including the local newspaper, were eager to see track laid to get the project moving. The Copper River and Northwestern Railway, now controlled by the syndicate, acquired the right-of-way through Keystone Canyon in January 1906 and began work leading to the rugged terrain of mountains and glaciers lying between Valdez and the Interior. Meanwhile, however, a railroad construction engineer named Michael J. Heney had secured the right-of-way for an alternate route running up the Copper River to the future mines. Heney was well known for having built the White Pass and Yukon Railroad from Skagway to Whitehorse in two years, beginning in 1899. Yet in southcentral Alaska he was faced with elements never before encountered in the history of railroading. The Miles and Childs Glaciers flowed down from the mountains and terminated with icy fronts facing each other from both sides of the Copper River sixty miles upstream from the mouth. Heney had studied this challenge and had determined that it was possible to bridge the river and run the line between the two glaciers. He became so convinced of the superiority of this route over the one beginning in Valdez that he invested his own money in construction of a line starting from the Native village of Eyak, where in 1905 he purchased an abandoned salmon cannery to serve as railroad headquarters. A year later, the town of Cordova had been established at the site, and Heney landed crews and equipment there to begin construction. This location had the advantage of its proximity to the Bering River coalfields. Soon the syndicate became convinced as well, with its motivation being to join the vast copper resources together with the unlimited supply of Bering River coal. The syndicate abandoned its work in Keystone Canyon, bought the right-of-way from Heney, moved to Cordova, and threw the resources of the Copper River and Northwestern Railway behind construction of a line following Heney's proposed route up the river to Kennecott.[58]

The Alaska Syndicate quickly became the most powerful economic force in the territory. In addition to the copper mines and the railroad, it controlled the Northwestern Commercial Company and its three subsidiaries: the Alaska Steamship Company, the salmon packing company Northwestern Fisheries, and a freighting company operating on the Seward Peninsula, the Northwestern Lighterage and

Development Company. It appeared, as one historian observed, that "the syndicate had a finger in every financial and exploitative venture in Alaska."[59] And its influence was felt in the political arena as well. When Progressives in Congress advanced a bill to federally subsidize construction of a railroad to the Interior, David Jarvis appeared in the nation's capital to voice the syndicate's opposition. He argued that such action would unfairly interfere with private enterprise and would bankrupt the companies that had already begun construction. Jarvis's lobbying efforts were so persuasive that he was credited with stopping the bill in its tracks.[60]

For Progressives in the era of popular antitrust sentiment, the expression of such economic and political power was an instant red flag. The Morgan-Guggenheim syndicate controlled mining, transportation, and fisheries in Alaska, and with affordable coal so vital to its railroad, the empire aimed to make that resource its next acquisition. The Bering River coalfield was open to access under the US homestead laws, which had been extended to Alaska in 1900.[61] However, Congress, in order to thwart monopoly control of the resource, limited private claimants to tracts no larger than 160 acres, rendering large-scale coal mining essentially uneconomical. The restrictions imposed by this law were unrealistic and unworkable, and across the West, wherever large coal deposits were found on federal lands, corporations and railroads had for years either ignored or openly defied them. Coal operators were forced to engage in what one historian has labeled "necessary fraud" by buying up individual holdings and combining them to gain access to a tract large enough to make mining profitable.[62]

President Roosevelt found the situation intolerable, and he believed that it was Congress's responsibility to craft new legislation to provide a legal avenue for corporations and railroads to mine coal on federal land profitably and under government oversight. Furthermore, from his standpoint as both a conservationist and an antimonopoly Progressive, Roosevelt was alarmed by the threat posed by the Morgan-Guggenheim trust, which he suspected intended ultimately to buy up and consolidate coal claims and prevent construction of competing railroads. On November 11, 1906, he took action, completely withdrawing from entry all coal leasing on federal lands. His intent was to stop the process and give Congress time to enact a new, fair, and workable system of leasing. Recalling the issue years later in his autobiography, Roosevelt wrote that under the old system, coal lands were being leased to developers, mostly big corporations and railroads, for "wholly inadequate prices," often as little as $10 to $20 per acre, and without assurance against monopoly. "When this condition was brought to my attention," he explained, "I withdrew from all forms of entry about sixty-eight million acres of coal land in the United States, including Alaska."[63]

If newspaper coverage can be considered a gauge of public opinion, the move aroused little response across the territory. Papers generally reported simply that the president's action was needed to blunt monopolistic control of the Alaska economy. Newly elected congressional delegate Frank Waskey commented in the *Alaska Prospector* of Valdez, saying that the withdrawal was intended "to curb certain financial interests which are endeavoring to monopolize the coal deposits of Alaska and which are trying to grab all of the mineral deposits of the Copper River valley."[64] The effect and extent of the withdrawal were yet unknown. The staunchly pro-development Seattle-based *Alaska Monthly* magazine could only speculate that the action had the potential of stopping all railroad construction and that those companies that had already invested millions of dollars in Alaska's future were now left "holding the sack."[65]

As 1906 came to a close, no one in Alaska or Washington, DC, would have predicted that years would pass before Congress was able to enact legislation to resolve the problem of coal leases on federal lands. Before the issue was settled, it would cause bitter enmity among those who complained of the abuses visited upon Alaska by the federal government.

5

THE ALASKA SYNDICATE EMERGES AS AN ECONOMIC AND POLITICAL FORCE

First I'm in—and then I'm out.
The Guggys know what they're about.
Then I'm out—and now I'm in.
The Guggs, you know, have lots of tin.

⁓⁓

IN 1907, hard lines were drawn and the battle turned bloody. In January, Governor Hoggatt appeared in Washington, where the second session of the Fifty-Ninth Congress was getting under way, and Thomas Cale was taking Frank Waskey's place as Alaska's congressional delegate. Hoggatt's actions did not sit well with the proponents of territorial self-government back home. Working with David Jarvis, the governor lobbied as best he could to persuade congressmen and senators that home rule was bad business for Alaska. The *Daily Alaska Dispatch* of Juneau reported "a merry war" being waged, with Waskey and Cale fighting on one side of the issue and Hoggatt and Jarvis on the other. Senator Knute Nelson, who maintained his abiding interest in the needs of Alaska and who continued as a member of the Committee on Territories, "declared that he had the utmost contempt for Captain Jarvis, who was nothing but a paid lobbyist for certain interests in Alaska."[1]

There could be no mistake about who those "certain interests" were. "Back of Alaska's demand for more political autonomy is a fight to save the vast region from the clutches of the Guggenheims," the *Alaska*

Dispatch charged in an editorial. "Already the monopoly has placed its grasping hand on the territory. [It] is the menace which threatens the wealth and freedom of competition in Alaska, and it is ably aided and abetted by financial interests that center about J. Pierpont Morgan."[2]

President Roosevelt, for his part, was determined to protect Alaska and conserve its resources, especially with the Alaska Syndicate's formulation of plans for large-scale mineral extraction. He moved quickly to create vast tracts of National Forest lands, in July designating 5.4 million acres in southcentral Alaska as the Chugach National Forest, and in September creating the seventeen-million-acre Tongass National Forest in southeastern Alaska. Significantly, the Chugach included the Bering River coalfield, which the syndicate intended to exploit as a major source of fuel for the Copper River and Northwestern Railway running to the Kennecott copper mine. The two National Forest designations delighted Gifford Pinchot, the Roosevelt administration's chief forester. They fit perfectly with his philosophy, as he hailed Roosevelt's conservation efforts as "the most significant achievement" of his presidency. "The conservation of natural resources is the key to the future," Pinchot wrote. "The very existence of our nation, and of all the rest, depends on conserving the resources which are the foundations of its life."[3]

The trust-busting aspects of Roosevelt's Progressive agenda were well received among the pioneering settlers of the territory, but conservation measures of this kind were not met with such enthusiasm. Alaskans had three intertwined issues on their minds: unhindered access to resources with economic development based on mineral extraction, resistance to the economic strength and avarice of the Morgan-Guggenheim syndicate, and the demand for self-government through a local elected legislative body.

In Valdez, feelings ran especially high. Hopes for a railroad terminus in the city had been raised, and when the Guggenheims started construction through Keystone Canyon, a prosperous future seemed assured. In 1906, the *Valdez News* reported that the first twenty miles of the road would be completed by the end of the summer, predicting that "The people of Valdez will ride on a train through Keystone Canyon before snow flies in the fall. Hurrah!"[4] But before the end of that year, the syndicate abruptly shut down construction in the canyon and shifted its focus to Katalla, which had ready access to coal

President Theodore Roosevelt, left, and Gifford Pinchot in 1907. Pinchot was Roosevelt's friend and trusted confidant, who advised the president on conservation issues (Library of Congress Prints and Photographs Division LC-DIG-ppmsca-36197).

deposits. Eventually, the company settled on a terminus in Cordova and a route up the Copper River. The people of Valdez were left feeling betrayed by false hopes and bitterly resentful of the world of high finance represented by J. P. Morgan and the Guggenheims. And adding to the intensity of emotion was certainly the general antitrust sentiment of Progressive-era America. Suddenly, everything Alaskans hated was wrapped up in one entity called the Alaska Syndicate, which not only monopolized key industries but stifled competition and controlled employment as well.

The people of Valdez come out to lay the first rails for construction of the Alaska Home Railway in 1907 (Alaska State Library ASL-P192-17).

As further insult, the syndicate exerted its influence in an effort to kill Alaskans' favorite political cause, representative territorial self-government. Like the Juneau paper, the *Alaskan* of Cordova reported on a "fierce fight" being waged over the issue, with the Morgan-Guggenheim syndicate said to be backing the opposition. The paper identified Hoggatt as a leader of the forces against, saying that he "insists that the real business men of Alaska do not want territorial government."[5] The *Fairbanks Evening News* reported an even stronger comment: "Hoggatt says that self-government by Alaskans is advocated by only saloon-keepers, saloon bums, and demagogues," adding that the differences between the governor and the territory's congressional delegation were growing. "Every day shows them to be more and more diametrically opposed on the question of the needs of Alaskans."[6]

The people of Valdez, meanwhile, had not given up on dreams for a railroad, and in the summer of 1907 the town eagerly welcomed a fresh proposal by businessman Henry Derr Reynolds and his associate, former territorial governor John Brady, to build one. Reynolds sold shares in a new company, capitalizing on the public's intense animosity toward the hated Guggenheims. Even the name of the enterprise, Alaska Home Railway, evoked an aura of can-do confidence in defiance of the evil syndicate. At a public meeting held on a Saturday evening in August, the townspeople collectively purchased $105,000 in stock at a dollar a share. "The great corporate interests of the East have been gradually extending their sphere of influence with the obvious intention of absolutely controlling the transportation facilities of Alaska," the *Alaska Prospector* said. "It is high time that the people were aroused to the danger of the situation." The paper praised Reynolds for leading "a fight of the people for their rights."[7]

James Wickersham, who happened to be holding court in Valdez at the time of the excitement, remained outwardly noncommittal, primarily because he had heard rumors that the company had been paying dividends out of income derived from new stock sales. Privately, however, he scoffed at Reynolds, Brady, and the entire enterprise. From outside the meeting hall on the night of the mass meeting, he heard "swelling applause" as the two promoters "gave vent to abuse of the trusts." The next morning Wickersham wrote that the town was "feverish" and that the meeting was "a most skillful game to get the citizens of the town bound to the Reynolds-Brady scheme." The two men "denounced the trusts in the name of the Bible," he wrote. "The whole revival meeting is so ludicrous and funny to one who is able to stand aside and look on; but the gullible flocked to their mourners' bench with subscriptions."[8]

Reynolds promised to start construction immediately upon sufficient investment from the public stock offering, and indeed the project got under way in the summer of 1907. On August 15, the *Alaska Prospector* reported that a large crowd had turned out "to see the first dirt fly on the Alaska Home Railway" as Valdez citizens grabbed picks and shovels and volunteered to help clear the first mile. "The town is united as never before, and every petty difference is buried beneath a whirlwind of enthusiastic activity," the *Alaska Prospector* wrote. "It is as though a wizard's wand had aroused the dormant energies of a mighty people."[9] As the *Cordova Alaskan* put it, Valdez had a severe case of "Reynoldsitis," adding that "the people have almost gone nutty, running around town with hats on and estimating their wealth by the millions."[10]

Within days, however, workers witnessed the first signs of trouble. The Alaska Syndicate, while it had stopped construction work on the line out of Valdez, had not abandoned its ownership of the right-of-way through Keystone Canyon. Having no intention of allowing access to a competing railroad, syndicate bosses sent a small crew to maintain a presence in the narrow passage through the mountains seventeen miles out of town. The action set up an inevitable conflict with Reynolds and his backers who, according to the *Alaska Prospector*, "really mean business." Alaska Home Railway crewmen vowed that if confronted with opposition, "we shall meet it and go anyone one better that tries to make us trouble in any way." One Home Railway construction engineer expressed the crew's resolve. "We are going to have trains running on real iron rails before winter and that is all there is to it," he said.[11] The Cordova paper smelled trouble as well, and when the syndicate sent "a gang of men" into the canyon to see that their part of the right-of-way was not infringed, the paper predicted that a "scrap" between the Guggenheim and the Reynolds factions was inevitable.[12]

A sign prominently posted on August 28 warned Alaska Home Railway workers that they were "forbidden" from entering or trespassing on the right-of-way owned by the Copper River and Northwestern Railroad. Reynolds responded by posting a notice of his own to the men in his employ. "You are working for the people of Alaska who will protect you," it said. "Pay no attention to the trust or any of its schemes to block progress. The citizens of Valdez are standing back of you."[13]

On September 25 the tense situation came to a head in what the *Seattle Post-Intelligencer* reported as a "bloody fray."[14] A crew of unarmed Home Railway workers who entered the canyon were told to stop. They ignored the order, and the guards opened fire. Six men were hit, and one later died of his wounds. The results were immediately disastrous for the Alaska Syndicate as its public image, already at a low level among Alaskans, dropped even further. "There was no sort of excuse for the brutal attack on certain railroad employees," the *Post-Intelligencer* editorialized three days after the incident. "They cannot be shot down in cold blood." The paper added a reminder about laws preventing monopoly as well as a subtle dig at Hoggatt, warning the governor, well known for his pro-syndicate leanings, that he would "fail woefully" if he did not demand full prosecution of the men responsible for the shootings.[15]

A mere three weeks later, the Alaska Home Railway was out money and out of business. As the *Alaska Prospector* reported on October 17, "word was received that all hopes of raising the amount necessary to continue operations was gone and consequently all work has been stopped and the men will be in town today."[16] The editor of the Cordova paper could not resist gloating, writing that the sudden end of the Reynolds plan came as predicted. "Valdez is the latest town to have the wool pulled over her eyes," the *Cordova Alaskan* said. "The schemer has financially ruined her. The $106,000 raised by subscription has faded away and nothing to show for it except a few miles of graded road bed—minus the rails—that leads nowhere and is essentially useless."[17]

The loss of the Alaska Home Railway coupled with the violence perpetrated on unarmed workers at the hands of Morgan-Guggenheim guards intensified hatred of the syndicate and everything it stood for, especially its opposition to Alaska self-government. The *Seattle Post-Intelligencer*, a strong and consistent supporter of the movement, vilified Governor Hoggatt for his contention that the businessmen of the territory stood against it. On the contrary, the paper editorialized, they "seem to be willing to shoulder the burden, and they should be allowed to do so." As American citizens, the paper concluded, "they are entitled to the American system of public administration, fashioned after the well-known and long-tried American model."[18]

While the issue of self-government remained at the forefront of public opinion, Republicans across Alaska were preparing to convene in Juneau in November. One predominant piece of business was the selection of delegates to represent the territory at the next year's national party convention. In preparation for the Juneau convention, Republicans meeting in Valdez early in the month provided a good indicator of the mood of the party membership. In the words of the *Cordova Alaskan*, they gave Governor Hoggatt "a good dressing down." They endorsed President Roosevelt's efforts to control "the illegal combination of capital known as the trust," they urged Delegate Thomas Cale to introduce legislation to give Alaska territorial government, and, in the most strongly worded declaration of all, they asked the president to investigate the conduct of Governor Hoggatt, who, they contended, had been biased in his examination of the shootings in Keystone Canyon and had interfered with the prosecution of those charged in the incident. "An investigation will show that Gov. Hoggatt is not a suitable person for the high office of governor of the territory," the resolution stated.[19]

For the Seattle paper, the Juneau convention was an opportunity for Alaskans to make their issue known to Congress. The *Post-Intelligencer* urged Republicans to select delegates who would demand that the national party insert home rule for Alaska in its platform. "Then Congress will give heed," the *P-I* concluded.[20]

As the territorial convention came together on November 14, the proceedings were overshadowed by a deep division among party members centered on Hoggatt's administration and the governor's stand on the home-rule question. Within the party, one faction pushed for a strong resolution in favor of self-government while a smaller group supported the governor and his opposing position. It immediately became clear that, with the issue so divisive and the sides so entrenched, no compromise was possible. From the outset, the anti-Hoggatt forces were in control, and with little delay the governor's supporters, numbering about thirty-five, bolted in protest, leaving the remaining members free to craft resolutions and choose delegates. "The anti-Hoggatt party would refuse to be swerved from their determination to put the convention on record as strongly against the Hoggatt administration," the *Post-Intelligencer* reported. "The adoption of a strong home-rule declaration is, of course, a foregone conclusion."[21] Editorially, the *P-I* praised the Alaska Republicans for their strong and persuasive stand. "The opposition has shrunk to nothingness," the paper said. "The representatives of the federal officials and outside corporations, who alone opposed the granting of self-government to the territory, finding themselves in a petty and hopeless minority, withdrew from the convention to save their faces." The writer concluded that the remaining question was "whether the desires of the people or those of outside investors" would prevail.[22]

Within weeks, the stinging rebuke of Hoggatt from the governor's own party cut even deeper, this time following a blow delivered by the president himself. On December 3, with the opening of the Sixtieth Congress, Roosevelt delivered his annual address, and in it he announced his backing of the home-rule movement. "Some form of local self-government should be devised for Alaska, as simple and inexpensive as possible," he stated. The president also reiterated at great length his position in regard to corporate monopoly, making it clear that he was not against the partnering of big corporations in all instances, but that antitrust regulation was necessary to protect the public and consumers from unfair practices. He advocated a policy of "discriminating between those combinations which do good and those combinations which do evil."[23] The *Seattle Post-Intelligencer* was delighted with Roosevelt's words. "If Alaskans and the friends of the northern country at the nation's capital will do what they ought to do," it said in an editorial, "Alaska will soon come into full possession of the territory's undoubted constitutional rights."[24]

In the midst of this commotion, the political waters were stirred further by James Wickersham's announcement that he was resigning his appointed position as federal judge. Wickersham had always been considered to be a likely candidate for congressional delegate, and his sudden resignation only heightened that speculation. The judge had routinely been reappointed at the end of his terms by President Roosevelt, but he had always faced tough confirmation battles. Opposition to him in Congress was led by Senator Knute Nelson, who could not forgive Wickersham for his role in 1904 in defeating a favorite cause of Nelson's, that of establishing a fourth judicial district in Alaska. Since then, Wickersham had been retained not through the normal congressional confirmation process but by a series of recess appointments initiated by the president between sessions. Nelson had plenty of support from Fairbanks residents who accused Wickersham of dishonesty and favoritism in his court, and in a letter to Wickersham written at the time of confirmation hearings before the Senate Judiciary Committee in 1906, Nelson enumerated a list of ten charges. The first of those accusations centered on the judge's association with E. T. Barnette, his acceptance of a gift from Barnette of a prime piece of real estate in Fairbanks, and his subsequent actions in deciding court cases in Barnette's favor. Nelson cited a case involving a disputed mining claim in which a jury had found against Barnette but Wickersham had set aside the verdict, allowing Barnette to turn a handsome profit. In that and many other cases, Nelson wrote, "you have manifested a disposition in judicial proceedings to favor Capt. Barnette." The senator also detailed a pattern of tolerance for illegal and immoral activities in charges supported by statements made by reliable people of Fairbanks. They contended that an establishment known as the

Horse Shoe Saloon was operating with Wickersham's "knowledge and implied consent" on the lot Wickersham had received as a gift from Barnette. Nelson also presented charges that Wickersham had a record of favoring lawyers who supported him politically "while you are disposed to embarrass and obstruct in various ways the attorneys who you think are not friendly to you."[25]

In September 1907, Wickersham, knowing that he was headed for another fierce confirmation fight, had made his decision, and he began drafting his resignation letter. "It seems hopeless to expect those senators who have opposed my confirmation to ever cease to do so," he told the president. "I have greatly desired confirmation by the Senate of your action of reappointing me as judge in this frontier district, but I now think it is vain to expect it."[26] In reality, Roosevelt had lost patience with the judge and with the unrelenting criticism and incessant confirmation fights, and he expressed despair over what he saw as pervasive corruption and lawlessness among federal appointees in the frontier boomtowns of the north. "Several years of experience of Alaskan officials makes me feel that if we get one who cannot be successfully accused of breaking say seven out of the ten commandments, we have done rather well," he said in a letter to the attorney general.[27] In past years, the president had stood by Wickersham, believing that hostility toward him had come primarily from bitter losing contestants in cases decided by the judge. "[I] came to the conclusion that while there were things in his past which were not what they ought to have been, yet that on the whole he had been sinned against rather than sinning," Roosevelt recalled in a letter written years later. By the fall of 1907, however, his confidence in the judge had dwindled to nearly nothing on evidence that Wickersham was "showing great laxity" in enforcing liquor laws and laws against gambling and prostitution.[28] He responded to Wickersham's resignation letter with a terse two-sentence note, accepting it "with regret" and adding, "I appreciate fully, however, why you feel you must leave."[29] The *Seattle Post-Intelligencer* reported the resignation in a front-page story on September 28, citing opposition to Wickersham in the Senate along with opportunities for him to earn more income as a private practice attorney as the reasons.[30]

Another factor contributing to Wickersham's action was undoubtedly his relationship with Governor Hoggatt. The two men, both direct presidential appointees, had worked together in a cooperative and friendly manner for more than a year, but in recent months the relationship had soured. The source of the conflict dated from that summer, when Wickersham issued a legal decision with which Hoggatt disagreed. The judge had refused to disbar a lawyer and political foe of the governor after a criminal conviction. Hoggatt was incensed, and when he made his opinions public, Wickersham knew that the days of social and professional collaboration with the governor were at an end. In his diary he noted that Hoggatt and others were "tearing their hair and rending their garments" following issuance of the decision, but that he would not bend. "They can go to the devil," he declared. "Finis, Governor."[31] In his resignation letter, picked up and reported by the press, Wickersham wrote that Hoggatt's views were "unjust and presumptuous, but his opposition and his refusal to support the court added greatly to my burden."[32]

Over the course of the few months following his resignation from the federal bench Wickersham's political persona evolved, especially in regard to the fierce hatred of the Morgan-Guggenheim syndicate that defined his career as Alaska's delegate to Congress. His stance on territorial self-government at times appeared solid, especially following a speech he delivered in Fairbanks in October at a banquet held to commemorate the fortieth anniversary of the 1867 purchase of Alaska from Russia. After giving a long and detailed interpretation of Alaska's legal status within the federal government, he concluded his speech with an unequivocal statement in favor of self-government. "It is the first step in the progressive evolution of a constitutional form of government," he stated. "The highest ideal of government is one 'of the people, by the people, for the people'."[33]

Yet in early 1908, as he was setting himself up in private practice in Fairbanks, he continued to nurture a friendly relationship with Stephen Birch and David Jarvis, two Alaska Syndicate officials who were enemies of the cause. In a letter on February 1, he asked Birch to continue to write with the latest news concerning syndicate business. "I am always greatly interested in your success," he wrote, "and I try to keep posted in relation to transportation matters and railway building in the neighborhood of the Copper River."[34]

Birch responded in early April with a query about Wickersham's availability as a legal representative of the syndicate in Alaska.[35] The prospect did indeed interest Wickersham, and he replied with a pro-

Stephen Birch of the Morgan-Guggenheim Alaska Syndicate (Alaska State Library ASL-P277-019-45).

posal to serve as general counsel, with an office in Seattle and a contract for $15,000 per year. However, an entry in his diary indicates some hesitation in giving up the opportunities that had presented themselves in Fairbanks. "I don't care whether they accept it or not," he wrote, "for my business here is proving very much better than I expected and I am free."[36] By the time Birch received Wickersham's letter, the syndicate had held its annual meeting and had made the decision to retain another law firm. Birch informed Wickersham that both he and Jarvis believed that his prospects would prove to be greater in private practice. "I want to do for you that which is best for your interest," Birch wrote. "After reviewing the entire situation, I believe that at this time the general counselship of the Alaska Syndicate has not a good future in it, nor the opportunities of making money, as a free-lance like yourself will have in Alaska."[37]

To this news Wickersham expressed neither disappointment nor bitterness. He noted that the syndicate's contract with the law firm was for just $1000 per month, much less than he had proposed. "Things may come around in time so that I can assist Birch," he noted, "but I am not inclined to hurry the situation for I can make more money as I am."[38]

Still, the former judge found the lure of politics irresistible, especially with Election Day, August 11, only two months away, and Thomas Cale sounding uncertain about his willingness to return for another session as Alaska's congressional delegate. In early June the field included Cale, an independent; John W. Corson, a Republican who had secured the backing of the Hoggatt wing of the party; John Clum, who was supported by strident anti-Guggenheim Republicans; and John Ronan, the only Democrat in the race. Cale was widely considered to have been ineffective in his term as congressional delegate. Despite his tireless efforts, he had failed to make any progress toward passage of legislation for self-government. Wickersham had helped him draft legislation for Alaska home rule, which he introduced in the early days of the congressional session, but it had gone nowhere. Governor Hoggatt traveled to Washington and made every effort to defeat any such proposal, and his efforts were seriously detrimental to the congressman politically. According to the *Fairbanks Daily News*, Cale's reelection depended on convincing the voters of his accomplishments "in spite of the bitter opposition of the governor and the indifference of Congress to Alaska's needs."[39] The paper was pleased that all four candidates stood firmly for home rule, and that no matter which of them was elected, "the federal government will be given to understand that the people of the territory are insistent in their demand for a form of self-government."[40]

As Wickersham inched closer to announcing his entrance into the race, he actively sought an endorsement from the Alaska Syndicate, and the cordial association he had maintained with Birch and Jarvis led him to believe he would get it. He knew that the Hoggatt Republicans were backing Corson, but he remained skeptical about how effective Corson could be given Corson's loud promises to run a home-rule campaign. "How he can work in harness with Hoggatt remains to

Wilford Hoggatt, Alaska territorial governor, who opposed
Wickersham on major political issues in 1908, including the
establishment of an elected territorial legislature (Alaska
State Library ASL-P01-2285).

be seen," Wickersham observed.[41] The *Fairbanks Daily News* commented bluntly that Hoggatt's name was so reviled among the electorate that his endorsement of Corson would spell doom for the
candidate. "That alone is sufficient to defeat him," the paper said.[42]
Cale still had not returned to Alaska following the close of the congressional session, and it appeared uncertain as to whether he was willing
to make a serious run for reelection.

On June 23, Wickersham responded to calls for his candidacy at an
enthusiastic political rally in Fairbanks and agreed to enter the race.

Immediately, he focused on offering a fresh alternative in the field, capitalizing on his strong name recognition and a home-rule platform. Through his travels during his tenure as federal judge, he was easily one of the most widely known men in Alaska. Two days later, Fairbanks newspapers were reporting Wickersham's "positive declaration" that he was indeed a candidate for the office of congressional delegate.[43]

The *Fairbanks Daily Times* was initially quiet, but on July 2 it opened an unrelenting attack on the Wickersham campaign. As ammunition the editors used a letter written by Wickersham to Hoggatt eighteen months before in which the judge had told the governor that he agreed with his assessment that Alaska was not ready for territorial self-government. Dated January 9, 1907, when the two men were still on friendly and cooperative terms, the letter proved to be a major embarrassment for Wickersham when it was made public and printed in the *Times*'s lead editorial column. It was exactly the opposite of the message he wished to convey to the voters in the last days leading up to the election of 1908. In the letter he had told Hoggatt that promoting home-rule legislation as Alaska's highest priority was "certainly a great mistake and one which will cost the territory dear. You are right in opposing it." Alaska's population was too sparse and the tax base too small to sustain self-government, Wickersham wrote, adding that the majority of the populace opposed it. He acknowledged the popularity of the issue but said that most of its support came from "a small number of people with nothing else to do and are simply good-naturedly mistaken."

The *Times* jumped on that concluding statement with mocking sarcasm. "Now, good-natured but mistaken fellow citizens, what do you think of that?" the editor asked. "How does it compare with his present vote-catching speeches? Continue to be good-natured, fellow citizen, but don't allow yourself to be mistaken so easily."[44]

Four days later, the *Times* printed the letter again, this time under a bold headline asking its readers "To Whom Did He Lie?" In one column the paper printed a quotation from Wickersham's letter to Hoggatt, and in the adjacent column the judge's statement in favor of territorial government given in his acclaimed speech to a Fairbanks audience the previous October.[45] It was a stark juxtaposition, and it hit dead center, painting Wickersham as a political opportunist who was willing to adopt any opinion to suit his best advantage.

Wickersham had no defense. The attack left him feeling weak and beleaguered, and he knew he could not run a campaign from a standing such as that. To complicate matters, Corson arrived in Fairbanks, and in the midst of Independence Day activities he campaigned aggressively and dominated the news. "I am drifting along in an embarrassing and weak position," Wickersham lamented. "I hate a weak man, and now I appear in that role."[46] When many of the people he had counted on for help in Valdez, Skagway, and Nome announced their support for Cale, rumors of his withdrawal from the race spread broadly. The newspapers pestered him for a statement of his intent, and on July 6 he summoned a reporter to his office to announce his decision to withdraw.

On July 7, the *Times* reported Wickersham's announcement, along with the more surprising news that Cale was also pulling out of the race. The latter item proved to be a bit premature, as Cale still wavered, and a spokesman insisted that he remained a viable candidate even though he still had not returned to Alaska after the end of the congressional session. Within a week, however, Cale made a formal statement of his withdrawal, citing his wife's ill health as the reason. This left Cale's supporters out in the cold, and they immediately turned to Wickersham, imploring him to reconsider his withdrawal. Especially in southeastern Alaska, where the judge enjoyed widespread popularity, former Cale men promised him their votes. Wickersham resisted until his friends in Fairbanks organized a campaign committee and promised to work for his election. On July 14 he agreed and once again became a candidate. The *Times* could not resist expressing its contempt in sarcastic verse:[47]

> *First I'm in—and then I'm out.*
> *The Guggys know what they're about.*
> *Then I'm out—and now I'm in.*
> *The Guggs, you know, have lots of tin.*

The paper's editors went to all lengths to tether Wickersham to the hated Alaska Syndicate. But now as a candidate once again he focused his energies on proving he had no such connection. He built his political platform on two essential planks: advocacy of territorial self-government and opposition to the Morgan-Guggenheim trust and all it stood for. This latter position placed him at odds not only with the syndicate but also with the mainline Republican Party, which backed Corson in the contest for delegate. It was a purely political stand, prompted by a letter Wickersham received from Jarvis on July 17 with the statement that the syndicate would not support him in the race and that Corson remained its candidate. The letter came just as Wickersham was preparing an address outlining his positions on various issues, and with the news from Jarvis he quickly added his strong anti-syndicate plank, vowing to "oppose in every way possible the control of transportation or mining business within Alaska by the Guggenheims or any other dangerous combination."[48] The letter with its refusal of support offended Wickersham personally. His subsequent public anti-Guggenheim pronouncement was the first expression of spitefulness he had ever aimed at the syndicate,[49] and from that day forward, that remembered slight motivated his life in politics.

As Election Day drew near, Wickersham's critics exploited every weakness they could find. One of those was his status as an independent, running without affiliation with either major political party. Cale also was an independent, and the press blamed his failure to advance home-rule legislation on this absence of party loyalty. "Independent candidates have no legs to stand on," one paper asserted, adding that an independent delegate from Alaska would continue to be ineffective in Washington because Republican and Democrat members of Congress would feel no obligation to help him.[50] Wickersham's record as a judge came into play as well. "He will be fought by the many personal enemies he won while on the bench," the *Times* said. "Do we want a candidate who will meet nothing but hostility, opposition, and obstruction in Congress?"[51]

In the end, however, Wickersham's positive name recognition around the territory served him well. He won decisively in Fairbanks, Nome, Valdez, Skagway, Juneau, and Sitka. In Cordova, where the Alaska Syndicate exercised considerable influence, the voters overwhelmingly chose Corson, but the overall total favored the former judge by a considerable margin.

Still, in the rough world of frontier politics, Wickersham's critics would not be silenced. "We are not going to fall over ourselves to congratulate him," the editor of the *Times* declared. "An election cannot turn black into white or make an angel of a sinner. As to Wickersham the politician, we shall bury the hatchet only in his vitals."[52]

In December, just before leaving Fairbanks for the start of the congressional session, a letter from Cale's secretary warned Wickersham of the hostile elements that awaited him in the nation's capital. Hoggatt, the secretary wrote, had been in town for three weeks working to discredit the newly elected delegate within Congress and the Roosevelt administration, asserting that he had been elected by the "saloon, whiskey, and gambling population" to advance their interests. Hoggatt is "using all the despicable methods and false arguments his fertile brain can concoct," the letter writer said, urging Wickersham to make his way to Washington as quickly as possible to "assist in relegating the governor to the realms of quiescent somnolence."[53]

Collier's magazine, November 13, 1909. The cover story by Louis Glavis, with the subhead "The Whitewashing of Ballinger," exposed corruption in the Taft administration surrounding coal leases in Alaska. The portrait of Interior Secretary Richard Ballinger is encased in a question mark (Shutterstock 787303192).

6

ALASKANS FIGHT
FOR TERRITORIAL
SELF-GOVERNMENT

The pestilence that walketh in darkness;
the destruction that wasteth at noonday

⁓Ⅳⅼ⁓

CONFLICT, GREED, and corruption were the staples of the Progressive-era national muckraking press, and resource-rich Alaska provided them in plenty. On November 13, 1909, *Collier's* magazine hit the streets with a screaming cover headline asking, "Are the Guggenheims in charge of the Department of the Interior?" The story, beginning on page 15, was written by Louis R. Glavis, a former employee of the federal agency in charge of investigating applications for patents on coal claims on federal lands. Glavis had been dismissed from his job in September 1909 after issuing a report recommending denial of thirty-three claims totaling about five thousand acres in Alaska's Bering River coalfield. Glavis had turned up evidence that these claims, filed in the name of Clarence Cunningham, were fraudulent on grounds that the applicants had conspired to consolidate them when approved and sell them to the Morgan-Guggenheim syndicate. Such an action would violate the intent of Roosevelt's coal land withdrawal order of 1906, which aimed to conserve public lands and prevent monopoly control by large business conglomerates.

William Howard Taft, Roosevelt's close advisor and handpicked successor as president, had taken office in 1909, and the controversy that grew from Glavis's accusations turned the former president and the sitting president, who once had been close political allies, into bitter rivals. *Collier's* editors drew a sharp distinction between the two men, stating in an introduction that Glavis's findings showed that Roosevelt's ethical standards were far higher than those that had been exhibited by members of the Taft administration. Roosevelt, the magazine said, "lent energy to the belief among men that to do right and seek justice was the course required of public servants." Glavis's article, it continued, showed those principles to be "in sharp contrast" to those of the current secretary of the interior, Richard A. Ballinger. The subhead above the story summed up the editors' view of the entire affair, labeling it bluntly "The whitewashing of Ballinger."[1]

At the time of Roosevelt's withdrawal of federal coal lands from further entry, there were about nine hundred claims filed and pending approval by the federal General Land Office. Roosevelt had modified the withdrawal order to allow those claims already filed to be considered for approval. At the same time, however, he asked Congress to pass legislation to change the current laws in a way that would expressly disallow consolidation of the 160-acre claims under a single owner.[2] As Glavis explained in the *Collier's* article, Roosevelt's motivation was to prevent monopoly by requiring that each claimant must use the land in his own interest and for his own advantage. The intent, Glavis wrote, was to "forbid speculating in coal lands before entry either by dummy entry men or by previous agreement to consolidate claims after entry."

Glavis's most serious charges were directed at Ballinger, who, he asserted, had used the power of his office to push the Cunningham claims through to patent even though he knew they were fraudulent. Prior to his appointment as secretary of the interior under Taft, Ballinger had been commissioner of the General Land Office in charge of investigating coal claim applications. He resigned from that job in March 1908 and went into private legal practice in Seattle. One of his clients was the Cunningham group of coal claimants. In March 1909, upon Taft's inauguration, the new president appointed Ballinger as his secretary of the interior, and a short two months later the department officially ordered the Cunningham claims to be accepted and patented. Suddenly, Glavis found himself in what he described as "a very difficult position," knowing that his recommendations were in direct opposition to his superiors. "If I accepted their ruling," he wrote,

"10,000 acres of Alaska coal lands were slipping from the United States with no hope of recovery and were going to claimants, many of whom were fraudulent. The chance for wise regulation of Alaska coal lands urged by President Roosevelt would be gone."

Glavis then took the only action he knew could stop Ballinger's rush to approve the claims. Without consulting his superiors, he presented his evidence to US Attorney General George W. Wickersham, who ten days later overruled the Department of the Interior. This marked the end of Glavis's career in federal service. His dismissal came directly from Taft, who, Glavis realized, had "seen in this nothing but overzeal and insubordination on my part."[3]

With half of the Cunningham claims lying within the Chugach National Forest, Glavis directed his concerns to the nation's chief forester, Roosevelt's close associate and advisor on conservation issues, Gifford Pinchot. There Glavis found a sympathetic ear in a man who shared Roosevelt's passion for conservation of the nation's resources but who found that he had much less influence with the new man in the White House. Writing years later, Pinchot recalled that he immediately believed the details of Glavis's story. "The material he submitted satisfied me completely that the Cunningham claims were fraudulent," he wrote. "I wanted the fraud stopped. . . . Through the Guggenheim Syndicate the natural resources of Alaska were in danger of monopoly."[4]

Taft and Ballinger questioned the constitutionality of Roosevelt's actions setting aside large tracts of land for national forests and parks without Congress's approval.[5] Clearly, neither man was an enthusiastic conservationist. Taft quickly moved to support Ballinger and condemn Glavis, firing him for "impeaching the official integrity of his superior officers."[6] The president's message of support for his interior secretary was the basis of *Collier's* "whitewashing of Ballinger" streamer. Taft concluded that Glavis's charges amounted to "only shreds of suspicions without any substantial evidence to sustain his attack." He told Ballinger that he considered him to be a man of "the highest character and integrity" and that he believed that he had held no information that would have been of benefit to the Cunningham group of claimants.[7]

By January 1910, events swirling around the Alaska coal claims had raised a furor that reached to the highest levels of government, and the uncompromising Pinchot found himself at its center. A special investigating committee composed of six senators and six representatives was scheduled to begin hearings before the end of the month into what would come to be known as the Ballinger-Pinchot Affair. However, before the committee convened its first meeting, Pinchot stirred the waters further with a letter to Senator Jonathan Dolliver, chairman of the Senate Committee on Agriculture and Forestry. In it, Pinchot presented evidence gathered by two US Forest Service employees, Overton Price and Alexander Shaw, about the fraudulent nature of the Cunningham Alaska coal claims and Ballinger's role in the efforts to rush them through to patent. Price and Shaw, direct subordinates under Pinchot, had for weeks been feeding information about the affair to the press, and they knew that their criticism of the secretary of the interior could well put their jobs in jeopardy. But they explained to Pinchot that they were compelled by a sense of duty to try to protect "the property of the people and government of the United States against claims which we believe were fraudulent and in respect to which there was a grave and immediate danger of public loss."[8]

Pinchot, in turn, took the material gathered by Price and Shaw and made it the basis of his letter to Dolliver. He defended his two subordinates' actions in exposing the corruption within the Department of the Interior and went even further in publicly criticizing the president of the United States for decisions he had made in dealing with the controversy. Pinchot, Price, and Shaw believed firmly that they held the moral high ground—that they were right, and Taft was wrong. "A public officer is bound first to obey the law and keep within it," Pinchot's letter to Dolliver read. "But he is also bound, at any personal risk, to do everything the law will let him do for the public good." When Pinchot's letter was read on the Senate floor, Taft had had enough. The next day, January 7, he fired the chief forester, saying that the Dolliver letter was "an improper appeal to Congress and the public" before the whole evidence could be considered by the congressional investigating committee. "By your own conduct you have destroyed your usefulness as a helpful subordinate of the government," Taft told Pinchot, concluding that it was his duty to remove him from office.[9]

ALASKA SELF-GOVERNMENT

Meanwhile, James Wickersham focused his first year in Congress on fulfilling the promise he had made to voters to achieve self-government for Alaska. On June 7, 1909, soon after being sworn in as Alaska's delegate, he introduced such legislation, and he found that the measure would become intertwined with the controversy swirling around Ballinger and Pinchot as the committee looking into that affair began its hearings. Looming behind both issues—self-government and Ballinger-Pinchot—stood the powerful and ever-present Morgan-Guggenheim syndicate. Wickersham's political foes included not only Wilford Hoggatt, Wilds Richardson, and Stephen Birch, whom the delegate labeled as syndicate lobbyists, but also a group of powerful senators, along with the president himself. Taft was all in favor of a local legislative body for Alaska, but his idea about the makeup of that body was abhorrent to Wickersham and, for that matter, to most Alaskans. In 1900, President William McKinley had appointed Taft governor of the Philippines and charged him with overseeing the new US possession until the people proved themselves able, in the eyes of the United States government, to govern themselves. Ten years later, Taft, as president, drew on that experience and applied it to Alaska. Part of the Philippine model was a local self-governing legislature, the members of which were not elected by a vote of the people but appointed by the governor. The Alaska bill written by Taft and introduced in the Senate by Albert Beveridge of Indiana on January 18, 1910, called for an eleven-member legislative body consisting of a governor, an attorney general, a commissioner of the interior, and eight members representing each of the four judicial districts in the territory. All were to be appointed by the president.

Wickersham was enraged, and as the Senate Committee on Territories began hearings on the bill two days after it was introduced, his emotions were barely contained. The people of Alaska want to have a say in the membership of the legislature, just as every other territory in the country has had, he told the committee. "I was elected upon that platform, and I am going to stand here and insist upon the proposition earnestly and honestly, and I am going to show that what this bill proposes is in violation of the will of the people of Alaska and is open to so many objections that it ought not to pass." He presented a telegram addressed to Taft and signed by the mayors of every incorporated town in Alaska and sixteen of the territory's newspapers pleading for an elected legislature in conformance with Wickersham's bill.[10]

The provision for an appointed rather than an elected legislature met resistance on the Senate floor as well, especially among western-state senators who had a personal understanding of the issues facing territorial residents and their relationship with the federal government. William Borah, a Republican from Idaho, quickly voiced his opposition following Beveridge's introductory speech. "This is a peculiar and extraordinary bill," he asserted. "The right of self-government, the power of the people of Alaska to express themselves, is effectively cut out of the entire scheme of government." This is "the colonial doctrine of England in its simplest form."[11]

Coe Crawford, a Democrat from South Dakota, added his voice to Borah's in opposition. Crawford was a Progressive-minded former governor who supported Theodore Roosevelt's antitrust and conservation efforts. He had backed Taft for president in 1908 on the strength of Roosevelt's endorsement, but two years later, in the wake of Ballinger-Pinchot, he had begun to have doubts about Taft's true Progressive credentials.[12] Crawford thoroughly rejected the proposal for a presidentially appointed legislature in the style Taft had fashioned for the Philippines. His resistance was grounded in ten years of living in a US territory to which judges, commissioners, and the governor were appointed and sent in to exercise authority over the people. "I know there is no condition of things that so stings the pride and awakens irritation as to have presiding over them men who are not responsible to the people over whom they preside," he stated.[13]

Borah demanded an explanation of the reasons such a proposal had been brought forth, suggesting that "there must be peculiar and extraordinary conditions in Alaska to warrant this kind of legislation." Beveridge responded that the authors of the bill had considered making the legislature elective, but they rejected the idea because "the sparse population and enormous extent of the territory, the difficulty of communication, in physical hardship, in time and expense make the question of an elective legislature impracticable." Borah was not satisfied. "I am still at a loss to know why it should contain the provisions which it does," he said. "There must be some controlling and imperative reason in the minds of the committee."[14]

Wilds Richardson, head of the Alaska Road Commission. Wickersham accused him of being a lobbyist for the Morgan-Guggenheim Alaska Syndicate (Alaska State Library ASL-P20-022).

In Wickersham's mind, the answer was simple: it was what the Morgan-Guggenheim syndicate and its team of Washington lobbyists wanted. In testimony before the Senate Committee on Territories, Wickersham charged that Wilds Richardson, head of the Alaska Road Commission, was present in Washington as a lobbyist for the syndicate. Richardson, he contended, was pressing for legislation that would provide for a commissioner of the interior who would be appointed as a member of the new legislature. Wickersham feared that the syndicate would control all such appointments, and the effect of the measure would be to "perpetuate" Richardson as part of the government of Alaska. "We do not want Major Richardson to get into the organization of government and attempt to foist himself on the people out there in this kind of way," he added.[15]

Wickersham then directed his comments at Hoggatt, who had resigned as governor the previous year and now was working in Washington as what Wickersham labeled "a head lobbyist for Guggenheims." He charged that Hoggatt, even while drawing a salary as governor, had acted in the interests of the syndicate in opposition to an elected legislature and now continued to do so. "Hoggatt came down here and said openly and publicly that the people of Alaska could not be entrusted to elect a local legislature," he testified.[16]

Wickersham resented Richardson and Hoggatt for representing themselves in Washington as spokesmen for Alaska. He himself was the elected delegate, he declared, and he spoke for all the people of Alaska except for "one or two big interests which hope to control the great undeveloped resources of the territory as well as its government."[17] As Wickersham's testimony came near the end, he found himself in a disagreeable exchange with the committee chair, Albert Beveridge. The Alaska delegate said in summary that neither he nor the people of Alaska wished to stop the Morgan-Guggenheims from developing the resources of the territory. Quite the opposite, he said. "We want them to develop the country. We want the coal mines and the copper mines opened. But we do not want the whole country turned over to the great corporation." At this Beveridge bristled, reminding Wickersham that the proposed legislation was the president's plan, and any notion that it "would in any sense turn this country or any advantages in it over to the Guggenheims or any other interests is not correct." Wickersham could not resist a parting comment as he left the witness stand. "You would have the people of Alaska bound hand and foot and the national resources of the territory in the hands of a few people," he shot back. "I beg you not to pass it."[18]

Richardson's testimony immediately followed Wickersham's, and committee chair Beveridge asked him directly if he had a relationship of any kind with the "Guggenheim interests." He replied that he had none except for personal acquaintances with some of the personnel and that he was representing himself only as an officer of the US Army in the best interests of Alaska.[19]

Finally, former Alaska Governor Hoggatt made his appearance before the committee, roundly denying Wickersham's assertion that he was a paid lobbyist for the syndicate. The charges "are unqualifiedly false," he contended, and his presence in Washington was at the request of the president and the secretary of the interior. He was explicit in his preference for the president's plan for an appointed rather than an elected local legislature. Any general election, including the one that put Wickersham in office as congressional delegate, was nothing more than "a farce," he said. "It is too big a country for any local general government," adding that he had never seen the need for any elective local lawmaking body.[20]

On January 26, 1910, the feud between Alaskans in the nation's capital reached the front page of the *Seattle Post-Intelligencer*. Under the headline "Wickersham is after scalp of Maj. Richardson," the paper reported that Wickersham had formally asked the secretary of war to order Richardson to leave Washington and return to his duties in Alaska. The delegate accused Richardson of lobbying in favor of the Morgan-Guggenheim interests and against the concept of an elective Alaska legislature. He charged that Richardson's motive was to secure for himself the appointed position of the territorial commissioner of the interior, effectively leading to military control of the lawmaking body in Alaska. A week later, the paper printed the full text of Wickersham's letter to the secretary. The appointed legislature as proposed in the Taft-Beveridge bill "would put practically all the power into his [Richardson's] hands," Wickersham charged. "He would become the dominant governing force and the dispenser of franchises, privileges and concessions of the public resources of Alaska," and he "would be in a position to aid the Guggenheims and other big interests." Wickersham concluded with a final plea to the secretary to do something to silence his adversary. "I protest" against his presence in Washington, he wrote, and his actions as "a lobbyist in favor of legislation which the delegate in Congress from Alaska is opposing as inimical to the interests of the people of that territory."[21]

As congressional hearings continued on the Alaska home-rule bill and on the investigation into the Ballinger-Pinchot Affair, both issues

were informed by a broad nationwide antitrust, antimonopoly sentiment. And conservation, as personified by Gifford Pinchot, was part of
the mix as well. In a lead editorial printed in the midst of these hearings, the *Seattle Post-Intelligencer* summed up much of the nationwide
popular opinion. The object of conservation, the paper said, was not
only to "save our natural resources from waste" but also to "rescue
them from monopolistic control." Monopoly, it continued, "assails the
purse in everything we buy." "Like the plagues of Egypt," it is "the pestilence that walketh in darkness" and "the destruction that wasteth
at noonday."[22]

Patents on new coal claims had essentially halted as a result of the
controversy over the Cunningham claims and the associated congressional inquiry, and at the same time the Taft-Beveridge plan for
an appointed Alaska legislature faced strong opposition. Some credit
must be given to Wickersham for successfully creating in the minds
of many in Congress, if not also among a segment of the general population, a connection between corporate monopoly and the fight for
Alaska self-government. As historian Jeanette Nichols insightfully
observed, "Conservation applied to the Guggenheims was manipu-
lated to popularize a local legislature applied to Alaska."[23] Congress
failed to reach any decision on the bill before the session ended.

In the meantime, however, a handful of national magazines discovered in Alaska a fertile field for investigation. Conditions in the
nation's northern possession illustrated perfectly the codependent
relationship between Progressive-era reform and muckraking journalism. Following on the heels of the *Collier's* piece by Glavis and with
the start of congressional committee hearings on two Alaska issues,
The Outlook, a leading national weekly, began a series of opinionated
reports. The February 26, 1910, edition of the popular journal led with
a piece by Atherton Brownell laying out the need for a form of self-
government. But the author as well as the magazine's editors reached
conclusions that were not pleasing to Delegate Wickersham and other
advocates of an elective legislature. Brownell's article expressed support for a form of the Taft-Beveridge bill based on the president's
Philippines model, proposing a seven-member commission of which
four people with "varied expert knowledge" would be appointed by
the president and three additional members would be locally elected.

Conditions in Alaska were different from the Philippines, the author asserted, in that it needed federal oversight but at the same time its population was fully capable of exercising some form of popular electoral rights. This mix of appointed and elected legislators would avoid "the suggestion of carpetbaggery that is abhorrent to Alaskans." The author downplayed the threat of a Morgan-Guggenheim monopoly and argued for a set of stringent land laws that would reach a middle ground to allow needed development by corporations "while at the same time checking undue greed."[24] *The Outlook*'s editors agreed with that assessment, but in their introduction to Brownell's piece, they added a warning against the threat of corporate greed. The obvious priority in Alaska was to establish "orderly, stable, and civilized conditions," the introductory piece said, but new legislation must also make impossible "the wasteful exploitation and monopolization of its enormous natural wealth." The magazine editors noted Senator William Borah's objection to the provisions of the bill based on Taft's experience in the Philippines, but they insisted that the realities of Alaska's size, sparse population, and lack of facilities as detailed in Brownell's article "render any form of self-government by the people of Alaska as a whole difficult, if not virtually impossible."[25]

Hampton's Magazine weighed in with two lengthy pieces by Benjamin Hampton in April and May. The first addressed the question of who in the end would come to control Alaska's vast natural resource wealth. Would it be "the Morgan-Guggenheim combination," the author asked, or would it be "the whole people"? At the forefront of the question was the fate of the self-government legislation pending in Congress. Hampton presented Delegate Wickersham as the leading opponent of Taft's Philippines-style appointed legislature in a fight against powerful forces led by Senator Beveridge of Indiana. He explained Beveridge's motivation as one of pure politics. With his term ending that year, Beveridge found himself at risk as a Republican in a state with a legislature controlled by the Democrats. (The Seventeenth Amendment was passed in 1913, providing for direct election of US senators. Before that, senators were appointed by state legislatures.) Beveridge desperately needed support from high places, and when Taft asked him to introduce the Alaska bill and push it through Congress, he saw his chance to earn the favor he needed from the president.

Throughout committee hearings chaired by Beveridge, the senator repeatedly cited Taft's knowledge and experience gained in other noncontiguous possessions as justification for the essence of his bill.[26]

According to the *Hampton's* article, in the first two months of 1910 Alaskans "swarmed all over" Washington, and most of them, like Richardson and Hoggatt, were lobbying in favor of the Taft-Beveridge bill. Wickersham, in response, continued to warn that an appointed legislature would make it too easy for powerful business interests to control everything of value in the territory. *Hampton's* insisted that it had no objection to corporations earning a profit through development of natural resources. But at the same time it opposed any system that "creates multimillionaires out of the development of the public property and gives these millionaires a chance to use their wealth and power to make our cost of living higher." Conservation of publicly owned resources was a "new conception," it said, and there should be "a persistent demand that it be made the motive of a new departure in national policy." Finally, the *Hampton's* article argued for the federal government to build and operate a railroad in Alaska. The corporations, it said, would oppose that idea because they want to use the transportation system to control the economy, but public ownership would ensure the government's power to regulate prices and would remove the threat of monopoly control by powerful business trusts.[27]

In May, *Hampton's* followed with a second article focusing on the wealth and control held by the Morgan-Guggenheim syndicate in Alaska, describing the value of the Cunningham claims, if they were consolidated and patented, as so great as to make the syndicate "richer and more powerful than the Pennsylvania Anthracite Trust or the Standard Oil Company itself." However, the key to development of Alaska was transportation, and specifically the territory needed a railroad starting at an ice-free southcentral harbor and running north to the Tanana Valley. "Whoever controls its transportation controls Alaska," the author said, and the only way to prevent the Morgan-Guggenheim trust from gaining such control was for the federal government to step in and build the railroad itself. Such a plan is "safe, sane, and feasible," *Hampton's* contended, but the public should expect fierce opposition from the syndicate bosses because "they want the railroads for themselves so that through them they may dominate Alaska and pour her great wealth into their own pockets."[28]

Richardson and Hoggatt were not the only Alaskans who caused trouble for Wickersham in early 1910. On March 22, Falcon Joslin appeared before the House Committee on Territories, favoring a hybrid legislature partly appointed and partly elected. Joslin, as builder and operator of the Tanana Valley Railroad in the Fairbanks area, held views on mining and transportation in interior Alaska that were of value to the committee. He was not seen as a Morgan-Guggenheim lobbyist and, in fact, had long promoted the idea of a railroad to the Interior constructed and run by the federal government. His argument in favor of a legislature split between appointed and elected representatives disappointed Wickersham. As a member of the committee, Wickersham challenged Joslin and reiterated his position, addressing him directly. "You know the platform I ran upon," he said. "You know I was pledged to secure an elective legislature . . . and you know me well enough to know I am going to try to do it."[29]

Joslin based his opinion on what he termed "expediency." Under questioning from Wickersham, he acknowledged that in principle Alaskans, like all peoples, are entitled to choose their own government and to govern themselves. "Nobody can deny that," he said, and he predicted that in time the legislature he envisioned would "evolve" into a wholly elective body. At present, though, there was too much opposition within the territory, he stated, especially among prominent leaders, noting especially Hoggatt's opposition to any kind of legislative assembly. Furthermore, the wide extent of the territory and the lack of efficient transportation were unsurmountable barriers.[30]

As the congressional session drew to a close, the House and Senate failed to draft a compromise on Alaska self-government, and the bill was set aside.

BALLINGER-PINCHOT

Meanwhile, the Ballinger-Pinchot Affair continued to dominate the news. *McClure's Magazine* printed a lengthy investigation in its January 1910 issue. Over the course of the previous five years, the article said, "control of Alaska has been drifting steadily into the hands of the Guggenheims," and it seemed "inevitable" that the company would eventually dominate everything of value in the district through ownership and control of the means of transportation. "Great masses of capital will not be denied," the authors observed. The assets held by the syndicate in Alaska "contain the greatest deposits of copper in the known world," and with the completion of the Copper River and Northwestern Railroad, the trust wished to gain control of the coalfields as well.[31] The article estimated that tracts filed by the Cunningham claimants would produce at least forty-five million tons of coal worth $22.5 million, yielding a profit to the developers of nearly one thousand times the federal government's selling price. The authors reiterated Glavis's charges that the claims were fraudulent but that, even so, Secretary Ballinger had urged a quick approval. Such action, the article contended, would amount to a "gift" given to "one of the ugliest and most dangerous monopolies in the country. . . . It is the familiar old double process of the robbing of the American people—by theft of their property and the resale of it at excessive monopoly prices."[32]

Collier's also continued to follow the story. With the congressional investigating committee scheduled to begin its work in late January, the magazine's publisher, knowing that Glavis as author of the "Whitewashing of Ballinger" article would face tough questioning, moved to stand behind its author. Collier's hired Louis D. Brandeis to represent both the magazine and Glavis for the hearings, which took on the atmosphere of a courtroom trial with committee members sitting as judges.

As the principal accuser, Glavis was the first witness called, and he endured the toughest and most extensive questioning. Pinchot later recalled that even amid attempts to "browbeat and confuse him," he remained unflappable. "Glavis as a witness was a marvel," he wrote.[33] Historian Nelson McGeary, who included a thorough summary of the entire Ballinger-Pinchot feud in his biography of Pinchot, noted that "the Glavis memory, encyclopedic and precise, made him a competent and impressive witness."[34] In his treatment of the congressional hearings, McGeary also emphasized the political overtones that hung over the proceedings, leading to a distinct prejudice in favor of Ballinger. Republican committee members recognized the damage that would result from ruling against a cabinet-level official who was supported by a president of their own party, while Democrats saw an opportunity to embarrass the Taft administration. "Members on both sides were quick to seize any possible political advantage," McGeary wrote.[35]

The long and tedious Ballinger-Pinchot hearings continued through May, after which the committee submitted three separate reports to Congress, all following political lines. Seven Republican members concluded that there was nothing wrong with Ballinger's actions in the affair. They found Ballinger to be "a competent and honorable gentleman, honestly and faithfully performing the duties of his high office with an eye single to the public interest." However, the majority report was also a partial victory for the Pinchot side in that it recommended that the coal leasing process should be taken out of the Department of the Interior and the outcome of the Alaska claims should be decided by an appropriate court. It added that it would be "the height of unwisdom" to allow the Alaska coalfields "to be monopolized or gathered into the private ownership of a few for speculative purposes." On the other hand, the four Democrats on the committee highly praised Pinchot and Glavis and criticized Ballinger, saying that the secretary "is not deserving of public confidence and that he should be requested by the proper authority to resign his office." The third report was written by Representative Edmond Haggard Madison, a Progressive Republican, who also sustained the accusations against Ballinger and concluded that he was unfit for the position he held. As a result of the affair, Ballinger resigned within a year; the Alaska Cunningham claims were never approved, and they remained in the public domain.[36]

In Alaska, public opinion regarding Cunningham, Ballinger, Pinchot, Glavis, and the entire affair was mixed. Generally, people in the North were amused by the sudden national attention the territory was attracting, but to them conservation was an unwelcome concept. Economically, Roosevelt's coal lands withdrawal had been bad news for the territory, especially in Cordova and Katalla, where hundreds of workers sat idle. Development of coal resources meant jobs and a ready source of fuel for a badly needed railroad system. The public was on Wickersham's side when he blasted the trusts and decried the dangers they posed through monopoly control of resources and transportation, but as for Pinchot's appeal to save the forests, the people had lost patience. In four years since the withdrawal order, Washington had done nothing to create a system of coal leasing that would put workers on the job and get the territory moving. Progress was within reach, but congressional action was needed to make it possible. Progressive-minded Alaskans were uncomfortable with the idea of corporate monopoly, but they despised the idea of conservation over employment, and they condemned "Pinchotism" as a hindrance to progress. They took Cunningham's side, while newspapers praised Ballinger as an honorable public servant who had been mistreated by overly ambitious accusers. Pinchot was blamed for the lack of progress and the loss of jobs in Alaska, and the concept of conservation was labeled as a crackpot idea or a "utopian scheme" that had no relevance or applicability in the North.[37]

The Seattle-based *Alaska-Yukon Magazine* took particularly hard lines in its defense of Cunningham and its condemnation of Pinchot. The publication charged that the federal government, through Glavis and others, was determined in the name of conservation to deprive the coal claimants of their rights, and the result was industrial and commercial stagnation. "This story of the bad faith of our government in regard to Alaska ought to stir up the indignation of every manful American," the writer asserted. "To an age of steam and steel, coal is what lifeblood is to the body. Alaska and the whole Pacific Northwest feel . . . the evil results of the arbitrary handicap the government has placed on progress by tabooing the coal of the North." It was nothing more than the latest abuse of Alaska handed down from Washington. "To say that our government has proved an unkind and negligent stepmother to Alaska would be a tame and inadequate euphemism."[38]

In the midst of these tensions, Congress continued to grapple with a long-term fix for the Alaska coal lands dilemma. In the House, Representative Frank Mondell of Wyoming sponsored a bill that would set up a system by which individual claimants could lease up to 2,560 acres and pay an annual fee per acre as well as a royalty on coal extracted. Wickersham, though eager to see new enabling legislation pushed through Congress, objected fiercely to Mondell's plan on grounds that the royalty proposed was far too small. More central to his objection, however, was the overall system of leasing rather than sale of the coal claims. He wanted to see the claims sold to developers while the federal government retained the power to fix, control, and regulate prices and profits derived from coal mined in Alaska. In Wickersham's view, a leasing arrangement was essentially "a communistic form of government in a territory" and would reduce Alaskans "to the status of tenants upon the estate of the national landlord."[39]

As floor debate continued, tensions between Mondell and Wickersham escalated, with the Alaska delegate complaining loudly that the bill did not give the people of Alaska "a fair opportunity" to acquire and operate coal claims. Tempers reached the boiling point when Wickersham charged that the Mondell leasing law was designed to give preference to big operators, such as the Cunningham group, who had already filed claims. In fact, he said, even while the Ballinger-Pinchot investigating committee was in the midst of hearing evidence of corruption in the federal leasing system, the local land office in Juneau was busy issuing patents to these claimants "at the back door . . . just as fast as it could be done." And, he added, Mondell's denial of these facts "shows how little the gentleman knows about the true situation in Alaska."

Mondell had reached the limit of his patience, and, turning to the congressman seated next to him, he uttered in a voice loud enough for Wickersham to hear, "He is a liar, that is all." Those words brought the volatile Alaskan to a fit of rage. He rushed toward Mondell, shouting, "You are a liar if you say that," while trying to grab him and strike him with his fist. The *Congressional Record* indicates that at that point, "the Sergeant at Arms, bearing the mace, appeared." Order was restored and both men apologized. Mondell explained for the record that his comment was not made in debate but as an aside to dispute certain assertions made by the Alaska delegate. Wickersham contended that receipts for payment on coal claims issued to large corporations by the General Land Office in Juneau were considered by the Department of the Interior to be equivalent to a patent. Mondell maintained that receipts issued were only acknowledgments of payments made and nothing more. He said that "it is well known" that a receipt for money paid on a coal claim application is not the same as a final patent.[40]

Wickersham was joined in opposition to the Mondell bill by several congressmen, including notably Edmond Haggard Madison of Kansas and Irving Lenroot of Wisconsin. Madison, who had held a seat on the Ballinger-Pinchot investigating committee the year before, charged that the proposal amounted to a gift of publicly owned resources to the Guggenheim conglomerate. "I sat too long in that case and read it too many times not to know what the evidence is," he said, adding in conclusion that the bill as it stood was a "mockery."[41] Lenroot objected on grounds that the proposal gave the secretary of the interior the right to grant coal patents by favor. It "robs the government of control over its own property," he asserted. The whole purpose of the Mondell bill "is to put the coal lands in Alaska in the hands of the favored licensee of the Secretary and to tie the hands of the government in their management and disposal."[42] The *New York Times* reported that opponents, led by Republican conservationists joined by several Democrats, "proceeded to denounce [the bill] from every standpoint," and it died by a vote of 32 to 151.[43] Wickersham was exultant. In his diary, he noted his own hand in defeating two of President Taft's "great schemes." The appointive legislature bill and the national coal leasing bill as applied to Alaska would have been "ruinous and un-American," he wrote.[44]

In the year to come, cries for action on Alaska matters came to be heard with greater urgency in Washington, and Congress began to take seriously its role in the territory's affairs. The needs in the North had been well articulated: a workable coal lands law, a form of territorial self-government, and aid for construction of a system of efficient transportation. These three issues were so closely related that legislation on any one of them required action on the others as well. They could not be resolved separately.[45]

A WIN FOR SELF-GOVERNMENT

Alaska wants her rights;
she wants home rule;
she demands territorial government

～❦～

IN THE MIDST of these rising tensions in Washington, the widely popular Alaska author Rex Beach weighed in with his view of conditions in
the territory when the *Saturday Evening Post* led its February 25, 1911,
issue with a highly opinionated article entitled "What Is the Matter
With Alaska?" Beach had earned a reputation as a fiction writer, but
he held strong feelings about economic and political problems in
Alaska as well, and with this piece of investigative reporting he hoped
to convince a nationwide audience that the federal government had
an obligation to step in and fix them. Beach broke away from the slant
prevalent among muckrakers of the day and argued against the notion
that the corporate trust known as the Alaska Syndicate was the evildoer that gobbled up competition and stood in the way of the common
people's access to vast coal and mineral resources. His observations,
he explained, were based on inside information gained by his years of
residency in the North and his status as a "sourdough by temperament
and experience."[1]

As an Alaskan, Beach had indeed earned his stripes. In 1897, at age
nineteen, he left Chicago, where he was studying to become a lawyer,
and joined the rush north when news of gold in the Klondike hit the
streets. Over the next five years, he worked the ground near the middle

Yukon River village of Rampart and on the beaches at Nome, toiling in the muck and finding barely enough color to avoid starvation. Though he never earned his fortune in mining, he did strike what one biographer described as "a lucrative vein of literary gold."[2]

By 1903, having decided that he had no inclination to make a career of either the law or gold mining, he began to write short stories drawing on his experiences in Alaska. He sent his first composition to S. S. McClure in New York, and the editor was immediately hooked, paying fifty dollars for the work. "The Mule Driver and the Garrulous Mute" appeared in the November 1903 edition of *McClure's Magazine*, launching the fledgling writer's career. In the next two years, *McClure's* published six more of Beach's stories, "The Shyness of Shorty," "The Colonel and the Horse Thief," "North of Fifty-Three," "The Thaw at Slisco's," "The Test," and "Pardners."

Beach had clearly found his calling, and he loved it. "Sundays, evenings and holidays I spent in riotous living with my fiction characters," he recalled years later. "I wrote on railroad trains, in waiting rooms, or wherever I could hold a suitcase on my knees."[3] But in addition to this proliferation of short fiction, Beach's early compositions included a forty-thousand-word fact-based account of graft and claim jumping in the goldfields of Alaska. "The Looting of Alaska: The True Story of a Robbery by Law," published in *Appleton's Booklovers Magazine* in installments in the first five months of 1906, involved an array of corrupt politicians, judges, and other public officials reaching to the highest levels of government. The work was based on firm evidence, solid research, and impeccable reporting of events, and it placed Beach within the fold of the best traditions of muckraking journalism.

It was the story of the stampede to Nome and the attempt by certain men to render invalid the claims of the first prospectors to file on the rich gold-bearing ground. The "three lucky Swedes" who had made those original discoveries were not US citizens. With no official authorities present in the district, laws were passed by consensus at miners' meetings, and it was quickly decided at one of these that the claims of noncitizens were invalid. Through the course of his five-part article, Beach laid out the details of the plot and named the federal judges and powerful politicians who tried to carry it out. When the great Republican political boss of the Northwest, the "senator-maker" Alexander McKenzie, got word of the riches to be had in Nome, he quickly formed a corporation, the Alaska Gold Mining Company. Among the stockholders was US Senator Henry C. Hansbrough, who used his influence in Congress to benefit the company. McKenzie was able to secure the appointment of his good friend Judge Arthur Noyes to the bench in Nome, and Noyes dutifully ruled against every gold claim filed by a noncitizen. "With laws of their own draughting, administered by courts of their own making, McKenzie and his friends did not see where they could lose," Beach wrote. He went on to show "how it is possible in this enlightened day for a band of determined and unscrupulous men with political backing to rape a whole country."[4] Beach contended that the conspirators knew that such actions would be found illegal and possibly unconstitutional, but by the time such a ruling took effect, "they would have gutted the mines, floated the big company and sold out."[5]

Beach had arrived in Nome in the summer of 1899 and had witnessed events for himself as the plot unfolded. McKenzie took possession of mining claims as well as the property of the original owners. "Within a week his system was running smoothly, his court was grinding out orders unheard of in law, in decency, or in dreams; and the stream of gold dust had been diverted from the Swedes into pockets whose bottoms reached to Washington."[6] As the culprits were well aware, the scheme could not last forever, and soon McKenzie was sentenced to jail and Noyes was deposed. This marked the end of the Alaska Gold Mining Company and what Beach termed "the most brazen, high-born, daring political robbery that has come to light in years."[7] He concluded the final installment of this series with a plea to the federal government to pay more attention to the needs of Alaska and to ensure that only honest and incorruptible judges and public officials be sent to administer the territory.

With the publication of this work in *Appleton's Booklovers*, Beach earned recognition as a muckraker intent on exposing graft and exploitation.[8] Editors, including S. S. McClure, begged Beach for more of such hard-hitting journalism, but he declined, letting it be known that he much preferred to compose fiction. The material Beach had collected in Nome was ready-made for creative embellishment, and he soon produced his first novel, *The Spoilers*, set in the gold rush town of Nome and with the action surrounding the corruption he had exposed in his lengthy article. The novel's plot was ready to use, he noted.

"About all I had to do was add a little imagination, flavor with love interest, season to taste, and serve."[9]

In his 1909 novel, *The Silver Horde*, Beach adhered to a theme popular among Progressives as well as muckrakers of the day, that of a man at war with a powerful corporate trust. The work told the tale of the salmon canning industry in Alaska and the efforts of an independent operator to compete against overwhelming forces. Many of the tactics Beach portrayed in the story were actually used by the corporate cannery owners of the day. These included the sabotaging of equipment and fixing prices below the level at which independent operators were able to survive.[10] He presented the trust as a cruel exploiter of natural resources as well as the human labor force, using every weapon to crush its opponents. It pressured banks to withdraw loans, and it incited a strike and a riot against the challenger. As one reviewer observed, "The hounds of greed will stop at nothing to eliminate competition."[11]

However, in his 1911 piece in the *Saturday Evening Post*, Beach turned his back on the notion that Alaskans were suffering at the hands of the all-powerful and ubiquitous trust. In addition, he scolded a collection of writers, magazines, and politicians, whom he charged with exaggerating conditions in Alaska to serve their own selfish ends. Clearly, he had Wickersham in his sights. Alaskans send a delegate to Congress, he said, but no one knows the reason why "for he has no vote and is about as useful to his constituents as a tailfeather to a frog."[12] He argued that the people had no interest in debating the merits of an elected versus an appointed territorial legislature. The question of self-government was irrelevant, overshadowed entirely by the urgency of settling the coal lands controversy. Until that matter was resolved permanently, development—including transportation and jobs—was at a standstill, and no capitalist would be foolish enough to invest in future prospects. The only positive economic activity cited by Beach was Morgan-Guggenheim's completion of the Copper River and Northwestern Railway, which was essential for the working of the copper deposits north of Cordova. And the success of even that, he said, hinged on a political settlement of the coal lands withdrawals. The Morgan-Guggenheim investment was, in his words, "the one and only permanent improvement that Alaska will have for some time to come."[13]

Clearly, Beach was not an adherent of Wickersham's vendetta against the syndicate. In his view, the only bright future for Alaska depended on encouraging industry to increase its investment in mineral extraction and transportation, and the success of the railroads depended on access to coal. The coal lands withdrawal created an absurd situation. "It is laughable," he wrote, "to think of a country that is so badly in need of transportation forcing a railroad to import inferior coal from Canada at a higher price when its own trucks run over coal beds of infinitely better quality."[14]

Beach concluded with a plea for a government-built railroad to provide efficient transportation to the Interior. "Once the land laws are properly framed and the coal made available, it is the railroads that will lend Alaska the secret of bloom, the magic of economic creation. Without them she must remain locked away in the dark of her mountain shadows, her potentiality sealed in the womb of something that never was and never will be."[15]

In Washington, Senator Simon Guggenheim of Colorado, son of Meyer Guggenheim of the famous mining and refining company, was so pleased with Beach's *Saturday Evening Post* article that he had the piece entered into the *Congressional Record* in its entirety and referred to the Senate Committee on Territories. The pro-development *Alaska-Yukon Magazine* responded favorably as well, although it quibbled with Beach's assertion that Alaskans did not care "a tinker's hoot" about territorial self-government and the question of whether representatives to a legislative assembly would be appointed or elected. That misstatement, the magazine said, "spoiled" one of the best articles ever written about Alaska land laws. "Real sourdoughs" want to participate in local government, the editor charged, and in three elections for congressional delegate, they had "very emphatically" voted for the candidates who represented that stance.[16]

Congress's failure to resolve these critical Alaska issues brought tensions in the territory to a boiling point. On May 2, 1911, the *Cordova Daily Alaskan* reported on a mass meeting where "there was considerable dissatisfaction expressed" with the treatment Alaskans were being given by the federal government. On the opinion page, the editor blamed the government, conservationists, and coal barons of the East for holding back development. "Men of the North have lost all patience," the writer warned, "and are now demanding their rights."[17]

Workers in Cordova protest the withdrawal of Alaska coal lands from leasing by dumping imported coal into the harbor in 1911. The action was portrayed in the press as a reenactment of the Boston Tea Party (Alaska State Library ASL-MS220-01-03-01).

Two days later, the crowds that had packed the Cordova meeting hall took to the streets and to the Alaska Steamship Company dock, where tons of coal imported from Canada were stockpiled. Armed with shovels, the mob began to pitch coal into the bay in a sign of protest. Within hours, the afternoon edition of the local *Daily Alaskan* hit the streets with a screaming headline calling the event Cordova's own Boston Tea Party. Below that, the paper reported that the previous night, protesters in Katalla met on the beach to "show their hatred for the man responsible for their ruin." After building a bonfire, the men "burned Gifford Pinchot in effigy and held general jollification over the event."[18]

The coal protest was front-page news in Seattle as well, with the *Post-Intelligencer* also playing up the Tea Party angle. The *P-I* reported that some of Cordova's most prominent citizens took part, with the president of the Chamber of Commerce urging on the protesters, shouting, "Shovel away boys. We want only Alaskan coal."[19] On its editorial page, the *P-I* sympathized with the protesters and the citizens of Alaska "who have been bled through the denial of the privilege to use the fuel which lies at their feet."[20] The *Daily Alaskan* regretted the use of illegal tactics, but its editorial writer said the action was completely justified. A week later, the Cordova paper ran a five-column banner headline declaring "Pinchotism Is an Injustice" and reported that at a town meeting the people of Chitina condemned the delay in opening the coal lands and congratulated Cordovans on their protest.[21] The paper lamented the "long train of evils in the form of official misrule from the nation's capital." The coal-day incident showed that finally "Alaskans, having already smarted so long, did not propose to sit idly by and twirl their thumbs the same as on former occasions."[22]

Later in May, Wickersham reiterated Alaskans' mood before a meeting of the Senate Committee on Territories in Washington. He extolled the wealth of resources, including coal, copper, gold, timber, and fish, but he said that development and prosperity were being held back by federal government neglect. "We have every element of permanence and growth," he told the senators. "We have everything necessary to make a great country out there if we can only get a little sympathy from Congress." The two primary needs, he explained, were a territorial legislature and congressional action to open Alaska coal lands to mining. "Give us a chance to develop that country and we will do it," he said, charging that "Congress has done nothing to aid in developing Alaska but much to prevent it." The result of the coal lands withdrawal and the establishment of the Chugach National Forest has been "stagnation and retrogression." But at the same time, he reminded the committee of its duty to protect Alaska from falling into the hands of corporate monopoly control. "Only the people can develop a new country," he concluded. "Neither great monopolies nor a paternal government can or will do it."[23]

Theodore Roosevelt made his opinions on the subject of Alaska coal known as well. In a pair of articles penned for *The Outlook*, the former president called on Congress to enact laws immediately to provide for development of the resource. He said that Congress's failure to act on the matter was entirely the fault of "the Guggenheims and their apologists and backers" and their "effort to secure special privileges and illegal favors to which they had not one shadow of claim." If they had not pursued these attempts to get around the law, he wrote, Congress would already have passed the needed legislation instead of taking up its time with the Ballinger-Pinchot investigation. Roosevelt's argument was grounded in pure Progressive philosophy. It was pro-business but fiercely antimonopoly while it promoted conservation and protection of land and resources "in the interests of the settlers of Alaska and in the interests of the people of the United States and not in the interests of the Guggenheim Syndicate." He advocated a law that would not prevent big corporations from working and making a profit, but he insisted that work must be done through a system of leasing, not ownership, of tracts large enough to make mining practical. He put the federal government at the center of the solution, saying that regulatory oversight was essential. "Alaska must be developed," he concluded, and Congress would be "guilty of criminal negligence" if it failed to act immediately.[24]

Slowly, Congress began to respond to the upwelling of events and the urgent cries for attention to Alaska matters that were regularly appearing in the press. On August 19, 1911, the Progressive firebrand of the Republican Party, Senator Robert La Follette of Wisconsin, introduced a resolution calling for government ownership and control of railroads in the territory. The resources of Alaska belong to all of the people of the United States, the resolution stated, and without changes to land laws, they were destined either to be turned over to private monopoly or to remain undeveloped. Both possibilities were unacceptable, La Follette declared in Senate floor debate. The time had come for Congress to enact legislation that would ensure conservation of resources, provide for responsible development, and guarantee that the true owners of those resources—the citizens of the United States—would be the beneficiaries of development. At the core of his proposal was, of course, the need to control and regulate the Morgan-Guggenheim syndicate, which represented "the enormous power of the greatest concentration of capital that the world has ever known."[25] "Will the American people be so blind, so dull, as to permit this enormously rich field of Alaska to become the property of Morgan and those allied with him?" he asked, before charging that if the syndicate were allowed to control railroads in Alaska it would only be a matter of time before it would "take over every valuable mineral property in that country." The first step to be taken in preventing such monopoly control was for the federal government itself to build and operate a railroad and to own and operate a coal mine to supply the needs of the railroad as well as the US Navy. Such action, La Follette concluded, would establish at last the policy of governmental ownership and "see to it that this great storehouse of wealth shall be used for the benefit of all the people."[26]

In the House of Representatives, Democratic Representative William Sulzer of New York took a leading role in pushing the cause of Alaska self-government. Sulzer, who owned a number of mining operations in the territory and had traveled there extensively over the previous twelve years or so, had long argued that Congress had neglected Alaskans' needs and that it was time to grant them the ability to make their own laws. "It is a shame the way Alaskans are treated," Sulzer wrote in a piece published in the *Alaska-Yukon Magazine.* While the government received more than a half-million dollars a year in revenue from Alaska, it appropriated only "a paltry pittance" in return. "That money properly expended by the people in Alaska would open up and develop this vast territory," he said. "That money should be spent by Alaskans for Alaska, and the only way this can be accomplished is through the agency of territorial government."[27]

The Outlook continued to focus on affairs in the territory as well. In a four-part series starting in December 1911, author W. D. Hulbert offered a detailed look at "What Is Really Going on in Alaska." In Hulbert's view, the core of the issue lay in the fact that nearly all of Alaska belonged to the whole nation collectively, not to individual landowners, and therefore any actions in Congress had to consider the interests of all citizens along with those of Alaskans themselves. "How about the people of the states," Hulbert mused in the introduction to his series of articles. "Alaska was bought with their money in their time of adversity. Must not their interests, too, be considered?" The dilemma, as he explained it, centered on the problem of providing access to resources to allow Alaskans to go to work and at the same time protecting those resources from falling into the hands of greedy corporate trusts. Only two entities were capable of overseeing development, he said: "Wall Street and Uncle Sam." And he suggested that if the federal government was unwilling or unable to do the job, it should get out of the way and allow private industry to operate under "proper limitations and restrictions."[28] At the very least, Hulbert concluded, Congress owed it to Alaskans and to the nation to open the coalfields under a workable leasing system. To Alaskans, this meant not only jobs but also the building of railroads and smelters, which in turn would "mean business activity and prosperity in a region that is now almost dead."[29]

On April 17, 1912, soon after the opening of the second session of the Sixty-Second Congress, Representative Henry Flood of Virginia called up before the House a bill to create an Alaska Territorial Legislature. Introduced by Wickersham and approved by the House Committee on Territories the previous August, the bill was a clear statement of Congress's intent to convey to the people of Alaska the power to govern themselves through a local elected legislative body. Flood, the chair of the House Committee on Territories, explained in detail the unlimited wealth that lay waiting to be developed in Alaska, but noted that, through actions such as the coal lands withdrawal, the government had continually thwarted every effort toward economic activity. It was past time, Flood continued, to permit Alaskans to elect their own legislature and enact their own laws. "The land is there, the people are there, the development, so far as we have permitted it to go forward, is there," he stated. "Fairness and justice and common sense and right demand that we should give to these people what they ask."[30]

Sulzer was, of course, an eager supporter, and he was joined on the House floor by Representative William Wedemeyer of Michigan, whose impassioned and dramatic plea quoted lines from Robert Service, the widely popular Bard of the Yukon:

> It's the great big broad land way up yonder,
> It's the forest where silence has lease;
> It's the beauty that thrills me with wonder;
> It's the stillness that fills me with peace.

Wedemeyer contended that this proposal for Alaska was consistent with the rights that had been given to other US territories. Congress would retain ultimate control, but the initiative for local laws and regulations would be under a locally elected legislature, "the only body of men that can know the situation in detail as it actually exists." Wedemeyer's lengthy speech was greeted with enthusiastic applause from the House floor. "We owe something to the self-reliant pioneer," he concluded. "We owe them the privilege of self-government, a privilege we should be slow to deny men of our own blood."[31]

Sulzer followed in the same vein, focusing on the vast wealth of resources and saying that in gold and silver alone Alaska had produced more than twenty-nine times the cost of its $7.2 million purchase from Russia. It was, he stated, "the cheapest bargain in land in the annals of time." He spoke in detail of the territory's potential for development not only in mining but in fisheries, timber, and agriculture as well. But it was the appeal for full rights of citizenship for the Alaskan people that formed the core of Sulzer's argument, "a right which should no longer be denied to the hardy men who have gone to the northland and made their homes." His dramatic conclusion also brought long applause from the full House. "Alaska is the wonderland of the world," he intoned. "No words can adequately describe it. The time is at hand when this vast territory will be developed by American genius, American capital, and American enterprise, and take my word for it there will be no more prosperous section in all our progressive country for American brawn and American brain. Alaska wants her rights; she wants home rule; she demands territorial government."[32]

Representative George White of Ohio was less enthusiastic. Although he declared his support for the bill and pledged to vote in its favor, he expressed doubts about the optimism voiced by Sulzer and others, especially in regard to agriculture. White's skepticism was based on his two years living in Alaska and working a placer claim. "My partner and I sank a 72-foot shaft near the Yukon and were forced to thaw every foot of the dirt the entire depth," he said. And based on his experience, the House should "understand why I question to some extent the immediate rush of home seekers and farmers that is promised as the result of the enactment of the pending bill." He suggested that the current population did not justify a fully elective legislature and expressed a preference for the partly elective and partly appointive plan as proposed by Senator Albert Beveridge in the previous session of Congress. In the end, however, White indicated his intention to vote for the bill much in the same way a parent buys for his son a suit that is several sizes too large "with the certain knowledge that [he] would grow into it at some period of the wearing."[33]

One week later, it was Wickersham's turn to state the case in House floor debate. In a one-hour speech, the Alaska delegate presented a history of the legislation going back twenty years to 1892, when both major political parties at their national conventions endorsed the concept of self-government for all US territorial possessions. Since then, he said, it had repeatedly been incorporated into party platforms and supported by presidential candidates. Wickersham then presented a wide array of editorials from more than twenty newspapers from Seattle and all across Alaska. They were typical, he said, of the "great mass of editorial comment in favor of the bill now before the House." With the president, Congress, and the general public all in support of self-government, the only remaining question, according to Wickersham, was whether members of the governing body should be appointed by the president or elected by the people of the territory.[34]

Wickersham found himself working to debunk the notion that because the territory's population was small and transient, an appointed body was justified. This was the position taken not only by President Taft but also by his appointed Alaska governor, Walter E. Clark. The governor had testified weeks earlier before the House Committee on Territories, reiterating his objections to the elected form of territorial legislature. He was widely quoted in newspapers across Alaska as telling the committee that the sparse and scattered population made the cost of electing representatives and maintaining an elected territorial legislature too burdensome.[35] Governor Clark resisted Wickersham at every turn, including in his annual reports to the secretary of the interior. There, in 1911, he had quarreled with the very idea that a legislature in any form would benefit the territory. Those in favor of such a body, he wrote, "either deny the truth or question the sufficiency" of three major points that rendered self-government impracticable: that the population was not only too small but also "unstable" and "lacking in homogeneity"; that the total amount of taxable property was insufficient to cover the expenses of the new government; and that the territory would lose more in federal benefits than it would gain through local control. Clark concluded his report for that year with a list of nine legislative measures that he viewed as urgent for Alaska, including a coal lands leasing law, sanitation and public health, supervision of banks, and compulsory school attendance, but he made no mention of territorial self-government.[36]

Wickersham argued doggedly against stereotypes and images of Alaska and its people that he believed to be entirely wrong. He took particular exception to the word "migratory" when used by an administration official to refer to most Alaskans. "Migratory?" he exclaimed. "Certainly. Of what earthly use would a prospector be who is not? He travels from stream to stream digging shafts and scraping the rim in search of colors. Disappointed for ninety-nine times, often in the hundredth hole he finds the colors which bring the stampede."[37] He presented statistics that demonstrated the stability and permanence of the population and the growth of communities. Furthermore, he said, Alaska's population was not small when compared to the populations of several states when they were admitted to the union. In 1912, Alaska had, according to Wickersham's figures, a larger population than sixteen territories when they were given an elected legislature and larger than nine states when they were granted statehood.[38] Wickersham was forceful and persuasive, and his arguments were having a positive effect as members expressed their belief that Alaskans should enjoy the right to conduct their own business through an elected legislative body. Representative Richard E. Connell of New York was one of many who spoke up in favor of the bill, saying that he was expressing the sentiment of all Americans in demanding that the people of Alaska be given the right to govern themselves. "Indeed," he continued, "even Russia has shown more concern for her subjects in desolate Siberia than our government has shown for the people of Alaska."[39]

The bill creating the Alaska Territorial Legislature was easily passed by the full House on April 24, 1912, and by the Senate on July 24. Finally, on August 23 President Taft, giving in to popular demand for an elected rather than appointed legislative body, signed it into law. There had been hints for some weeks that Taft, despite his personal preferences, would not block the bill. The *Seattle Post-Intelligencer* had reported in early April that prospects for passage had never looked better, and the paper indicated that with near unanimous support in Congress the president would not be seriously opposed to any measure that was presented to him for his signature.[40] Wickersham was exultant, noting the "glorious victory" with an exclamation point in his diary on the day the bill passed the House (April 24).[41] The day the president signed it into law was also Wickersham's fifty-fifth birthday, and the Alaska delegate commented that he could not have received a better gift.

The new law was far from perfect, however. It was very much the product of compromise, and the opposition was able to write in many restrictions on the power and authority of the new legislative body.

For example, Congress reserved the right to repeal any act of the territorial legislature, and the legislature was forbidden to change or repeal any laws passed by Congress. The territory could not establish its own court system and could not alter the structure of taxes on business and trade as established by Congress. It was, as Ernest Gruening pointed out in his history of the territory, "a very limited form of self-government."[42]

FRONTIER POLITICS IN 1912

Caesar will be James Wickersham

PROGRESSIVES roiled the waters of presidential politics in election year 1912. Theodore Roosevelt burst onto the scene with all the bluster and tact of a bull moose, challenging his party's incumbent president for the nomination and then mounting his own third-party bid when the Republicans stuck with their man Taft. Roosevelt had handpicked Taft for the presidency in 1908, but two years into his successor's term he had lost confidence in his credentials as a true Progressive. The core of Roosevelt's discontent was Taft's persistent support of Secretary of the Interior Richard Ballinger. While hunting in Africa and touring in Europe, the former president had kept abreast of affairs in Washington mainly through communication with Gifford Pinchot. He was outraged at Taft's unfailing backing of Ballinger and his refusal to dismiss him even in the face of overwhelming evidence of corruption and incompetence in the handling of the Cunningham Alaska coal claims controversy.

But that was not all. Taft, in his time in office, had been far too timid a reformer for Roosevelt's liking. Not only in the area of land conservation but also when it came to antitrust legislation, support for labor laws, and strengthening government regulation of railways, Roosevelt believed that Taft had betrayed—or at least failed to advance—the Progressive cause. On his return to the states in June 1910, the former president was greeted, as one historian observed, "like a conquering hero."[1] During his time away from the country, Roosevelt's Progressive philosophy had deepened and taken on an even stronger form, which would guide his campaign for the presidency in 1912. While on safari in Africa, he had read Herbert Croly's book *The Promise of American Life*, which laid out the concept of the "new nationalism," extolling the need for a strong federal government to step in when needed to ensure justice for the individual. The book had a compelling effect on Roosevelt, and he told Croly in a letter that he would "use [his] ideas freely." Croly's argument was that the fortunes of the individual and those of the nation were intertwined and that strong intervention by the federal government was called for when necessary to remedy social ills. Individual effort was highly valued, along with a strong central national government to control big business in the best interests of workers and consumers. "The national advance of the American democracy does demand an increasing amount of centralized action," Croly wrote. State governments were not able to deal with the social and economic ills that accompany what Croly called "the aggrandizement of corporate and individual wealth." They could not be expected to address national issues such as regulation of interstate commerce and the organization of labor.[2] "The millionaire and the trust have appropriated too many economic opportunities formerly enjoyed by the people." Roosevelt, he concluded, was the first American statesman to realize the connection between the national interest and continuous broad-based reform to restore power and opportunity to the people.[3]

Returning to the states in the summer of 1910, Roosevelt was deluged with requests to speak. He was the object of so much attention and his style grew so strident in its anti-Taft tone and content that, in fact, he had an infuriating effect on the president. "I am bound to say," Taft wrote to his brother, "that his speeches are fuller of ego now than they ever were, and he allows himself to fall into a style that makes one think he considers himself still the President of the United States." Roosevelt promptly embarked on a speaking tour across sixteen states, which Taft remarked was "one continual ovation" to himself.[4] It was on this tour in Osawatomie, Kansas, that Roosevelt made his first public proclamation of the "new nationalism" and what it meant to him. It went beyond the conservation and trust-busting efforts of his presidential administration to include a comprehensive array of reforms such as direct primaries, welfare reform, a graduated income tax, worker's compensation, and increased federal regulation of business. "The man who wrongly holds that every human right is secondary to his profit must now give way to the advocate of human welfare," he told his Kansas audience. "Every man holds his property subject to the general right of the community to regulate its use to whatever degree the public welfare may require it."[5]

Suddenly, Roosevelt found himself cast as the nation's leading Progressive, more closely identified with the cause than even Robert La Follette. Early in 1912, Roosevelt's popularity was on a fast ascent while La Follette's bid for the Republican nomination was losing steam. The party was being torn apart at the seams; the Progressive wing turned against Taft and the "standpatters," refusing to support the party doctrine. As Roosevelt moved closer to announcing his intentions to seek the Republican nomination, he began to articulate additional reform measures, including women's suffrage and direct election of US senators to replace the practice of appointment by state legislatures. One reform measure would prove to have an effect on that year's Republican Party National Convention: a change to direct primaries to choose delegates in place of the brokered conventions that had characterized national conventions in the past. Because Taft largely had the support of party regulars in most states, adoption of the primary system was Roosevelt's only route to the nomination, and he cleverly turned his own nomination into a campaign issue consistent with his appeal for "the right of the people to rule."[6] These were radical departures from the doctrine of a party that had identified itself as the protector of big business, and Roosevelt's attacks stunned and outraged traditional Republican leaders, including Taft.

As the Republicans convened in Chicago on June 7, Roosevelt arrived with victories in nine of the twelve states that held primaries. This left the Republican National Committee with the task of distributing the delegates chosen in the primaries to the three candidates—Roosevelt, Taft, and La Follette—while also distributing delegates chosen by state conventions and caucuses. In the end the committee, made up mostly of old-guard Taft supporters, awarded the majority of the delegates and the party's nomination to the incumbent Taft.

Roosevelt was not inclined to step aside quietly, and his supporters—Progressive Republicans—were not about to allow the Democrats to lay claim to their reform policies without a fight, especially with the leading Democratic prospect, Woodrow Wilson, coming forth as a prominent advocate of the Progressive cause.[7] Amid outraged cries of unfairness and outright theft of delegates, Roosevelt's backers promptly bolted and began to follow through on plans to form their own party and put forth their own candidate. In fact, Roosevelt had anticipated exactly this scenario even before the party convention came to order in Chicago. Addressing a raucous rally, he vowed to battle to the end and defy the interest of the party bosses and the privileged. "We fight in honorable fashion for the good of mankind," he shouted before wildly enthusiastic crowds, "fearless of the future, unheeding of our individual fates, with unflinching hearts and undimmed eyes; we stand at Armageddon, and we battle for the Lord."[8]

Roosevelt's Progressive Republican loyalists proceeded out the door of the Chicago Coliseum and into a nearby meeting hall, where they solidified plans to form a third party and scheduled a national convention in the same city. Later that month, the National Progressive Party was formed, and after Roosevelt declared himself as fit as a bull moose, the press promptly nicknamed it the Bull Moose Party. The convention was set for August 5 in Chicago, and as that date approached the organization took shape, attracting members from the ranks of both major parties. Significantly, Roosevelt's nomination was seconded by the renowned Chicago reformer Jane Addams, who in her speech lauded the Progressive Party as "the exponent of that great American movement which is seeking the betterment of social conditions."[9]

The heart of the party's platform was the need to provide opportunities for the working class, to improve working conditions, and to regulate big business in such a way as to distribute wealth more fairly and equitably. The prominent position taken by Addams at the convention was seen as an indication of the party's commitment to women's suffrage. Traditional Republicans viewed the movement with outrage, with the *New York Times* going so far as to label the Progressive Party platform as "socialist doctrine."[10]

Meanwhile, the Democrats met in Baltimore amid feelings of confidence that their candidate would run successfully against a sundered Republican Party. The leading Progressive in their ranks was Woodrow Wilson, the former college president who had been elected governor of New Jersey in 1910. Wilson biographer A. Scott Berg characterized the platform adopted by Democrats in 1912 as "moderately progressive," focusing on lowering the protective tariff, strengthening antitrust laws, initiating a progressive income tax, and amending the Constitution to provide for direct election of senators.[11] Wilson himself articulated views that landed him to the left of Taft but in many ways aligned with Roosevelt. The trust question became the main issue of the campaign, with the two Progressives agreeing on the dangers of business consolidation but differing on the method of dealing with it. Roosevelt believed that monopoly was inevitable but that it could be controlled, regulated, and made useful to the public without being broken up. Wilson argued that, under Roosevelt's policies, government would never be able to effectively regulate monopoly and that government must step in to ensure that active competition was allowed to thrive.[12] He proposed to regulate competition in order to prevent the very formation of monopolies. Louis Brandeis, the highly respected lawyer who became Wilson's campaign spokesman and trusted ally, explained to the press that the candidate wished "to regulate competition instead of monopoly, for our industrial freedom and our civic freedom go hand in hand."[13]

Wilson carefully made clear that he had no complaint with big business so long as the corporations engaged in fair competition. The real danger, he said, was that the same groups of investors monopolized the banks and the railroads as well as manufacturing, mining, and utilities. Existing laws were powerless to prevent the powerful from crushing labor and consumers.[14] "The old political formulas do not fit the present problems," Wilson wrote. Big business is "necessary and natural, but that is a very different matter from the development of trusts," which are "indefensible and intolerable" in that they are established by men who wish to eliminate competition. "When we undertake the strategy to overcome and destroy this far-reaching system of monopoly, we are rescuing the business of this country, not injuring it."[15]

Wilson was immediately aware of Roosevelt's public appeal and his own comparatively dull, bookish persona. "He is a real, vivid person," he confided to a friend. "I am a vague, conjectural personality, more made up of opinions and academic prepossessions than of human traits and red corpuscles."[16] In September and October, the Democrat embarked on a campaign tour of several western states, addressing issues of concern to rural America and reiterating his reform-minded policies. In Lincoln, Nebraska, Wilson stood before approving crowds with the Nebraska "prairie populist" William Jennings Bryan at his side. "In coming to Nebraska," he proclaimed, "I am coming to the Mecca of progressive democracy," and he went on to lay out the need for strict control and regulation of corporate monopoly. "The hands that are being stretched into the bowels of the earth to take possession of the great riches that lie hidden in Alaska and elsewhere in the incomparable domain of the United States are the hands of monopoly. Are these men to continue to stand at the elbow of government?"[17]

And in St. Louis, a month before Election Day, Wilson brought up Alaska again, this time blaming Congress for failing to resolve the vexing problem of coal land leasing and charging that the impasse was due entirely to the threat of a monopoly controlled by Alaska Syndicate bosses. Why, he asked, were "great mountains of coal" sitting and waiting in Alaska unsalable under the government ban? His answer: "It is because the government doesn't know how yet to prevent the Guggenheims and men like them from closing their hand over the resources of Alaska."[18]

In Alaska, meanwhile, election year 1912 was shaping up to be another bruising affair, with James Wickersham standing at the center of the same kind of divide that had rendered the national Republican Party into two warring factions. Wickersham had so alienated himself from party loyalists—those who remained committed to President Taft and Territorial Governor Clark—that a Republican nomination for a third term in Congress appeared to be an impossibility. He made it clear to party leaders in Alaska that he would never "accept a nomination from a convention which would nominate Taft delegates [to the national convention] and endorse Taft's policy toward Alaska."[19]

In the days and weeks before Congress passed and President Taft signed the bill establishing an elected Alaska legislature, the rancorous debate was still very much alive in territorial politics. In March, the head of the Alaska Republican Party, Louis P. Shackleford of Juneau, foresaw the danger of a Roosevelt election, and in a speech before a gathering of his party he predicted serious consequences for the territory in such a case. "Roosevelt is the mouthpiece of Gifford Pinchot," he warned. "In the event of Roosevelt's election to the presidency, the policies of Pinchot would be carried out to the letter. Alaska would get nothing but stagnation and feeble development of its resources."[20] Shackleford did not mention Wickersham by name, but clearly he perceived the delegate's connection to the Roosevelt-Pinchot organization, and he had no intention of seeing him return to Washington to represent Alaska.

Early in the election season, many political observers were already tiring of the eternal feuding. A Juneau newspaper expressed relief in the emergence of local Democrat and lawyer Robert W. Jennings, calling him "the people's choice" for congressional delegate and giving him an early endorsement. "He is known to be upright, broad-minded, and above petty political practices," the paper's editorial page read. "He is too broad and too brainy to permit continuing squabbling and bickering, the curse of Alaska in the past. His election means death to factions and petty bickering and ensures harmony, advancement, and prosperity."[21]

At its territorial convention in Valdez at the end of March, the Alaska Democratic Party nominated Jennings as its candidate for congressional delegate.[22] But the Democrats were not immune from divisive and raucous infighting of their own. After party members nearly came to blows amid arguments about credentials and the seating of delegates, a dissident group walked out and reassembled in a nearby hall in a so-called "rump" convention. This group of "rump" Democrats put forth its own candidate, Martin Harrais, and thus, with the territorywide election set for August 13, the field of candidates for the seat held for two terms by James Wickersham suddenly included two Democrats—Jennings and Harrais.[23]

The Alaska Democratic Party adopted a platform that laid the blame for Alaska's ills on the shoulders of the Republicans, who had failed to make any progress toward the issues that all sides agreed were in the best interests of the territory. From the president on down to the appointed territorial governor and the elected congressional delegate, the Republican Party had mishandled every opportunity, the Democrats contended. Congress "ought to have given Alaska an elective legislature," the party platform said. "On the contrary, it has attempted to foist upon the people a commission appointed by the President." Self-government was described as a sacred right. "The power to make laws which are to govern us in our social affairs is but the application to Alaska of a right sanctified by the blood of our fathers." The cause of the lack of success has been "the internecine quarrel between the two factions of the Republican Party," the document concluded, and the people of Alaska are "sick and tired" of it. The Democratic platform also called on the federal government to construct and operate a railroad from tidewater to interior Alaska and to develop and maintain a coal mine to provide fuel both for the railroad and for the general public, strictly regulating prices and preventing monopoly.[24]

At the same time, the Republicans convened in Cordova and followed through on their rejection of party incumbent Wickersham, nominating Nome mayor William A. Gilmore as their candidate for congressional delegate. Wickersham knew that he would never earn the Republican endorsement so long as Shackleford and Clark maintained control, but news of Gilmore's rise within the party caused him to question his own political future. Gilmore was an old ally, friend, and supporter who had worked to elect Wickersham in years before. "I am in a hole," Wickersham despaired. "I cannot and will not fight him. It puts me out of touch for I cannot join with Shackleford and his crowd in turning the territory over to the Guggs."[25]

Fortunately for Wickersham, the same forces that had torn the national Republican Party down the middle were at work in Alaska as well. An insurgent wing of the party, loyal to Wickersham, vowed to stay away from the Cordova convention, reasoning, as one Wickersham Republican explained, that independent Republicans had nothing to gain by taking part. "That will be a Shackleford convention," he complained. Neither had Wickersham any intention of attending. A Valdez paper quoted him as reiterating the charge that Taft had personally made certain promises to Shackleford, Clark, and former Governor Hoggatt: if they delivered committed Taft delegates to the national Republican convention, they would then be allowed to control appointments to the forthcoming Alaska Territorial Legislature.[26]

At Cordova, the Republicans adopted a predictable platform, which promoted all the issues that Alaskans across the territory universally cared about. They insisted on full territorial self-government with a legislature elected by the people, and they demanded a solution to the coal lands impasse by granting patents to all leaseholders without delay under a law "that will be equitable and just but will prevent monopoly." The Republicans also called on the federal government to build, equip, and operate a railroad from the Gulf of Alaska to a terminus in the Interior.[27]

The independent wing of the Republican Party immediately began to plan for a convention of its own, where members intended to nominate Wickersham and persuade the two-term incumbent to enter the race against Gilmore and the two Democrats. By the middle of April, the independents' cause received a boost with the House passage of the Wickersham bill calling for an elected territorial legislature. Even Wickersham's strongest opponents were forced to give him a measure of credit. The *Valdez Daily Prospector*, for example, streamed the news from Washington across its front page. Yet it was faint praise. Immediately below the blaring headline announcing the bill's advancement there appeared another story that unabashedly painted a glowing picture of the paper's favored candidate, Robert W. Jennings, who had given a speech in Valdez the day before. In his lead, the *Prospector* reporter informed his readers that the Democratic candidate presented "a masterpiece of logic" that "reached far up in the realm of eloquence." Jennings attacked both arms of the Republican Party, charging that Wickersham, if reelected as an independent Republican, would be an outcast in Washington and that Gilmore, if elected, would represent the home-rule position of the hated President Taft. Jennings predicted that the Democrat Woodrow Wilson's election to the presidency in November was a certainty, and therefore he as a member of the president's party and the party of the majority in Congress would be more effective than either of his opponents. "An independent representative has no standing," he said in reference to Wickersham. "He takes no part in party caucus, and he is not taken into the confidence of party leaders." As for Gilmore, Jennings was equally dismissive. He is the candidate of Shackleford and the special interests, he said. And furthermore, the Republicans exhibited a glaring contradiction. They claimed to support an elected territorial legislature, but at the same time they were sending committed Taft delegates to the national party convention. "Taft wants the territory run by a bureau appointed by himself," Jennings charged. One could not in sincerity support Taft while also advocating for elected self-government for Alaska. "The day of judgment for the Republican Party has come," he concluded. "The people

are sick and tired of the bombast of a Roosevelt and the weak and vac-
illating spirit of Taft."[28]

On the editorial page of the same day's edition, the *Prospector* gave
Jennings its full endorsement, praising the Democrat's "masterful
exposition of the political situation as it exists today in Alaska." The
paper reiterated the inconsistency inherent in the Republicans' stand
in favor of home rule and yet backing Taft's candidacy. That action
alone, the editor wrote, revealed "the hidden plans of the Republican
Party masked behind a platform of fair words and promises" while
their real intent was to kill home rule entirely.[29]

The independent Republicans convened in Valdez on May 29 and
wasted no time in voicing their support for Roosevelt and Wickersham
while denouncing the Shackleford, Hoggatt, and Clark faction, which
they labeled "a cabal commonly known throughout Alaska as the 'Rule
or Ruin Gang.'" They praised Wickersham for his work in shepherding
the home-rule bill through Congress and for "the courageous stand
taken by him against the commission form of government for Alaska
proposed by President Taft." The independents went on to condemn
the "silly inconsistency" of the regular Republican Party platform and
denounce Taft for his failure to carry out Roosevelt's promise to provide an elected legislature.[30] The *Valdez Daily Prospector*, which had
"nail[ed] the banner of Robert W. Jennings to her masthead,"[31] welcomed Wickersham's candidacy. It "adds zest to the game," the editor
wrote, but "it will worry no one, save perhaps Shackleford's unfortunate candidate." The *Prospector* predicted that if Wickersham were to
return to Washington, he would be severely weakened by politics. "In
case Taft is elected," the paper observed, "Wickersham will be compelled to remain without the storm door; in case the Democrats triumph, he will not be in harmony with the dominant party."[32]

As the home-rule bill continued to make headway through Congress
in the summer of 1912, Alaskans across the political spectrum were
forced to acknowledge Wickersham's success in securing a measure
that all agreed was in the best interests of the territory. The strongly
pro-Jennings *Daily Alaska Dispatch* in Juneau ran a front-page story
reporting on a resolution passed by the local city council, which
expressed that body's "pride and satisfaction" in seeing the bill
approved by the House of Representatives. It was, the resolution said,
"a victory which restores to us the heritage of every American citizen,

the right of self-government."[33] In Nome, the *Daily Nugget* was a staunch supporter of the city's mayor, William Gilmore, in his race to win the delegate's seat in Congress, yet the paper was effusive in its praise for Wickersham when the home-rule bill was recommended for passage by the Senate. Should the measure become law, the editor conceded, "we will have to give credit where it belongs and render unto Caesar the things that are Caesar's, and in this particular case, Caesar will be James Wickersham."[34] A month later, when the home-rule bill received final congressional approval and was headed for the president's signature, the *Nugget* again gave credit where it was due. The front-page headline proclaimed "Delegate Wins Again for the Territory." And on the editorial page of the same edition, the *Nugget*, while noting its differences with Wickersham in his "methods of politics," recognized the delegate's "staying qualities" and added that "Alaskans cannot help but admire a man with the tenacity to hold on with a bulldog grip and win out in the end."[35]

Meanwhile, however, Wickersham's successes in Washington did not deter his opponents in Alaska from continuing attacks that sometimes turned vicious and personal. The Democrat Robert Jennings focused his campaign on two issues that he contended made Wickersham unacceptable as Alaska's delegate to Congress: his close association with Roosevelt and his combative, self-centered personality. Addressing a crowded rally in Juneau, Jennings pointed out that Wickersham had endorsed Roosevelt and that Roosevelt was "the great prime mover of the two greatest ills from which Alaska suffers." Those ills were the withdrawal of coal lands from development and the establishment of a national forest reserve in southeastern Alaska. As for Wickersham's temperament, Jennings charged that the man had "no tact" and that he quarreled with everyone who could be of help to the territory. "He hollers 'Guggenheim' and 'corporate hireling' at all who do not shout his praises," he said. "He opposes everything for the benefit of Alaska which he himself does not originate."[36]

In May, the Socialists of Alaska met in Fairbanks, hammered out a platform, and put forth a congressional candidate of their own, Kazis Krauczunas of Ketchikan. By 1912, socialism had gained a strong presence in the mining camps and small communities of interior Alaska and fishing towns in Southeast. Krauczunas's advocacy of unionism and reform of labor laws resonated well with workers who resented the power of the Morgan-Guggenheim syndicate and had become dissatisfied with working conditions and low wages.[37] A native of Lithuania, Krauczunas was like many first-generation European immigrants who had crossed the ocean with expectations of prospering in the New World but had become embittered when they found conditions no better than what they had left behind. For many in the North, their dreams of staking a claim and earning a living by working their own ground had dissolved, and their only option was to toil under what one historian called "the profit-gorged capitalist and his tentacles of monopoly."[38]

The tenets of socialism promised some relief for discontented workers. The party convention in Fairbanks demanded immediate establishment of territorial self-government in Alaska with an elected legislature. It called on the federal government to build and operate a railroad to access resources in interior Alaska and to develop and operate coal mines, which would furnish fuel for the railroad and provide coal for the people of the territory at the cost of production.[39]

The left-leaning Fairbanks paper *Alaska Citizen* was on board with the socialist agenda. It complained in its editorial columns that, in six years of representation in Congress, Alaska delegates had accomplished little and changed nothing. In the *Citizen*'s view, Wickersham had been wholly ineffective, due largely to his combative temperament. In his two terms in office, the delegate had "given more heed to the venting of his personal animosities than he has to the wants of the territory," the paper said. It went on to charge that he had "not in the slightest degree facilitated in the building of a mile of railroad" and that because of his hatred for the Guggenheims he had "allowed rancor to cloud his better judgment." The editor suggested that Krauczunas was a man whom Alaskans could trust. He would "accord to their wishes a greater amount of importance than to his personal squabbles."[40]

As Election Day drew nearer, Wickersham's association with Roosevelt and Pinchot loomed large in the campaign. And in early August, when the Bull Moosers convened in Chicago to nominate the former president as a third-party candidate, newspapers across Alaska were quick to heap scorn on the proceedings. In their view, Roosevelt and Pinchot were the cause of every ailment that afflicted the nation's northernmost citizens. Their conservation policies had locked up resources in the territory, stifled development, and robbed workers of jobs. On August 3, Wickersham boarded a train in Washington, DC, headed for Chicago, where he was seated as a Roosevelt delegate at the national Progressive Party convention. He was greeted by Gifford Pinchot, and immediately he called on this old ally in the fight for territorial self-government to insert a plank for Alaska home rule in the national party platform. Two days later, Wickersham met personally with Roosevelt, who informed him that he had instructed the platform committee to add such language.[41] Wickersham then hurried back to Washington, where final passage of his home-rule bill was still not certain. In Fairbanks, the *Daily News-Miner* was outraged. "Is Wickersham looking after our interests when he is today in attendance at the Bull Moose convention in Chicago?" the editor asked. "Is he looking after our interests when he deserts the home rule bill at a critical stage to play politics with the Bull Moose?" But it was not only Wickersham's neglect of his responsibilities in Washington that angered the editor; it was the fact of his cozying up to the hated conservationists. Roosevelt, if elected, would extend his policies "until every resource in Alaska is tied up," he wrote. "What excuse can James Wickersham have as delegate from Alaska for stultifying himself and working against the interests of his constituents?"[42]

The *Cordova Daily Alaskan* predicted that Wickersham would "pay a severe penalty" for his participation at the national Progressive Party convention, even suggesting that his association with Roosevelt and Pinchot would lead to the end of his political career. Alaska's delegate had "allowed himself to get tied up with the one man who, more than any other, is responsible for the unhappy, discontented, and impoverished condition of the people of this northland," the *Daily Alaskan* said. Swayed by Pinchot, Roosevelt had "tied up the resources of Alaska and discouraged capital from seeking investment and undertaking development in this territory."[43]

Stuck in Washington as the congressional session dragged on through the summer, Wickersham was unable to meet the voters face-to-face and respond directly to mounting criticisms in the press. Gilmore, Jennings, Harrais, and Krauczunas seemed to be gaining in strength as they swept across the territory speaking to packed houses.

In Nome, the *Daily Nugget* had for weeks been guaranteeing a win for Gilmore, explaining that "the miners and prospectors scattered here and there over the peninsula" would come out in force on Election Day to support their hometown mayor.[44] The *Daily Nugget* further predicted that Gilmore would carry Wickersham's hometown of Fairbanks, where none of the three local papers endorsed the delegate for reelection.

But on Election Day, August 13, with Wickersham celebrating the imminent signing of his home-rule bill, voters across Alaska were not inclined to argue with success. The incumbent won handily, and the *Fairbanks Daily Times* admitted that "the mass of Fairbanks rejoiced." Early counts showed the Socialist Krauczunas polling second in the territorywide tally, followed by Gilmore and then the Democrats Jennings and Harrais. Wickersham's victory was accomplished with the backing of Progressive Republicans along with a great number of Socialists, who obviously found much to admire in the Progressive agenda. It was a clear popular rebuke of Shackleford and Clark and their brand of partisan politics. "The people have had more Republicanism than they have had good government," the *Times* concluded. "They refused to be dictated to by the autocrats of the party machine and have drifted steadily over to the delegate and into the ranks of the Socialists."[45]

Still, the results left many partisan Socialists disappointed. The Fairbanks-based *Tanana Valley Socialist* newspaper commented that Wickersham's win meant that there would be no change in the conservative coalition that stood in the way of progress for the working class. "We now have a Repo-Demo-Wicko combination," the *Socialist* complained, and "windy Jim will undoubtedly act as the bellwether for the triple alliance." Workers must "emancipate themselves from their industrial bondage," the paper declared. "The people, the wealth producers, must rule or be ruined."[46]

For his part, Wickersham, savoring a decisive win at home, prepared for his return to Congress with the support of a majority of the voting public in favor of a Progressive agenda.

PROGRESSIVISM AND THE ALASKA RAILROAD

This national devilfish

～✲～

PROGRESSIVISM was the incubator of the Alaska Railroad. In 1912, it created the ideal climate and provided the perfect conditions that allowed the project to take form until a living being was born two years later. The prospect of financing, constructing, and operating the railroad gave Progressives in Congress plenty of reasons to lend their support. It would open up vast areas of mineral and agricultural wealth in a land that was owned collectively by the American people but many believed had been managed poorly. It would build an efficient means of transportation from a tidewater port to the Interior, creating jobs and opportunities for the working public. It would demonstrate the Progressive conviction that government at its best was an agent for progress and improvement in people's lives. The government railroad made a statement of the strength of federal regulatory control in the era of popular reaction against the power of corporate trusts. It would occur in a place where the giant Alaska Syndicate owned by some of the richest financiers in the world threatened to monopolize every sector of the economy. This project would be a model of Progressive democracy at work.

Woodrow Wilson captured the electoral win in November when most political predictions proved true: Theodore Roosevelt's third-party campaign split the Republican vote down the middle and handed the victory to the Democrat. A fourth candidate, Socialist Eugene V. Debs, won 897,011 votes, nearly 6 percent of the total in the most successful campaign ever run by a member of that party. Never again would a Socialist receive such a large share of the total vote. Historians have noted that it was a remarkable showing, considering that Roosevelt's and Wilson's Progressive platforms probably took a considerable number of votes away from Debs.[1]

Alaska voters seemed optimistic about the prospects of legislation that would advance the causes they cared about. They had elected James Wickersham for a third term in Congress based on his promises to build on past successes. "He probably will have a Progressive Democratic administration to deal with," a Fairbanks newspaper noted, "and what has been denied Alaska in the past may be secured easily from a paternal government which promises much."[2] As it turned out, the nation had put into office not only a Democratic administration but also Democratic majorities in both houses of Congress.

This appeared to be Alaska's time. Public opinion and the mood in Washington were clearly growing in favor of doing something to aid in building up the nation's forlorn northern frontier. A series of events that occurred prior to the excitement of the 1912 elections served to bring an Alaska railroad bill closer to the fore. Early in the year, the Senate introduced a bill calling for construction of a government-funded line from coastal waters to the Interior, and the measure was received favorably. The *Saturday Evening Post*, a weekly magazine with a circulation of more than one million, praised the project for its potential to "open up" Alaska and for its place in protecting against the power of corporate trusts at work in the territory. "This is an intelligent and admirable bill," the *Post* said in its opinion column. "A government railroad is desirable in the highest degree for the free development of Alaska because a monopoly of transportation will mean a pretty effectual monopoly of mineral resources."[3]

At the same time, Secretary of the Interior Walter L. Fisher expressed his belief that the project was vital to progress for Alaska. Fisher, whom Taft had appointed as successor to the embattled Richard Ballinger, wrote in his annual report to the president that conditions in the territory called for "immediate action by Congress." His conclusions were based not only on official reports but also on his personal tour to Alaska the previous summer. He had come away from that visit con-

A four-member commission appointed by President William Howard Taft in 1912 was directed to travel to Alaska to examine possible railroad routes in Alaska from a southcentral port to coal lands and extending to the Interior. The commissioners included Colin Ingersoll, Alfred Brooks, Leonard Cox, and Chairman Jay Morrow (Alaska State Library ASL-P277-006-005).

vinced that the first and most vital need was a railroad, constructed by the federal government, running from tidewater to the Tanana-Yukon River system. Fisher was enthusiastic about the role of the railroad in developing mineral resources as well as the agricultural potential of interior Alaska. He said that the Department of Agriculture, after conducting experiments in Rampart and Fairbanks, believed that conditions there compared favorably with productive agricultural areas of northern Europe.[4]

Taft agreed and made the case as strongly as he could for immediate construction. In a message delivered to Congress on February 2, 1912, he called for a railroad system that would "reach from the coast into the heart of Alaska and open the great interior valleys of the Yukon and the Tanana, which have agricultural as well as great mineral possibilities." The president added that it was only on account of the special and unusual conditions prevailing in Alaska that he was advocating a railroad to be funded and built by the federal government. He explained that he would not support such a project if private enterprise were able to offer the same level of service, but an exception must be made in Alaska "for the purpose of encouraging the development of that vast and remarkable territory." Therefore, Taft proposed a plan in which the government would build and own the railroad but lease its operation to a private contractor. "The United States owes it to Alaska," he concluded, "to take an exceptional step and to build a railroad that shall open the treasures of Alaska to the Pacific."[5]

In March and April, committees in both houses of Congress opened hearings to address the transportation issues in Alaska. Representative William Sulzer of New York, a longtime critic of the federal government's treatment of the territory and persistent advocate of home rule, spoke at length about the need for the government to fund railroad construction. Sulzer described the mines of gold, silver, coal, and copper as "practically inexhaustible," and he promised that once the government supplied adequate transportation, families would "begin the cultivation of the soil, the production of lumber, the raising of cattle, and the development of its wonderful resources."[6] He was backed up by Falcon Joslin, owner of the Tanana Valley Railroad, who testified first before the House Committee on Territories and then one week later before the equivalent committee in the Senate. "Railroad building by private enterprise has proven absolutely a failure," Joslin told the House committee. "Work has stopped." He said that Alaska was like every other unsettled country in the world in that the population was too small to produce enough income to support private enterprise. According to Joslin, it takes "five to ten years of colonization" before there is sufficient population and traffic to pay operating expenses and interest on investment. "Private capital cannot wait for returns," he concluded, and therefore it was up to the government to step in and bear the initial cost burden.[7]

Addressing the Senate Committee on Territories, Joslin promised sweeping prosperity for Alaska if only the federal government would plant the seed. Just one thousand miles of railroad were needed to get the project started, he explained, and after that it would support itself. "A railroad system is like a plant; once you lay down the trunk line, it grows." After all, he stated, the government subsidized the Union Pacific and other railroads in the West, and from that beginning grew a network consisting of more than fifty thousand miles of track, none of which was aided by government. Joslin predicted the same future for Alaska. "I have no doubt that in forty or fifty years there will be ten thousand miles of railroad, and the government would never need to aid any except for the first thousand miles."[8] In addition, he predicted that with the growth of railroads, the population of Alaska would boom as well. He expressed his belief that within a year of the announcement of the government's intent to build a railroad, the eight thousand residents of the Tanana Valley would grow to sixteen thousand and very quickly swell to a hundred thousand.[9]

Such optimism was a common thread that ran through the testimony given by proponents of the railroad, and it had its effects on congressmen. One sign that Washington was listening to the needs of the territory showed itself in a provision in the Alaska home-rule bill passed by Congress and signed by the president on August 23, 1912. Section 18, which was added by amendment in the Senate after the House had already passed the bill, called for creation of an Alaska railroad commission appointed by the president and charged with the task of examining possible routes from a suitable harbor to the coalfields and extending to a terminus in the Interior. The commission was expected to recommend a route that would best facilitate the construction and operation of a railroad and coal mine. It was to be made up of engineers from the US Army and Navy and a civil engineer who had no connection with any railroad in Alaska. A fourth seat on the commission was narrowly specified for "a geologist in charge of Alaska surveys." This provision was clearly intended to secure a place on the commission for Alfred H. Brooks, the geologist at the head of the Alaska Division of the US Geological Survey, a man who was widely recognized as the nation's leading authority on Alaska's resources. President Taft acted quickly and within a week had named the four commissioners, with Major Jay Morrow as chair, Alfred Brooks as vice chair, and engineers Leonard Cox and Colin Ingersoll as members. The four men determined that with the summer nearly over they would have to depart for Alaska without delay in order to meet the December deadline for submitting their report to Congress. They assembled in Seattle and sailed north on September 10. On the 15th they reached Seward, where they examined the terminal and structures of the Alaska Northern Railroad.

The Alaska Northern was a failed attempt by private investors to construct a line from Seward to the banks of the Tanana River at Nenana. It began life as the Alaska Central in 1900, when developer John E. Ballaine chose the harbor on Resurrection Bay as the base for his operation. There he established the town of Seward and built the terminus for a railroad he envisioned as extending north to Cook Inlet, then to the Matanuska-Susitna Valley and across the Alaska Range to the Interior. Ballaine was banking on his belief that Alaska would develop resources, including gold, coal, timber, and agriculture, and that with the growth of these industries the territory's population would swell. His intention was to have his railroad ready in time for the boom and to provide the needed transportation; he was especially counting on tonnage from the Matanuska coalfield to his docks at Seward. But the enterprise faced a hard slog. By 1905, the track extended less than twenty miles out of Seward, and Ballaine, his cash reserves depleted, sold out to a group that renamed it the Alaska Northern. The new owners struggled to continue construction but by 1909 had reached only mile 71 at the head of Turnagain Arm where, as historian William H. Wilson described it, "the tracklaying of the financially exhausted railroad ceased forever."[10]

However, even though Ballaine's visionary railroad failed, his prediction of development and economic growth was not entirely wrong. Mining and farming did, in fact, prosper and attract several thousand people to the central part of the territory where Ballaine intended to do business. The 1910 census pegged the total number of permanent Alaska residents (not counting seasonal workers) at 63,700, and in the region encompassing Southcentral and the Interior, permanent residents numbered 32,500.[11] But, as historian Wilson pointed out,[12] the Alaska Central-Northern failed as a result of two unrelated factors. The first, completely unforeseeable, was Theodore Roosevelt's withdrawal of coal land leasing in 1906, which stopped coal production in the Matanuska and everywhere on federal land and took away a major source of revenue. The second was a fundamental misreading of the economics of railroading in Alaska. Success depended on access to a giant extractive resource akin to the fabulously rich Kennecott mine, which supported the Copper River and Northwestern out of Cordova. Lacking such a storehouse, a railroad would require a level of financing that could be had only with the backing of a private conglomerate the size of the Morgan-Guggenheim trust or through subsidies from the United States government. Ballaine had neither.

In Seward, the four commissioners looked closely at the Alaska Northern as a possibility for the start of a government-built route to the Interior. They traveled up the line to the end of the track and then by boat to the head of Knik Arm. From there, they moved with packhorses over a rough road to the headwaters of the Little Susitna River in the Willow Creek mining district to inspect conditions for new railroad construction. They returned to Seward by the same route and then by steamer to Katalla and Valdez. From there, the commissioners began an arduous journey of nearly two weeks, traveling by horse-drawn buckboard, stagecoach, and for the last forty miles by automobile, arriving in Fairbanks on October 12. In the Interior, they inspected the Tanana Valley Railroad and toured mining operations on Cleary Creek before turning south again by stagecoach and arriving on October 24 in Chitina to examine the Copper River and Northwestern Railway. They returned to Valdez and arrived in Seattle on November 17.[13]

The commission submitted its report to Congress on January 20, 1913. It was explicit in urging Congress to fund railroad construction to "be undertaken at once and prosecuted with vigor." In Alaska, the commissioners noted, the United States possessed "a frontier territory of great size and of wonderful industrial possibilities." The report described a climate that was favorable to permanent settlement and to agriculture. It cited mineral resources that were vast but little exploited and a population that was sparse only because of inadequate transportation facilities.[14] For access to the Interior, the commission recommended purchasing and extending the Copper River and Northwestern Railway, which was already in service from Cordova to Chitina. From there, it would construct 313 miles of track to Fairbanks. On the Cordova route, it said, the initial investment would be less than from Seward because the line as far as Chitina already existed, resulting in fewer miles of new track. Additionally, the commission found the harbor at Cordova to be superior to that of Seward, and coal resources were more accessible at Bering River than at Matanuska. However, the commission was not satisfied with this route alone, as it would leave unserved the large areas of rich agricultural lands and mineral wealth in the Matanuska-Susitna region and the valley of the Kuskokwim River to the southwest. As a solution, the commissioners proposed a second route, which would acquire the track abandoned by the Alaska Northern at Turnagain Arm and extend it first 115 miles to the Susitna and then an additional 229 miles to the Kuskokwim. The Cordova-to-Fairbanks line would be connected to the Bering River coalfield, and the Seward-Susitna-Kuskokwim route would have access to the Matanuska coalfield.[15]

Taft, in a message conveyed to Congress along with the commission report, firmly agreed with these conclusions, saying that the railroad system was "not only justified but imperative if the fertile regions of inland Alaska and the mineral resources are to be utilized. A large region will be opened up to the homesteader, the prospector, and the miner." Taft said that such progress could be realized only if the federal government stepped in to fund construction and ownership. However, he reiterated his opposition to government operation, saying as he had in his message to Congress one year before that operation should be done under lease with private enterprise.[16] By this time, of course, Taft was a lame-duck president, and the man chosen by the voters to succeed him, Progressive Democrat Woodrow Wilson, had no such reservations. In his first year in office, the scholarly Wilson— former Princeton University president and New Jersey governor— would forcefully endorse government construction and operation of the Alaska Railroad and sign the legislation that made the massive project a reality.

Early in 1913, there was no lack of advocacy in Washington. As the Sixty-Second Congress was nearing adjournment in February, Representative Sydney Anderson of Minnesota took to the House floor to promote legislation to fund construction of the railroad. "I was the pioneer in advancing the idea" that the railroad was the key to proper conservation and development of Alaska's resources, he said. His bill called for construction of a line beginning at Seward and running to Fairbanks with access to the Matanuska coalfields. To Anderson, it was important to "safeguard against monopoly" because history had shown that control of transportation had been the greatest force in the monopolies of coalfields. "If we are not in earnest in our desire to prevent the control of natural resources of Alaska by a few, there is no reason why the government should build a railroad," he concluded. "Most of us agree, however, that it is not good economic policy to permit the ownership of transportation facilities by corporations principally engaged in the development of other industries."[17]

On Inauguration Day, March 4, Wilson dedicated his presidency to a course that was founded on the core ideals of Progressive Democrats. His inaugural address noted the great advances the nation had made in achieving material wealth and industrial strength and in building up a system of government that had become a model of liberty. Yet along with such progress there had been a human cost. Too often, he said, "there has been something crude and heartless and unfeeling in our haste to succeed and be great," and the government had forgotten the people. "The groans and agony of it all had not yet reached our ears, the solemn, moving undertone of our life coming up out of the mines and factories and out of every home where the struggle had its intimate and familiar seat." He pledged to institute a proactive government that would have justice and service to humanity as its focal point. It was a statement of belief in the power and duty of government to be a force for good in people's lives.

Wilson did not mention Alaska in his address, but clearly he and his fellow Progressives saw the northern frontier as a place where their lofty ideals could be put into practice. It was a storehouse of wealth where a population of hardworking Americans were destined to live and prosper, and only the United States government had the means to make it happen. The resources were owned collectively by the nation's citizens, and Wilson was determined to see to it that they were used for the common good. A key position in his administration, therefore, would be the secretary of the interior, and for that position he required a committed Progressive and a person with expertise and experience with issues surrounding transportation, public lands, and resources. Four days before his inauguration, Wilson named just such a man to the position: Franklin K. Lane, a former lawyer, newspaper reporter and editor, and politician who had been appointed as commissioner of the Interstate Commerce Commission by Theodore Roosevelt in 1905 and reappointed by Taft in 1909. As head of the ICC, Lane became intimately involved with railroading, especially with federal regulation and oversight of trusts and the laws that had been put in place to prevent monopoly control of the industry.

Lane threw his weight behind the Alaska Railroad from his first days in office. In May 1913, committees in both houses of Congress were heavily engaged in hearings on bills working their way through the legislative process. In a letter of support to Senator Key Pittman, chairman of the Senate Committee on Territories, Lane based his reasoning on a belief in the unlimited resources waiting to be extracted and the benefit of that wealth to the whole people of the United States. He said that the one and only way to make an unsettled country "part of the real world" was by construction of railroads and that the ownership of those railroads determines "the future of that country, the character of its population, the kind of industries they will engage in, and ultimately the nature of the civilization they will enjoy." Without government help, he continued, Alaska would remain "little more than a land of natural wonders, here and there dotted with mining camps and fishing villages." However, with federal assistance Alaska would progress into "a land not only of mines and fisheries, but of towns, farms, mills and factories supporting millions of people of the hardiest and most wholesome of the race." Lane acknowledged that government-funded construction and operation of a railroad would be a departure from past policies for the United States, but he believed that the conditions prevailing in Alaska called for new ways of thinking. With federal ownership, he said, the government would be free of any selfish influences. "We can only secure the highest and fullest use of Alaska by making her railways wholly subordinate to her industrial and social life and needs—true public utilities."[18]

Lane's comments were noted in the press. *Literary Digest* responded by commenting that "the dark forebodings of those who said that too much conservation would be the ruin of Alaska seem to have come true."[19] The private capital that was needed in the early stages of the territory's development was driven out by a "hostile crusade," the magazine charged. As a result, no other investor had been willing to put time or money into the work, and "her development is slow and halting." The *Digest* went on to suggest that the Wilson administration's remedy calling for government ownership might prove to be the "salvation" of Alaska, citing the success of the government-owned Panama Railway Company as an argument in favor of the project so earnestly touted by Lane in his letter to Pittman.

In August, Lane, on a tour of western states, continued to plug Alaska as a center of great population in the future if only the government would take the lead in providing railroad transportation. "I have faith that my boy will see Alaska when it shall contain five, six, seven, or ten million persons and be one of the richest parts of the United States," he declared to a public gathering in Seattle. "We must build railroads in Alaska."[20]

While such optimism resonated well with audiences in Seattle, it was not always greeted with enthusiasm in the East. The *New York Times*, for example, huffed at the concept of public ownership of railroads. The paper was convinced that Lane's advocacy of it was "the logical result of the theory, regarded as self-demonstrating, that it is the duty of the government to prevent private capital from making a dollar in Alaska." If the coalfields on federal lands were opened to leasing on a large scale, the paper suggested, railroads would be built by private investors without cost to the taxpayers. "There are 65 million tillable acres and more mineral wealth than is known," it continued. "There ought to be railways, but they ought not be political railways. A surer help than the levying of taxes would be the taking off of the drags. The railroads would build themselves if they were allowed."[21] *The Nation* magazine generally supported the railroad, calling it an "admirable proposal," but it urged its readers to accept Secretary Lane's "ardor" with caution. The magazine acknowledged Alaska's great potential for resource development, but it seriously doubted claims of large population growth in the near future. The American people do not fear the "rigors of a long winter," the writer observed, but they do not prefer "to go to places so remote in point of location and so peculiar in other respects as Alaska. The process of settlement will in all probability be a slow one at best."[22]

Skeptics were heard in congressional committee meetings as well, and Alaska Delegate James Wickersham was ready with his defense against those who held out in favor of private sector development. He aimed to prove that private construction would never occur because the powerful Morgan-Guggenheim conglomerate would not allow it. In lengthy testimony, Wickersham explained the situation in

Alaska as one in which for years no one could build a private railroad without the consent of the Alaska Syndicate. The failures of railroad starts in Valdez and Seward were proof of the syndicate's power to control the competition. The Morgan side of the trust, Wickersham stated, had under its control more financial power than any other business in the world. And the Guggenheims held a monopoly on mining and transportation in much of the North Pacific. Together, the two "have thrown out their tentacles along the coast in Alaska," he said. Not only had they secured a monopoly on coal, copper, and transportation, but they were also in control of the three principal gateways to the Interior, those leading from Cordova, Valdez, and Seward. Alaska is "in danger of being entirely monopolized by the combination of these two powerful financial interests," he told the House committee. "It is your duty as trustees of this estate to stand between this trust estate and this monopoly and prevent them from taking it over."[23]

John Ballaine, founder of the Alaska Central Railroad, speaking before a Senate committee in May 1913, told a tale of the strong-arm tactics used by the Morgan-Guggenheim syndicate to stifle railroad competition in Alaska. Ballaine testified that after he sold his interest in the Alaska Central, he approached a top representative of J. P. Morgan about financing a different plan, a narrow-gauge railway reaching from Seward to the Tanana River. This Morgan representative, G. W. Perkins, sent an expert to Alaska to assess resource potential along the proposed line, and the man returned with a favorable report. Perkins himself traveled to Alaska in the summer of 1909 and subsequently informed Ballaine that he was in favor of financing the railroad but that his opinion was subject to approval of the Guggenheim family. By November of that year, the deal was off, Ballaine said, killed by the Guggenheims "on the ground that they regarded the Tanana Valley as their field." Furthermore, the Guggenheims were not inclined to back any additional railroad construction in Alaska until patents to pending coal land claims were settled.[24] Essentially, the powerful syndicate had called on its connections within the banking community to stop any financing of the project and end the start-up of a competing railroad.[25]

Reports of this kind were exactly what Wickersham wished the senators to hear. His arguments in support of the government railroad were centered, first of all, on his strident resistance to the Morgan-

Guggenheim syndicate and, second, on his glowing, sometimes gran-
diose, descriptions of the stores of mineral and agricultural wealth
lying in the ground. He told the Senate committee that the territory
could be home to ten million people. The Tanana Valley he described
as "fifty miles wide and hundreds of miles long and as fertile as the
Mississippi Valley." Annual precipitation is very low, he explained,
but nature has provided a "subirrigation" system by which the frozen
ground thaws and gives moisture to the crops from below as needed.
It is a phenomenon that "beats any irrigation project or reclamation
scheme in any of your western states, and does not cost you and never
will cost you a nickel." He concluded by observing that "in connection
with the development of coal, copper, and gold resources of the country, which are practically inexhaustible, it is hard to tell how large a
population the country can support."[26]

With the Senate and House committees concluding their hearings
in the summer of 1913, the railroad bills moved swiftly. In December,
President Wilson reiterated his support for the project in his annual
message to a joint session of Congress. The Alaska Railroad fit well
with his Progressive belief that the nation's natural resources were
commonly held assets to be used for the good of all. "The resources in
question must be used but not destroyed or wasted," Wilson declared,
"used but not monopolized upon any narrow idea of individual rights
as against the abiding interests of communities."[27]

The next month, when the second session of the Sixty-Third
Congress convened after the holiday recess, bills calling for construction of the Alaska Railroad were brought to the floor of both houses of
Congress. Senate Bill 48, sponsored by Senator George Chamberlain
of Oregon, came up for debate on January 12, 1914. On that day, over
the course of three hours, Chamberlain presented an array of reports
and statistics meant to inform his fellow senators of the temperate
climate prevailing in Alaska and the territory's limitless potential
for supporting a large population and an economy based on farming
and mining. He compared Alaska to the Scandinavian countries and
parts of Russia, which supported eleven million people while the
population of Alaska numbered only sixty-five thousand. This, he
said, was "an astounding comparison" when considering that these
European countries are almost exactly the same latitude as Alaska,
"with conditions almost exactly the same." He cited research done by

C. C. Georgeson of the US Department of Agriculture at experimental stations in interior Alaska, estimating the farming and grazing lands in the Tanana Valley alone at 9.7 million acres. If agriculture in Alaska were developed to its full potential, Chamberlain predicted, it along with mining and fishing "should support a population almost equal to that of Europe north of 60° latitude and a commerce of equal or greater importance." The senator warned, however, that such progress depended entirely on adequate transportation. He said that if members of Congress thoroughly understood the situation, "they would be entirely satisfied as to the possibility of developing Alaska from an agricultural as well as from every other standpoint, if proper transportation facilities were afforded."[28]

Chamberlain continued his efforts in Senate floor sessions held intermittently over the next ten days, addressing lawmakers who generally received him favorably. On January 14, however, he ran into stiff opposition from Senator John Sharp Williams of Mississippi, who based his arguments on an article written by Captain James Gordon Steese in that month's edition of the *American Review of Reviews*. Steese, a civil engineer with the Alaska Road Commission, agreed with the often-stated assumption that it was the lack of a transportation infrastructure that was retarding progress and development of the territory's vast wealth of resources. But Steese was a road builder, and he held doubts about the long-term success of a railroad standing alone in an emerging frontier without a network of feeder roads to service the freight and passengers moving on the rails. Every attempt to develop railroad transportation in Alaska had failed, he said, for the simple reason that no connecting roads had been in place to distribute the goods once they reached the railroad platform. "No railroad can be successful without roads as branches or feeders any more than a tree can grow by its trunk alone without branches and leaves," he wrote. "The last connecting line between the railroad and its customers, the mine, the farm, and the factory, is a wagon or truck." Steese contended that an expenditure of $7.25 million for roads over the next ten years was a much wiser investment than spending up to $40 million on a railroad. A network of roads would satisfy all the transportation needs in Alaska until the territory was sufficiently developed to justify construction of a railroad. "Without road systems, no Alaska railroad need be expected either greatly to stimulate the development so much as to be desired or to be anything but a financial failure itself," he concluded.[29]

Senator Williams had long been a critic of the entire proposition, basing his opposition on two points: the Alaska climate and the impropriety of government involvement in what should be private enterprise. "I submit that no thousand miles of railroad can be built in Alaska with the climatic conditions and the labor conditions for any thirty-five million dollars," he cried. "Even if the entire scheme is to be a brilliant success, it strikes me as something unusual and unprecedented and something not altogether justified by our duties toward that territory." Williams suggested that if the government were to spend that amount of money to build, own, and operate a railroad, the line should run not in "an outlying territory like Alaska" but rather from the Great Lakes to the Gulf of Mexico. "But I do not want to do either," he added. "I do not know where the government construction of railroads is going to stop if it starts." Williams feared the increased power of the federal government and the resultant direct threat to the freedom of the citizenry. "There has been no government in this world that ever began, continued, and fell that did not fall by top-heaviness," he stated, "by gradually assuming to itself every interest and every industry of the people until the number of those in the employ of the government became a resistless power, naval, military, and civil."

Now, with the Steese article in his hands, Williams had a third weapon to use in his battle against the project. He proposed building a system of roads in the territory at a fraction of the cost of the Chamberlain bill. "Seven or eight million dollars put in Alaska as a loan," he estimated, "will do more good for Alaska than thirty-five or forty million put into one trunk railway."[30] Williams was not alone. Senator Porter J. McCumber of North Dakota referred to the railroad as "the first great step into the realm of paternalism. It is the beginning of the paternalistic or socialistic idea of complete government ownership of all public utilities," he said.[31]

Other senators quickly rose to defend the project in the face of these attacks. Senator Thomas Walsh of Montana dismissed as "irrelevant" any notion of the "adverse character" of government ownership of railroads in Alaska. It was one matter for the government to enter into the railroad business in a highly populated and settled part of the country, where private enterprise was willing and able to provide service, he contended, but it was quite another to enter into a frontier "for the primary purpose of the development and settlement of that territory to make available to the people the great wealth nature has placed there." Walsh went on to speak for three hours in an effort to sway the Senate in favor of the railway bill. He pointed out the benefit to the US Navy of the nearly unlimited coal supply in Alaska, saying that the railroad would make it possible to avoid shipping coal from the East Coast to fuel the Pacific Fleet and thereby save millions of dollars a year. Walsh touted the agricultural potential of the Tanana Valley in the most glowing of terms, comparing it favorably to the farming regions of Alberta and Saskatchewan in Canada and in his home state of Montana. "They have sunlight until 10 o'clock at night," he proclaimed, and in addition, "the frozen ground keeps continually giving up its moisture for the support of the plant life above. Thus the frost below actually aids in the growth of vegetation." The result, he said, was that "the growing season sprouts, grows, and matures at a pace that is scarcely conceivable to those who reside in regions farther south."[32]

A few senators were skeptical, but opposition to the bill was not as organized or vocal as the pro side. Senator William Dillingham of Vermont was one who spoke up in response to those who touted interior Alaska's great agricultural potential. As a member of the Senate subcommittee that spent the summer of 1903 on a tour investigating the needs of the territory, Dillingham had traveled extensively in the Interior and had seen conditions on the ground firsthand. The land is covered with "tundra," he informed the Senate. "Hardy vegetables can be raised but under adverse circumstances." He concluded that it was likely that farmers could produce enough of these crops to supply the local mining camps, but he remained "convinced that it would be utterly impossible to ever make an agricultural area of that region in the sense in which we speak of agricultural areas in other sections of the country."[33]

Meanwhile, in the House of Representatives, James Wickersham's dogged campaign for the railroad reached its climax on January 14, 1914. In a remarkable six-hour speech on the House floor, the Alaska delegate poured out every argument and every urgent plea he had espoused in hearings held by committees of the Senate and the House. His case boiled down to five main points, which he enumerated as:

development of agricultural and mineral resources in Alaska; settlement of public lands for new residents; transportation of coal for use by the army and navy; establishment of post roads; and efficiency in moving the mail. But underlying everything for Wickersham was, of course, the man's impassioned loathing of the Morgans and the Guggenheims and the corporate monopoly they held in the name of the Alaska Syndicate. From the beginning of his speech, he went after the trust with all the weapons in his possession, and he stuck to his message as a mantra. For Wickersham, the issue to be decided by Congress added up to one clear choice, and he shouted the question to the assembled members of the House. "Government or Guggenheim— which? Shall the territory be controlled by its constitutional trustee or by the trusts? Shall it be owned by the people or by monopoly? Shall its resources be opened to acquisition and use by the pioneer prospector and homeseeker or unfairly monopolized by one great syndicate?"[34]

He went on to give eloquent and detailed descriptions of Alaska's history and its current territorial status, along with glowing summaries of its climate, resources, and potential for development. The Tanana Valley, he said, lay at the same northern latitude as Norway, Sweden, and Finland, had "more hours of sunshine than sunny California," and was "filled with exactly the same rich soil as the Mississippi."

Only one great obstacle stood in the way of progress and growth, Wickersham continued, and that was the Alaska Syndicate. No competing private railroad could get a start in the territory because "the great overwhelming Alaska Syndicate, the Morgans and Guggenheims, would not permit it," he charged, and past events had shown that "they would kill you if necessary." In the previous ten years, he added, the syndicate had crushed every attempt made by competitors to create alternative systems of transportation, and he warned that if the current bill were to be defeated, the grip of the worst railroad monopoly in US history would appear to be gentle compared to the hold that "this national devilfish" would have on Alaska.[35]

The Democratic majority in the House greeted Wickersham's presentation with praise and enthusiastic applause. Representative Victor Murdock of Kansas commented on the Alaska delegate's wealth of knowledge, suggesting that no one else on earth could have supplied such complete information. Murdock supported the railroad bill on partisan grounds, citing both the Democratic and Progressive Party platforms in their "definite" and "unmistakable" endorsements of the Alaska project.[36]

Opposition in the House focused on the expense, estimated at $35 million, the questionable correctness of government involvement, and doubts about the extent and value of mineral and agricultural resources as claimed by advocates. Representative J. Hampton Moore of Pennsylvania labeled the bill an "altruistic experiment" and contended that the initial cost would grow to $100 million with long-term operation and maintenance. This "precarious enterprise," he said, would go forward at the expense of worthier projects of benefit to a greater number of people in more populous areas of the country.[37] Representative Aaron Kreider, also of Pennsylvania, feared that congressmen's thinking was clouded by sentiment rather than informed by practicality. Kreider was perhaps responding to a passionate speech given by Representative Albert Johnson of Washington, who invoked the romance of the advancing American frontier in his plea for passage of the bill. "Open Alaska and it will give our new population a chance," Johnson implored. "There prevails today the same spirit that started our ancestors west from the original colonies, occupying and making habitable the territory from ocean to ocean. In all the history of mankind there is nothing that bears comparison with it." With construction of the railroad, he concluded, Alaska would be "opened, peopled, and made prosperous to take its place as our sentinel and our key to the new Pacific."[38]

Kreider was not swayed. Claims of vast expanses of tillable acreage were unrealistic, he said, and large farms were "out of the question" because of the high cost of clearing ground and the difficulty of raising crops on frozen soil. What Alaska needed instead, he contended, was "many miles of cheap roads rather than a few miles of expensive roads." He proposed a system of wagon roads as a more economical proposition. "It is all right to appeal to our sentiment and patriotism on sentimental and patriotic matters," he said, "but this is a business proposition pure and simple and should be legislated on from a business point of view."[39]

The most eloquent arguments against government ownership of railroads were given by Representative John Small of North Carolina, who warned that this "dangerous innovation" was the beginning of the nationalization of all railroads. Small said that he had heard all the points made in favor of the bill, but that none—not even the evils of monopoly control—had justified such a departure from federal policy. He contended that there was no condition existing in Alaska that could not be remedied by congressional action. With passage of this bill, he said, the nation would be "entering a policy fraught with such danger to our institutions that it is a precedent which should be honored in the breach. Right in the beginning we should realize its great dangers; we should resolve that the Congress of the United States will embark upon a policy of ownership of railroads in no part of our country."[40]

The bill passed the Senate by what *The Outlook* magazine termed an "emphatic" vote of 46 to 16, and then cleared the House also by a large majority of 232 to 86; President Wilson signed it into law on March 12, 1914. The act appropriated $35 million for construction and operation of the Alaska Railroad and directed the president to choose a route from a coastal harbor to the Interior. Wilson was pleased with the measure and intimated that he was willing to accept some credit for the outcome. "I feel that we have at last reached out the hand of real helpfulness and brotherhood to Alaska," he remarked as he affixed his signature to the bill. "This is a consummation that I have been hoping might arrive in my administration."[41] In Fairbanks, the news from Washington touched off wild celebration. For the *Daily News-Miner*, it was a repudiation of eight years of injustice since the federal coal lands withdrawal in 1906. "You know all too well the story of our thralldom," the paper editorialized. "We have been slaves, our resources bottled, and our development hampered in every way since Roosevelt committed the crime of the century." With the coming of the railroad, a new day was at hand, the paper concluded. "The miserable past is dead, and the glorious future is bright with promise."[42]

Wickersham, for his part, was eager to praise President Wilson for his role in promoting the project while also downplaying any positive role the Taft administration might have played. Never one to easily forget a grudge or readily mend political fences, Wickersham refused to recognize Taft's contribution. In late January, when it was clear that the railroad bill was headed for approval, W. F. Thompson, editor of the *Fairbanks Daily News-Miner*, wrote to Wickersham seeking his view of the origins of the legislation. Thompson contended that the Democrats were wrongly taking credit for their party and for the president, and he told Wickersham that the *News-Miner* would take that editorial position. "We are declaring that it was a Republican measure, introduced for Republican purposes during Taft's regime," Thompson wrote. "The Democrats are not entitled to the credit for having originated it."[43] Wickersham responded quickly with a different point of view, saying that there would be no Alaska Railroad bill such as it stood without Wilson's cooperation and support. "The whole credit," he said, "is due to President Wilson."[44] The *News-Miner* never acknowledged Wilson or the Democrats in that way, even though it did heap praise on Alaska's lone congressional delegate for his work at the finish.

For its part, the Wilson administration, from the president on down, kept Wickersham at arm's length, knowing the gruff, often belligerent, nature of his personality. Secretary Lane had been acquainted with Wickersham since the late 1880s, when Lane was a newspaper editor in Tacoma and Wickersham was a rising star in the Tacoma legal and political community. In 1913, soon after Wilson took office, Wickersham met with Lane to discuss issues of common interest. Later, Wickersham noted his impressions of the meeting in his diary. "I called only to pay my respects and offer my assistance in Alaska matters," he wrote. "In his conversation he seemed to assume that there would be much difficulty with me, that I was a sort of bull in the political and legislative china shop and must be handled with care."[45]

With passage of the railroad act, a related piece of legislation, the coal lands leasing bill, was already in the works, and seven months later Congress passed a law designed to provide access to Alaska coal deposits while thwarting monopoly control. The new law allowed leases of up to 2,560 acres rather than the previous 160 but specified that no operator could hold title to more than one lease. The *American Review of Reviews* proclaimed this act as a "great practical triumph" of the Roosevelt movement toward conservation of public resources and concluded that if such a measure had been passed a few years earlier, the nation would have avoided the entire Ballinger-Pinchot Affair.[46] "A new Alaska will be possible," Interior Secretary Franklin K. Lane declared. "Coal and iron, coal and copper will be brought together, and where these come together, as all know, great communities arise."[47]

10

THE NEW LAND OF OPPORTUNITY

The Chicago of Alaska

⟶⟅⟵

ON APRIL 25, 1915, James Wickersham rode into Fairbanks in the passenger seat of an open-air stage drawn by four horses, ending a fourteen-day journey over the "big trail" from Chitina. As the rig turned off the muddy road and drove north on Cushman Street, the congressional delegate must surely have been reflecting on the changes in the mining camp since he first saw it twelve years earlier. The "pig sty" that he observed in 1903, before the town even had an official name, had grown into a respectable community of 3,500 with many of the accoutrements and conveniences of modern life. There were electric streetlights and a telephone system that served local homes and businesses and also reached to the mining camps on the creeks forty miles to the north. Modern hotels offered steam heat, electric lights, and flush toilets with power supplied by the Northern Commercial Company plant on First Avenue at the south end of the Turner Street bridge.

Fairbanks was the supply and banking center of interior Alaska. Its stores offered stylish clothing as well as complete "outfits" for every miner and prospector who cared to venture out to the goldfields. Merchandiser John O. Ellis ("The Pirate") advertised "everything from a needle to an automobile" at his Second Avenue store, including groceries, hardware, dry goods, and miners' supplies. Barthel Brewing Company on lower First Avenue produced bottled beer, advertising that it had the "largest and best equipped plant north of Puget Sound."

Local government comprised Mayor Andrew Nerland along with a magistrate, one attorney, and a six-member city council. There was a chief of police and a fire department staffed by a chief, a captain, three horsemen, two drivers, and a plugman. The public school at Eighth Avenue and Turner Street had a principal, six teachers, and enrollment numbering more than two hundred students. A modern well-equipped hospital served the residents' medical needs. Social and community life was active, with five churches, two theaters, and a variety of private clubs, civic organizations, and secret societies such as the Arctic Brotherhood, the Order of Odd Fellows, the Royal Arch Masons, the Knights Templar, and the Pioneers of Alaska. A public library, constructed by the Episcopal Church in 1909 at the corner of First Avenue and Cowles Street, provided books, magazines, and a place to relax. And along with these amenities, the community boasted a distinct air of civic pride, best exemplified by the Fairbanks Commercial Club, presided over by Antone J. Nordale and dedicated to promoting Fairbanks as an attractive place to live and do business.[1] "Compared to the remainder of the United States," the *Daily News-Miner* crowed, "this is the greatest and most prosperous camp of all, and the people who are in it are the luckiest people in the union or out of it."[2]

Yet Fairbanks was still very much a frontier town, and its character was stamped by conditions that prevailed nowhere else in America—its brutal winters and the "unspeakable isolation" as described by famed Alaska writer Margaret Murie in her memoir, *Two in the Far North*. Murie, who came to Fairbanks at age nine in 1911, wrote fond descriptions of a close-knit community peopled by lively personalities who helped each other endure the hardships of northern life. In the second decade of the century, the city limits extended south to Twelfth Avenue, and nearly all residents lived in small log houses, which consumed up to ten cords of wood a year as fuel for both heat and cooking. Murie's home on Eighth Avenue was typical. She depicted a one-level four-room dwelling with an attached woodshed and storage area, one corner of which "in those days sufficed for sanitary convenience." She recalled that the buckets that were kept discreetly in that woodshed were emptied by "the most heroic soul on the frontier," who hauled them away at night on a horse-drawn cart.[3]

Few residents enjoyed the luxury of hot and cold running water. Water from the pump was so highly mineralized and rust-colored

James Wickersham, Alaska's territorial delegate to Congress, poses with a construction crew for the Alaska Railroad in Eagle River in 1915 (Alaska State Library
P277-006-066).

that it was unusable, and residents relied on Fred "The Waterman"
Musgjerd of the Blue Crystal Water Company, who made home deliv-
eries in five-gallon buckets for ten cents each. The company owned a
deep well, "which poured forth pure sweet water," as Murie recalled,
and Musgjerd made his rounds from house to house with a freight
sled pulled by horses. The delivery tank was fifteen feet long, built
around a woodstove to keep the water from freezing. For baths, many
Fairbanksans found it convenient to use the bathhouse at First and
Cowles rather than heating water on a woodstove at home.[4]

Transportation and communication with the Outside remained the
greatest causes of the feeling of isolation in interior Alaska. Freight and
passengers arrived by stern-wheel riverboats for the five months a year
when navigation on the rivers was possible, and over the icy trail from
Valdez or Chitina the remainder of the year. The Mississippi-style riverboats provided an easy, comfortable ride compared to the ordeal of
winter travel in an open sleigh. The Northern Commercial Company's
Overland Stage Service operated between Chitina and Tanana through
Fairbanks, carrying passengers, freight, and mail. Roadhouses spaced

about twenty miles apart supplied fresh horses and provided meals and overnight accommodations for travelers. NC Company advertising proclaimed that all stages were "fully equipped with robes and carbon heated foot warmers, which are proof against the coldest weather." Still, the journey was long and arduous in the best of conditions, especially through Isabelle Pass, a sixty-mile stretch of the trail from Paxson to Donnelly crossing the Alaska Range.[5] Mail service in and out of Fairbanks was excruciatingly slow, with arrivals on Sundays and Thursdays, typically nine days en route from Chitina.

On his drive north in that spring of 1915, Wickersham reached Paxson on his fourth day out of Chitina. His trip had started in Cordova, where he boarded the Copper River and Northwestern Railway, which covered the 131 miles to Chitina in one day. There he looked forward to a ride in one of the modern automobiles that had recently begun to take the place of horsepower on the trail. His passage by car proved to be an ordeal, as spring runoff turned the road to mud, and stream crossings became dangerous torrents of water. Other travelers who reached Fairbanks by automobile in April had the same harrowing experience. "Autos had a hard trip," the *Daily News-Miner* reported. Two vehicles "arrived finally last night bringing in eight people who had been on the big trail for eight days." One passenger described the road as "just one mudhole after another all the way."[6] As the Wickersham party arrived in Paxson, the ground was still covered with snow and ice, and they switched to horses, two teams of four "each drawing a double ender sled in one of which I lay wrapped in robes," Wickersham noted.[7] At McCarty the trail became impassable. Wickersham telegraphed to Fairbanks for an automobile to come for him, but no driver was willing to venture out because of reports of conditions on the road. The party waited for four days before hitching up the horses again and making the final run into Fairbanks, arriving a full two weeks after leaving Chitina.

The mood in Fairbanks that spring was upbeat with the assurance that a new means of transportation would soon do away once and for all with the rigors and uncertainty of frontier travel and communication. A modern railroad was on its way, and the town was jubilant. The *Alaska Citizen* declared that "the new government railroad is the magic wand that is promising to change it all and make of this neglected land a country of almost unlimited opportunities."[8] The

The Alaska Engineering Commission was appointed by President Woodrow Wilson to oversee construction of the Alaska Railroad. The commissioners, pictured left to right, were Frederick Mears, William Edes, and Thomas Riggs. Their first task was to choose a route from a tidewater port to the Interior (University of Washington Special Collections UW39795).

Fairbanks Commercial Club proclaimed that the rail "will undoubtedly result in Fairbanks becoming the Chicago of Alaska."[9] Alfred H. Brooks, who was widely recognized as the nation's leading expert on Alaska resources, expressed his confidence in the venture in an article published in the *Quarterly Journal of Economics*. With the coming of a modern system of transportation, he wrote, this "much misunderstood and much neglected territory" would return far greater value in mineral and agricultural products than the $35 million price tag on the railroad. "Without railroads, the land is valueless," Brooks concluded. "With them it becomes an asset of importance." In his view, the act recently passed by Congress and signed by the president was "one of broad statesmanship."[10]

Preliminary construction activity began almost immediately after President Wilson affixed his signature to the Alaska Railroad bill. The massive project was considered to be equal in scope to construction of the Panama Canal, and appropriately the Wilson administration turned to engineers who were fresh off the completion of that job. The three-man Alaska Engineering Commission, appointed by the president, included the superintendent of the Panama Railroad, Frederick Mears, along with William Edes and Thomas Riggs. Edes had many years of experience building railroads in western territories, and at the time of his appointment he was chief engineer of a large railroad in California. Riggs was a mining engineer and surveyor who was well known in Alaska as chief surveyor of the International Boundary Commission, which located the border between Alaska and the Yukon Territory.[11]

In May 1914, Wilson directed Secretary of the Interior Lane to send surveying crews into the field with the first order of business to decide on a route from tidewater to the heart of the Interior. The three commissioners focused on two general routes: the eastern corridor, starting from Cordova or Valdez, and the western, starting at Seward and extending up Turnagain Arm and continuing through the Matanuska-Susitna region. Both were considered to be possible gateways to Fairbanks and the rich Tanana Valley. It was a mammoth undertaking. The three commissioners purchased supplies and equipment in Seattle and soon began shipping men and horses north from there. The workers were divided into eleven surveying parties, each with a horse-drawn pack train and assigned to a different section of the country. A main base of operation was selected at an obscure location on Cook Inlet informally called Ship Creek or Knik Anchorage, which was the head of navigation for oceangoing freighters. From that point, surveying equipment, camping gear, provisions, personnel, and horses could be unloaded and distributed to points on Turnagain Arm or up the Susitna River. A second main base was at Fairbanks, and from there survey crews worked their way south to Nenana and Broad Pass. Other crews examined the condition of three existing railroads to assess the possibility of purchase. They were the old seventy-one-mile Alaska Northern line out of Seward, the Copper River and Northwestern Railway starting in Cordova and owned by the Morgan-Guggenheim Alaska Syndicate, and the forty-five miles of narrow-gauge track known as the Tanana Valley Railroad stretching from the village of Chena to the placer mines on the creeks north of Fairbanks.

The Alaska Engineering Commission was intent on gathering as much useful information as possible during the short northern summer in order to give the president all he needed to make his decision as to the route the rail would take. In their report, the three commissioners—Edes, Mears, and Riggs—took note of the special conditions that made this endeavor worthwhile. "That Alaska is wonderfully rich in minerals has already been proven," they wrote. "That its agricultural resources are at least sufficient to sustain a large population can easily be demonstrated to those willing to listen. There is practically no limit to its coal supply." But progress had been held back for years on account of an absence of transportation, the engineers concluded. With a system of railroads, "rapid development is probable; without it, growth will be exceedingly slow." They cited the gold mines in Juneau as examples of the success that was achievable with efficient water transportation close at hand, while in the Interior deposits five times richer could not be worked because of the high cost of moving men and materials.[12]

This project was unlike any other that the federal government had ever undertaken. It appropriated $35 million of public money to an endeavor for which its own chief builders predicted only "probable" success. As railroad historian William H. Wilson pointed out, in terms of federally financed public works, the only venture comparable in size and scope was the recently completed Panama Canal. And that, in contrast, virtually guaranteed a positive return through heavy commercial and naval traffic.[13]

The commissioners focused most of their attention in the summer of 1914 on the western route. Much more was already known about the possibility of a line originating in Cordova because of the history of the Copper River and Northwestern Railroad. The corridor from Seward to Fairbanks was divided into three sections, with each of the commissioners responsible for overseeing investigation of one of the three. Riggs had charge of the northern sector from Fairbanks south to Broad Pass. Though the Alaska Engineering Commission's final report to the president had the veneer of objectivity and made no recommendation, it was clear that the western route held certain advantages in its favor. It accessed the Matanuska-Susitna Valley, an area of greater agricultural value than any of the lands lying north of Chitina. Also, it passed through two promising sources of coal: the Matanuska coalfield and the Nenana River coalfield, which could provide a ready and inexhaustible source of fuel for Fairbanks and for the railroad itself.

Laying steel rails for construction of the Alaska Railroad. Once the route was determined, crews began working north from Seward and south from Fairbanks. The route was divided into three sections with a commissioner in charge of each section (UAF Rasmuson Library Archives UAF-1984-75-8).

And finally, though unspoken, there were political considerations. The eastern route would have included the purchase of the Copper River and Northwestern Railroad, owned by the Morgan-Guggenheim Alaska Syndicate, which was tainted by the unpleasantness of the Ballinger-Pinchot Affair. The Democratic administration of Woodrow Wilson wished to steer far clear of that.

The Seward route also garnered the most support from Alaskans. The *Fairbanks Daily Times* touted it for its access to the best agricultural areas and the richest coal regions of the territory. "Land suited for tillage and grazing are estimated at five to seven thousand square miles," the paper said. "We want a railroad that will open up the most country."[14]

On April 10, 1915, the president obliged. He issued an executive order designating a route for the railway beginning in Seward and extending 416 miles to the Interior, including construction of a thirty-eight-mile spur eastward to the Matanuska coalfield. The president also directed the secretary of the interior to purchase the Alaska Northern Railway. For those facilities in Seward, and the Alaska Northern's seventy-one miles of track extending to Turnagain Arm, the federal government paid $1.15 million.

The executive order sparked a booming stampede at the mouth of Ship Creek on the tidal flats where the town of Anchorage had its beginning. The place became the headquarters of the Alaska Engineering Commission, and immediately a tent city of two thousand job seekers sprouted.[15]

PROGRESSIVES AND THE TANANA ATHABASCANS: 1915

All but forgotten in the midst of this excitement and activity was the impact on the lives of Native Americans. The designated railroad corridor passed directly through lands that had been occupied for perhaps eight thousand years by seminomadic bands of hunter-gatherers. Interior Alaska was—and is—home to eleven Athabascan groups, comprising the northern sector of a family of thirty-seven related languages and societies. Athabascan is the largest language family in North America in terms of area of occupancy. Linguists surmise that as recently as 2,500 years ago, the ancestral language, Proto-Athabascan, was spoken in a vast area from central Alaska to British Columbia. Over time, the people, and with them their language, have spread east and south into western Canada and in pockets as far distant as the Oregon coast and the American Southwest. (Navajo and Apache are Athabascan languages.) Cognates in present-day Athabascan languages prove that they are all genetic descendants of Proto-Athabascan.[16]

Athabascans are highly mobile and adaptable; their lifeways and subsistence are keyed to a seasonal round of harvest activities, depending on the resources available to them. At the time of their first contact with white explorers in the late nineteenth century, Tanana Athabascans probably numbered no more than seven hundred. They traveled constantly in small bands, harvesting salmon in the summer, caribou and moose in the fall and winter, and migratory waterfowl in the spring. The first white men to come into the Tanana country in the 1880s were fur traders, who met groups of people still wearing traditional ancient Athabascan clothing.[17] This was the start of an influx of settlers who brought sudden changes to Athabascan social and economic structures. First the fur trade and then the gold rush ushered in the modern world. Trading posts were established along the river system, and the opportunity to exchange furs for clothing, utensils, food, and firearms had a profound effect on subsistence patterns and the annual round of harvest. Permanent villages grew up around trading posts, and Natives were increasingly drawn there to take advantage of modern amenities and eventually schools, churches, and health care. The network of trading posts gave the Natives regular access to trade goods, and, as anthropologist James VanStone explained, the people became increasingly dependent on the posts as the material items that were initially regarded as luxuries soon became necessities.[18]

Engaging in trapping required dog teams, which increased the need for large supplies of salmon to feed the dogs. The fish wheel was introduced at about the turn of the century, giving dog mushers and trappers an increased ability to harvest large amounts of salmon. In 1905, the Episcopal Church established St. Mark's Mission with a boarding school for Native children at the confluence of the Nenana and Tanana Rivers. The village of Nenana quickly grew to a population of three hundred and became a center for education and health care as well as a place where Natives from the entire region could sell furs and obtain trade goods. By 1915, missions and schools were operating in villages established at Tanana, Minto, Nenana, Chena, Salchaket, and Tanacross. Including Fairbanks, the population of the Tanana Valley numbered twelve thousand.[19]

With railroad construction a certainty, the threat to Native lands became all the more acute. Two men traveling in interior Alaska under the auspices of the Indian Rights Association of Philadelphia in the summer of 1914 reported that "the march of progress" would cause problems for the Natives unless steps were taken to protect their land rights. The railroad, they said, will attract crowds of people who have been "deluded by the seductive literature" promising great opportunities in the North.[20]

Delegate Wickersham had long been sensitive to the needs of Alaska Natives, and during his time in the territory he had shown a keen interest in their languages and lifeways. In that early summer of 1915, Wickersham, just back from the nation's capital, serving his fourth consecutive term in Congress, was eager to get out and see as much as possible of the interior Alaska landscape he had grown to appreciate and love. He traveled to Minto Flats, where he visited Chief Charley's camp on May 19, and later he arrived at a small Indian village at the mouth of the Tolovana River. There he met Chief Alexander, and with most of the village out hunting and fishing, the two engaged in lengthy discussions over the next two days. Alexander had long been an advocate for the welfare of his people. In a 1910 letter to Wickersham, he had asked the delegate for help in getting education and health care for his village. Now his concern was the effect of railroad construction, and Wickersham spoke frankly with him about the demands of land-hungry miners, farmers, and settlers. "Chief Sta-tad-tuna" [Alexander] called on me today bravely arrayed in his paint, feathers, beadwork, and moose skin coat," Wickersham noted in his diary. "We had a long talk about game laws, reservations, schools, etc."[21] Wickersham related his grave prediction about the future of Indian lands, and he told the chief that he believed the best options for the Natives were either to establish reservations, where all could live in a large community, or take individual allotments of 160 acres each. To Chief Alexander, a man accustomed to roaming freely across lands that his ancestors had occupied for countless generations, neither alternative sounded particularly attractive.

Alexander spread the word of Wickersham's warning to Native camps and villages down to Crossjacket and Tanana and upriver as far as Salchaket. The chiefs were alarmed, and quickly they agreed to a meeting in Fairbanks to get the information directly from the delegate and to inform him of their intentions. The meeting came together without delay, and on July 5, fourteen unified Tanana River Athabascan tribal leaders assembled in the George C. Thomas Memorial Library and waited for word from Wickersham. "The chiefs proved to be unusually intelligent" and "diplomatic," one newspaper reported after the conclusion of the two-day conference. "The Indians knew what they wanted and how to get it."[22]

Jacob Starr of Tanana was the first of the chiefs to speak, telling the assembly that he wished to hear from Wickersham a full explanation of what he had told Alexander in Tolovana. "We want to understand what he meant by that talk," Starr said. "What you told Alexander the Natives did not believe and came here to find out. After we learn that, we will talk."

"Oh, Alexander told you the truth," Wickersham responded. "I talked to him and told him about homesteads and reservations just as he told you I did."[23]

The United States government was represented by three men besides Wickersham. They were Thomas Riggs of the Alaska Engineering Commission; his assistant, G. Fenton Cramer, who would inform the chiefs of future plans for railroad construction; and C. W. Richie of the federal land office in Fairbanks, who was present to explain the options available to the Natives under the homestead program and the allotment act.

Wickersham stressed to the chiefs the advantages of those federal land programs, pointing out especially the positive benefits of reservations, where an Indian agent would teach Athabascan hunters "how to plow land and raise potatoes and other crops." But the heart of his message was a dire prediction. "The white men are going to take all of this good land," he warned, "and when all the good land is gone, the white men are going to keep on taking more land. After a while the Indian will have no land at all."

In pushing for reservations, Wickersham was reversing a policy he had stuck with since his first days in Congress. As early as 1908, Episcopal Alaska Bishop Peter Trimble Rowe had appealed to the delegate to persuade Congress to confine Natives to reservations under the authority of the army. Rowe's intent was to isolate the Natives from the "vicious class of white men" who profited by selling liquor. Wickersham dismissed the idea, telling Rowe that reservations had "never worked satisfactorily outside and would work less so here."[24] In 1912, speaking to the House Committee on Territories, of which Wickersham was a member, Rowe testified to the "deplorable and shameful" condition of Alaska Natives as a result of easy access to liquor. He pled for reservations, where the government could provide health care and education away from the presence of intoxicating liquor. Wickersham gave Rowe little encouragement or support, noting that "it has long been the policy of the government not to establish reservations in Alaska."[25]

The Progressive view of federal Indian policy was, indeed, to keep the tribes separate from white society. But in addition it focused on providing education, vocational training, and homemaking skills while also preserving tribal identity. The pre-Progressive Dawes Act of 1887 was the federal government's attempt to transform Indians into individualistic citizens. Instead of establishing new reservations, the law created a system under which Native Americans could receive title to 160 acres of land along with the opportunity to turn away from traditional hunting and gathering customs and learn to be farm- ers. The Dawes Act was based on the assumption that advancement for the Indians was being held back by adherence to tribal customs and identity. However, by the early 1900s, advocates of this policy of forced assimilation had become disappointed in the rate of progress, and President Theodore Roosevelt sought to modify it according to Progressive lines. Now, rather than working to eradicate all vestiges of tribal life, the government began to recognize the worth of retain- ing traditional Native values and family attachments. Progressive-era Indian policy focused on self-reliance through education and training while allowing the Indians to hold on to their traditional customs and preserve their Nativeness.[26]

Wickersham believed in the wisdom of these policies, but in 1915, with railroad construction posing a certain threat to Athabascan lands, his options were limited. The best he was able to offer to the chiefs assembled before him that July day in Fairbanks was a return to the reservation system, which he himself had rejected three years before.

Another group with a vested interest in that day's proceedings was the Episcopal Church, represented by a young missionary named Guy Madara. The church's main concern was the need to prepare the Natives for the coming of the railroad and the influx of people who would arrive with it. St. Mark's Mission in Nenana had become, in its ten years of operation, the "model mission" that Bishop Rowe had hoped to build in the Interior, and the missionaries were well aware that its success was due to its isolation. But the factors that had made Nenana work well for St. Mark's also made it attractive to the railroad builders. It was centrally located on the Tanana River, a corridor that Athabascan travelers had always used as a primary means of transpor- tation. And now, as the place where the rail line crossed the Tanana, it was an ideal location for staging construction and surveying activities. Thomas Riggs, as lead engineer for the northern section of the rail- road, had already begun offloading crews and equipment at Nenana to begin work on the line north to Fairbanks and south to Broad Pass. Madara and others within the Episcopal Church feared that the Native residents of Nenana would soon suffer the same fate as those at the village of Tanana near the army's Fort Gibbon at the confluence of the Yukon and Tanana Rivers. There, as Archdeacon Hudson Stuck described it, the "low-down white population" had caused deplorable conditions, including the presence of nine saloons where "toughs and bad characters" had a disastrous influence on the Natives.[27]

As the July 5 meeting in Fairbanks progressed, it became clear to representatives of the federal government that neither homesteads nor a reservation was a viable choice for the chiefs. Paul Williams, who served as interpreter for those Athabascans who did not speak English, explained that the plan required Indians to abandon tribal traditions and live on a designated plot of land. "It would take them away from the old homes and habits where they have been used to living," he said. Thomas Riggs responded with a warning and urged the chiefs to take action soon. "After the railroad which we are building comes into this country, it will be overrun with white people," he told them. "They will kill off your game, your moose, your caribou, and your sheep." A reservation or a homestead, he advised, would provide the means to protect them.

The Indians were not persuaded. "We don't want to go on a reservation," Chief Ivan of Crossjacket said bluntly, "but wish to stay perfectly free just as we are now." Chief Charley of Minto charged that if white settlers were coming in as Riggs predicted, it was the government's responsibility to take action. "We expect you people to protect us," he stated. And, finally, Chief Alexander, the man whom Wickersham had met in Tolovana, summed things up, saying, "We are people who are always on the go, and I believe that if we are put in one place we would die off like rabbits."

Wickersham, meanwhile, held firm in promoting the idea of a reservation as the best option for the Natives, adding a final word of warning. "Mr. Riggs is going to build a railroad," he said, "and when Mr. Riggs' railroad is built, the people are going to come in here in great numbers and push and push until the Indians are clear off the best land. You must do something."

The chiefs' response was given by Paul Williams, who stated the people's wish for government-sponsored industrial schools to teach job skills for the modern economy. They told Wickersham that they had been denied work on railroad construction crews and for other jobs that they felt they could learn to do fully as well as white men. "This is why we want the schools, to learn these things," Williams concluded, adding that the three things the Indians desired were "school, a doctor, and some labor."

The meeting left Wickersham at a loss for answers. As a product of his times, he was fully immersed in the view of the frontier as explained by Frederick Jackson Turner. Like the Turnerian western frontier, Alaska was seen as an open country, mostly uninhabited and free for the taking. Wickersham went into the meeting expecting to mediate a settlement that would leave the Natives satisfied with the land occupancy options the government had to offer. When they rejected him at every turn, he was forced to come face-to-face with the complicated reality of Native claims. Where the government was concerned, there was no negotiating to be done. The railroad had its right-of-way, and the project was going through with or without the Indians' approval. But, for the first time, Wickersham saw the undeniable history of aboriginal occupation of the land and the Natives' close, intractable cultural and spiritual connection to it. Turner's ethnocentric view of the frontier proved to be too simplistic, and a land-claims solution that would be acceptable to Natives as well as non-Natives was nowhere in sight.

On July 22, Wickersham mailed a transcript of the proceedings to Interior Secretary Franklin K. Lane, along with a cover letter that expressed his ambivalence. "Will you not kindly read this record," he implored, "and consider what ought to be done for these people before all the good land and fishing sites are taken up by the white men?"[28] It was a dilemma that Wickersham would never solve. He was caught between the Progressive imperative for development of the frontier and his sense of sorrow for the losses that would surely be felt by the Athabascan people. He believed in the government's duty to open the frontier and allow miners and farmers to populate and develop the land, but at the same time he lamented the impact such progress would have on the Native way of life. It would be more than a half century before an agreement was reached with passage of the Alaska Native Claims Settlement Act of 1971.

Historians have noted that government relations with Native Americans and African Americans constitute the basic paradox of the Progressive era. Social and economic reforms were aimed at improv-

The historic meeting of the chiefs of the Tanana Athabascans with James Wickersham in Fairbanks, July 1915. Chief Alexander is in the middle row third from left. Wickersham is in the middle row fifth from left. Paul Williams is in the front row, far right. Thomas Riggs is in the back row fourth from left (Alaska State Library P272-011-072).

ing the plight of workers in the nation's factories and on its farms, on achieving a level of fairness for the masses of consumers and disenfranchised voters. Progressives' intent was to attack privilege, and they made remarkable gains in fundamental issues of justice. But their "critical blunder," as historian Michael McGerr pointed out, was in tolerating segregation and thereby leaving minorities out of the reform movement. Progressives, McGerr concluded, "showed little fear in dealing with problems of gender, family, class, and economy—but not of race."[29]

Wilson himself was conflicted and sometimes even confounded by the issue of race, especially where African Americans were concerned. A great deal of his base of support was made up of white southerners, and by far the majority of his political appointees represented that part of the population. Under his administration, several departments of the federal government moved to segregate black workers, and Wilson and his cabinet made no effort to reverse that policy. When the National Association for the Advancement of Colored People protested, the president responded by saying that he believed segregation to be in the best interests of African Americans. He saw no indication of discrimination. Rather, he said, segregation within federal government offices was a first step on the road to full assimilation. Whites and blacks first had to occupy separate sections of the same buildings, and over time they would become familiar and accustomed to one another, thus "rendering them more safe in their possession of office and less likely to be discriminated against."[30]

Similarly, fairness and justice for racial minorities was of no concern to most Progressives in the plan for progress and development of the nation's far northern territory. "It will be strictly a white man's country," a member of the House Committee on Territories proclaimed in hearings on the Alaska Railroad Bill. "The conditions there are such as will be most favorable to propagating and developing a race of white people, and the best blood of the world will thrive and find a natural home in Alaska."[31]

EPILOGUE

*A railroad in the Garden of Eden with nobody there
but Adam and Eve would be a poor investment*

~⟋⟍~

THE RAILROAD

Thirty-five million dollars was scarcely half the amount of money needed to lay track from Seward to Fairbanks. And even in 1923, with the 470-mile road completed and trains running its entire length, construction was still not finished. As President Warren G. Harding and his entourage of seventy arrived in Nenana on July 15 to commemorate the achievement, much work remained, especially in the section between the Tanana River crossing and Fairbanks. The Alaska Engineering Commission reported to Congress that year that an "enormous amount of track surfacing and ballasting" was needed to bring the railroad north of Nenana up to a normal standard. Additionally, from the beginning of the line to the end, hastily constructed wooden bridges and trestles were found to be incapable of holding up to spring flooding, river ice, and heavy summer rains. Through service was interrupted continually in the first year of operation when, among other incidents, bridges on the Cantwell and Nenana Rivers were carried away by high water and track was washed out where a bank collapsed near Mt. McKinley National Park. The work of replacing numerous wooden structures with concrete and steel would have to begin immediately.[1]

The original appropriation for the railroad had been exhausted by 1919, and the Alaska Engineering Commission went back to Congress that year, seeking $17 million more. Construction had started from both ends, with crews working north from Seward, where the AEC purchased the stalled Alaska Northern Railroad, and south from Fairbanks, where it had acquired the nearly dilapidated Tanana Valley Railroad. What it got for the $300,000 price for the TVR was its terminal facilities in Fairbanks and about eight miles of right-of-way from Happy to Fairbanks.[2] The Department of the Interior remained firmly behind the project and was not deterred by the cost overrun. Secretary Franklin K. Lane expressed as much confidence as ever about the possibilities offered in a northern utopia. "I would personally like to spend a few years of my life just dreaming dreams about what could be done in that huge territory," he wrote in a letter to a friend in 1918. He envisioned a place where soldiers returning from the world war could settle and prosper. "We ought to be able to send a great many thousands of Americans as stock raisers and farmers into Alaska," he continued. "The climate is just as good as that of Montana and in some places much better. If we can possibly get that road completed by the end of the war and know we have another national domain there for settlement, it would help out mightily on the returning soldier problem."[3]

The department urged Congress to approve the $17 million appropriation, reiterating the points that had been emphasized by proponents of the original railroad bill passed five years before. Alaska's agricultural possibilities assured a stable population, the department told Congress in an official statement, adding that climate was no barrier to development and "she has all the best resources essential to the upbuilding of a prosperous country." Completion of the railroad would guarantee "permanent industries and provide homes for a strong contented people, who will be the source of inestimable strength to the nation and assure the early return of the cost of the railroad."[4]

Those in Congress who backed the measure pointed out that under normal circumstances the original $35 million would have been enough to build the railroad, but because of the war, wages had increased by 50 percent and the cost of materials by 160 percent. Representative Charles Curry of California, in debate on the House floor, stated that it was absolutely necessary to spend the additional

$17 million "unless we wish to sacrifice the $35 million already invested."[5]

George Grigsby, now Alaska's delegate to Congress, placed the Alaska Railroad within the context of American expansion and the settlement of the West. "No pessimist ever built a railroad or developed a new country," he declared. On the contrary, optimists in Alaska believed that growth and prosperity would surely follow construction of a modern transportation infrastructure. Without that kind of optimism, he said, the nation would never have seen the kind of development it had. "What has been the history of the growth of the great West will be the history of Alaska." A questioner pointed out that railroads in the American West were built by private enterprise and asked Grigsby to explain why the federal government was being compelled to step in where the private sector would not go. His answer focused on Alaska's unique place in relation to the rest of the country. Private enterprise builds railroads as an extension of a system already shown to be profitable, he said. Alaska had no such connection by rail to the rest of the country, and therefore private railroad builders could not be assured of a return on their investment.[6]

Congress authorized the additional $17 million on November 4, 1919, and two years later the AEC returned with still another request, now for an additional $4 million to build two bridges and improve the roadbed between Nenana and Fairbanks. This time, the commission was met with a bit more reluctance on the part of some congressmen, who expressed skepticism about the worth of the entire project. One member of the House Committee on Territories charged that "certain positive statements" regarding the completion of the railroad had "turned out to be inaccurate." Additionally, the Matanuska coalfield had so far failed to produce the astonishing amounts of coal that railroad enthusiasts had promised from the beginning of the debate. Another committee member concluded that agriculture in Alaska had shown itself to be a failure, and he demanded to know if the government could ever expect to see a return on its investments. There to answer these questions and present the case for further appropriations was Assistant Secretary of the Interior Edward Finney, who stated that once construction was complete and was carrying freight and passengers between Fairbanks and the ocean, revenues would amount to nearly $1 million a year. Traffic would increase substantially, Finney promised. "There is no doubt of that."[7]

In the meantime, however, Congress was faced with growing expenses and a flood of red ink. Through 1923, construction costs totaled $57,896,248, and the next year railroad manager Noel Smith came to Washington asking for still another appropriation, this time for $11,878,781 to deal with maintenance needed, for the most part, to repair damage caused by harsh Alaska conditions. Because of the "hasty construction of the line," Smith said, insufficient ballast was in place under the ties, resulting in twisted and bent rails every spring when the frost came out of the ground. The added money would fund work to add ballast, widen cuts to decrease the need to clear rock slides, and bring the line up to a standard required for safety and efficiency. Smith predicted that the improvements would lead to the day when the government could expect to see an end to the deficits.[8]

Cost overruns, along with construction and maintenance challenges never before encountered by railroaders in the United States, recalled concerns about the project voiced years before. Coupled with these issues was an initial disappointment with coal and agricultural production. Early on, the Alaska Engineering Commission had suggested that it was quite probable that the pioneer railroad would have to endure "a few lean years" while the country was being developed but that its eventual success could not be doubted. The AEC held up the example of the many prosperous railroads of the American West. Those railroads, the AEC said, "started through a country in many instances much less promising than Alaska, and now who would dare question their success?"[9]

One such skeptic who did raise questions was Wilds Richardson, president of the Board of Road Commissioners for Alaska and James Wickersham's persistent adversary. Alaska has been "overadvertised," Richardson had written in 1917, "and some wrong impressions given concerning the opportunities for settlement and homemaking." Although he was understandably biased in favor of roads over rails as a system of transportation to develop the territory's resources, Richardson articulated a clearheaded and realistic assessment of conditions on the ground. Any comparison of Alaska to the American West was false, he said, and any hope that the Alaska Railroad would stimulate development in the way the railroads had done in the great prairies was "foredoomed to disappointment." He believed that a "romantic interest" and a lack of accurate information led to an excess of enthusiasm in people who "confuse scenery with the business of life." Snowcapped mountains and great glaciers are inviting attractions for tourists, but they pose unforgiving barriers to prospective farmers and settlers.[10]

Alfred Brooks observed this juxtaposition in the public mind as well, noting in a 1914 article that "Alaska has been pictured, on the one hand, as a barren polar waste valuable only to the gold and fur seeker, and on the other, as a veritable Eden with almost unlimited resources. Hence there has been much confusion of counsel as to our proper attitude toward it."[11]

Whichever the case—barren polar waste or veritable Eden—the Alaska Railroad struggled mightily in its first years. The harsh, forbidding North presented a host of unforeseen difficulties in construction, maintenance, and operation. But even if the fertile and limitless paradise that enthusiasts depicted were reality, success was far from certain. "A railroad in the Garden of Eden with nobody there but Adam and Eve would be a poor investment," the great railroader James J. Hill remarked in a speech in 1903. Hill, the builder of the Great Northern Railroad and one of the most successful tycoons of the Gilded Age, explained the economics of the industry in basic terms. The railroad must rely on the resources of the country, but fundamentally it must be certain that there is a ready market for those resources. The railroad has to furnish the transportation for the products of industry, whether they be minerals or wheat or potatoes or timber, but to earn a profit it must have a connection to a viable market.[12] Hill's Great Northern ran from St. Paul to Seattle, where an existing and growing population guaranteed success. His trains carried manufactured products westward from the industrial Midwest to the burgeoning cities and farmlands of the Dakotas, Montana, and Washington, and on the return trip they were loaded with timber to supply a never-ending demand for building materials as the forests of the Great Lakes region were being depleted.[13] The Alaska Railroad had none of those advantages. Instead of serving an established and growing market that demanded its services, it was built on the hope and the promise that its existence would create that market.

"Financially the railroad was a conspicuous failure," Edwin Fitch concluded in his history of the Alaska project.[14] That was true initially, but by the late 1920s the situation began to turn around when revenues rose steadily as a result of new gold mining activity in the Fairbanks area. The Fairbanks Exploration Company shipped massive amounts of material to build a power plant and a number of dredges on the creeks of the Interior. Deficits began to drop sharply, from $1.2 million in 1930 to less than $258,000 in 1933, prompting manager Otto F. Ohlson to predict that the railroad would be self-sustaining within five years. Revenues from both freight and passenger service rose steadily, and in 1938 the operation showed a surplus of nearly $77,000 with bright prospects for the future because of a pre–World War II construction boom.[15]

COAL

Hopes for a wealth of coal faded as well. The railroad was built not on the sound assurance of profits from already-producing mines but on the expectation that production would boom once the line was connected to known deposits. The coal was there in abundance, but the quality of the resource and difficulties of mining soon became evident. Some in Congress felt they had been sold a bill of goods. "In moments of enthusiasm, amounting almost to hysteria, these distant fields were painted in rainbow hues that did not represent their real color and quality," Representative Frank Mondell shouted from the House floor in the midst of debate on a $17 million appropriation to complete construction of the railroad. Still, the devoted believers did not lose confidence. It was "conclusively shown," Representative James Strong of Kansas argued, that the Matanuska and Nenana fields would "produce enough coal at reasonable rates to not only take care of Alaska and take care of our [naval] fleet, but to take care of the needs of our northwestern territory." Mondell was not persuaded. "I regret the Matanuska coalfields have been a very great disappointment," he said. "Up to date there is not a single successful mine of considerable tonnage under lease in the Matanuska field."[16]

The US Navy had a special interest in extracting Alaska coal to fuel its Pacific Fleet ships, but it required a high-grade product that met certain specifications. Such coal was plentiful and economical on the

Atlantic coast but not so easily accessible in the West. To accommodate the Pacific Fleet, the navy was forced to ship coal mined in the East by rail across the continent at great cost. Congress supported the navy's efforts to explore the Matanuska coalfields and evaluate the resource for its suitability for naval fuel. In 1919 and 1920, the navy increased its exploration in the Matanuska fields and explored the possibilities of building docks, coal bunkers, and handling facilities in Anchorage and Seward.[17]

Rail access to the Matanuska mines was provided by a nineteen-mile branch from the main line to Sutton and eighteen miles farther to Chickaloon. It was soon after the completion of these branch lines that serious mining began, with disappointing results. The coal proved difficult to mine and was laden with dirt and bone. Mining experts found that much of it was too fine for hauling, and the seams were folded and steeply sloping. Masses of rock interrupted the beds. No export market could be found for coal of that quality.[18]

The mines produced coal to run the railroad engines, and there was a steady market for home heating fuel in Anchorage, Fairbanks, and along the rail belt. Some small amounts were shipped out of Anchorage for export, but eventually even this market disappeared. In 1923, after testing by expert coal geologists, the navy decided that Matanuska coal was not satisfactory for use as fuel for its fleet, and it continued to ship coal to the Pacific by rail from the East. In the late 1920s and into the 1930s, the US Navy converted its Pacific Fleet to fuel oil, and as a result the massive amounts that were projected for sale there never materialized.[19]

AGRICULTURE

Likewise, the boundless future for Alaska agriculture as promised by railroad enthusiasts never developed. The Tanana Valley, touted by Wickersham as fifty miles wide and a hundred miles long and as fertile as the Mississippi Valley, never emerged as the new homeland that was certain to attract a population equivalent to that of northern Europe. Some in Congress had doubted such claims from the beginning of debate on the railroad, but their voices were overmatched by Progressives who were eager to demonstrate that government could lead the way to creation of a new land with limitless possibilities.

It was that word "possibilities" that bothered those few doubters. "It must be borne in mind," Wilds Richardson warned, "that with the exception of some very small and widely scattered areas of still doubtful value, the word 'possibilities' accurately describes the condition at the present time." He said that the conditions that the farmer needed to guarantee success did not exist in Alaska. These included "arable land which can be cleared and brought under cultivation without prohibitive cost, a market for his product, and transportation facilities to reach that market."[20] Representative Charles Sloan of Nebraska was another skeptic. "The gentleman from Alaska and the members who reside upon Puget Sound tell racy tales of the agricultural products of our great northern possession," he intoned on the House floor. "They would endeavor to convince us that the Equator is seized by the warm currents of the Pacific and bent up into the latitude of Alaska carrying with it almost a tropical clime, with consequent tropic productions, producing cereals, fruits, and forestry in profusion."[21]

Yet even though these doubts were well placed, a significant amount of farming did, and does to this day, occur in parts of Alaska. Agriculture in the Tanana Valley was active and successful beginning in 1903. The Rickert Farm on the edge of Fairbanks near today's South Cushman Street is one example of a farm that produced great amounts of garden vegetables, grain, and hay for the local market. Among the population of the frontier city there was a strong desire to achieve food self-sufficiency, that is, to grow enough vegetables and grain to feed the outlying homesteaders and miners and not be dependent on supplies brought in from the Outside. In 1917, the Tanana Valley Agriculture Association was formed with fifty-one charter members who pledged to make farming viable in the Interior.[22] However, despite determined efforts, the goal of food self-sufficiency was never reached. In 1929, Alaska farmers produced an outstanding potato crop, but other than that they were able to supply only one-tenth of the territory's food demand.[23]

The 1930 US Census showed five hundred farms in Alaska with a total of just under nine thousand acres of improved land for cultivation. Farming on the large scale predicted by railroad enthusiasts was not credible. The population of Anchorage that year was 2,277, and of Fairbanks was 2,101. Nenana, the biggest rail-belt community between the two, numbered 201. Predictions of an immediate massive population increase and a boom in agriculture in Alaska following railroad construction proved to be wildly unrealistic. The population did come, but it took many decades longer than predicted, and it never came close to the millions foreseen by Wickersham, Lane, and the many other Progressive proponents of the railroad. The realities of life on the last frontier were simply too harsh. To make matters worse, the government railroad was, in fact, a detriment to the farming economy that did exist. With low freight rates, food products could be imported from Seattle cheaper than they could be produced locally. Alaskan farmers could not compete.[24]

GOLD

Gold production in Alaska declined steadily after its peak year of 1906, when 1,066,030 ounces were mined across the territory. In 1917, production was 709,049 ounces, but the next year, with the country's entry in World War I and the movement of working men into the military ranks, it fell to 458,641 ounces. It stayed at about that level through most of the 1920s but dropped to 331,140 ounces in 1928. Alfred Brooks noted in his annual report for the US Geological Survey in 1919 that "the very marked decline in Alaska's mining industry" was the result of worldwide conditions brought on by the war. The price of gold had remained constant while a general inflationary trend had increased costs enormously.[25]

The cost of the war and the job of rebuilding after the armistice had forced many countries, including the United States, to abandon the gold standard and turn to paper money. The result was instant and serious inflation while the price of gold remained fixed at $20.67 per ounce. That figure had been established based on the gold dollar as the unit of value. Since there are 23.22 grains of pure gold in the gold dollar and 480 grains of gold in one ounce, the price of one ounce figures out at $20.67.[26] It remained at that level through the 1920s, with serious downward effects on the economy and population growth of Alaska. The price of gold simply had not kept up with the costs associated with mining. At the end of the decade, however, the head of the Geological Survey was able to report some encouraging developments as the Fairbanks Exploration Company was investing many millions of dollars to install dredging equipment in the Fairbanks district. The beginning of production would "mark an event of great significance," Philip Smith wrote in his annual report. These industrial dredges working the creeks would require an extremely large labor force.[27]

In 1933, President Franklin Roosevelt signed an executive order that effectively ended the period of a fixed price of gold. His order forbade the hoarding of gold and required all owners of gold to deliver their holdings to a Federal Reserve bank to be exchanged at $20.67 per ounce. In the midst of the Great Depression, prices of farm products, manufactured goods, and raw materials had declined as a result of deflation. The president's intention was to increase the money supply and allow the dollar to depreciate, and thereby achieve a rise in domestic prices. The price of gold rose immediately, and in 1934 the president specified a price of $35 per ounce.[28] It remained there until 1971, when President Richard Nixon ended the exchange of the dollar to gold at $35 per ounce, effectively removing the United States from what remained of the gold standard.

PROGRESSIVISM

By 1916, Progressivism had run its course, though in its twenty years of life it had accomplished much in the way of social, economic, and political reform across the nation. Antitrust legislation, regulation of interstate commerce, and federal oversight of banking practices were great strides toward fairness for consumers; child labor laws and the eight-hour workday improved the lives and welfare of the laboring classes; direct election of senators and primary elections to challenge the power of party bosses brought a stronger voice to the masses of voters; conservation of natural resources helped to preserve some of America's most valued public lands while curbing the power of industry to exploit them with impunity; and, finally, women's suffrage brought a measure of justice to half of the nation's electorate. The unending refrain underlying all these accomplishments was, as the prominent Progressive Robert La Follette wrote in his autobiography, "the encroachment of the few upon the rights of many." La Follette and other leaders of the era believed in the power and the duty of the federal government to effect these reforms, that the federal government represented a single people rather than merely a collection of independent states.[29]

In Alaska, the legacy of Progressivism is substantial as well. In 1899 and 1900, Congress responded to the sudden growth of population during the gold rush and enacted new civil and criminal codes for the territory; in 1906, it passed legislation giving Alaska residents a voice in Washington with a nonvoting delegate to Congress; in 1912, it established a territorial legislature with locally elected representatives, giving the people a voice in their own affairs; and in 1914, it passed the Alaska Railroad Act, providing support to settlement and growth on a scale not seen in any other territory of the American West.[30]

Railroad construction played a role in the establishment of Mt. McKinley National Park in 1917. The naturalist Charles Sheldon, whose book *The Wilderness of Denali* (1930) chronicled a year of explorations beginning in 1906 while he was living in a cabin on the Toklat River, was a highly effective lobbyist through his association with the Boone and Crockett Club. Sheldon also had a close personal friendship with James Wickersham, and in 1914 he began an intense lobbying effort to push his idea for a national park through Congress. Sheldon was motivated by the effect that railroad construction would have on wildlife populations, fearing that market hunters would harvest huge amounts of moose, caribou, and Dall sheep to feed workers and the growing city of Fairbanks. Wickersham and others, such as Thomas Riggs, supported the plan because they saw it as an aid to the railroad through increased tourist traffic. Coupled with the Alaska Railroad Bill, the national park, signed into law by President Wilson on February 26, was a Progressive win, allowing government to take the lead in the growth of Alaska while also conserving and protecting its unique scenic and wildlife resources.[31]

In the same way, the University of Alaska can be considered a Progressive-era accomplishment. The federal land grant was secured in 1915, but the actual birth of the institution came in 1917, when the territorial legislature approved funding for construction of facilities on a hill overlooking the Tanana Valley southwest of Fairbanks. The original name, the Alaska Agricultural College and School of Mines, reflected the commitment of government on the federal and the territorial levels to aid in the development of this northern frontier.

In the minds of many in Congress and the general public, Alaska was a new acquisition, purchased by the American people, and they believed it should be managed by Congress in the best interests of the people as a whole. This created a unique and oftentimes contentious relationship between Alaska and Washington. The economy was entirely resource-based, and Alaskans' jobs and lives depended on access to lands wholly owned and managed by the government. Progressive-era Alaskans contended that they alone understood the way things were in the North. They wanted the federal government to clear the way for development, not overregulate them or restrict access, and they wanted their voices to be heard through locally elected self-government.

After the war in Europe started in 1914, the cause of Progressivism took a back seat to military issues, and most of the attention and energy in Washington was focused on preparedness. Theodore Roosevelt, still one of the nation's leading and most outspoken Progressives, was intent on swaying his party toward preparation for war, and this became the Progressives' main issue in 1916.[32] Military strength and nationalism were an easy fit for Progressives, especially those who were followers of Roosevelt. In the 1916 election year, the party platform essentially merged with the Republicans, leading to the end of the Progressive Party as a political entity. The Progressive platform was "indistinguishable" from that of the Republicans, historian William Leuchtenburg concluded. As the party "merged with Republicans on nationalist grounds, they adopted the social ideology of the Old Guard too."[33]

Woodrow Wilson himself turned his attentions away from the Progressive reform movement after 1914. The midterm elections that year resulted in big losses for the Democrats, and many Progressive Party members returned to their Republican roots as reform issues were overshadowed by talk of nationalism and preparedness for war.[34]

WICKERSHAM

James Wickersham forged his political persona on one of the tenets of national Progressivism: the fight against monopoly controlled by the strength of corporate trusts. He articulated the heart of the movement: the danger posed by unregulated big business and the power and duty of a centralized government to exercise control. In Alaska, his war on the trusts was waged against the Morgan-Guggenheim Alaska Syndicate. Still, for Wickersham and other Progressives, this battle with the private sector was a bit unnatural. It seemed socialistic to urge government to interfere with commerce and trade, yet at the same time unfettered capitalism presented a greater threat. Wickersham relished his role as the champion of every struggling Alaska miner, farmer, and small businessman against the greed and power of the trusts. It was a popular position to take, and it won him a seat in Congress in six consecutive elections. But the bruising campaigns and the razor-thin, contested races he endured every two years are an indication of conflicting views in the minds of the voting public. The syndicate was evil, true enough, but at the same time it actively worked to develop resources, and it brought opportunities to workers who were desperately in need of jobs. Newspaperman John Strong, who supported Wickersham and was later appointed territorial governor, stated it succinctly in an editorial in the Iditarod *Nugget*. The "Morganheims," he wrote, should drop their campaign of misinformation and "attend strictly to building and operating railroads and mining copper and coal. Alaska needs their money, but it does not need their brand of political domination."[35]

Wickersham won reelection in 1916 and 1918, but the results of both races were contested, and he was seated in the House of Representatives only after long, bitter, and contentious challenges to the vote counts. In 1916, Wickersham ran against Socialist Lena Morrow Lewis, who had earned a reputation within the national party as a tireless and powerful advocate of women's rights, and Democrat Charles Sulzer, brother of Representative William Sulzer of New York. The outcome was in dispute as soon as the results began to come in on Election Day in November. There were many irregularities. For example, military personnel were ineligible as voters, yet it was evident that in places such as Tanana, where there was a nearby army installation, many soldiers had cast ballots. Additionally, many Alaska Natives had voted, though in 1916 they had not yet been granted US citizenship. Sulzer was declared the winner in early 1917, but immediately after Sulzer took his oath of office and his seat in Congress, Wickersham filed a formal protest, and a House investigation was launched. Sulzer served as the Alaska delegate while the investigation dragged on through that year and the next, and in fact it was not resolved before Election Day came around again in 1918. As the final results of the 1916 election remained in doubt, the 1918 race was marred by the same irregularities. Again it was Sulzer versus Wickersham, with Sulzer being declared the winner by thirty-three votes. Meanwhile, the 1916 election was finally resolved in Wickersham's favor. He was seated and sworn in on January 7, 1919, for the few days remaining in the session, while a new investigation began to probe the uncertainties surrounding the 1918 results.

Sulzer died on April 15, 1919. Two days later, he was reaffirmed as the 1918 election winner, and a special election was set for June 3 to fill the seat vacated by his death. Alaska Democrats put up George Grigsby of Juneau while Wickersham, continuing his challenge of the results, refused to run, placing his faith in the certainty that eventually Sulzer's win would be overturned and he would be seated. Grigsby, with his victory in the special election, traveled to Washington and was sworn in as Alaska delegate on July 1, as Congress ignored Wickersham's request to postpone the seating until the challenge was resolved. Grigsby served nearly two years before, at last, the congressional Committee on Elections completed its report and declared Wickersham the winner of the 1918 election. He made his way to Washington, was sworn in on February 28, 1921, and served as Alaska delegate for three days before the session ended.[36]

The grueling contests had taken their toll. Wickersham biographer Evangeline Atwood concluded that at the end the delegate showed little enthusiasm for the job and that he took to venting his anger in a number of attacks against old political foes. "Moved by bitterness and frustration," Atwood wrote, "Wickersham resorted to personal revenge, lashing out against any and all whom he considered his enemy."[37]

Among his targets were Thomas Riggs, now serving as Alaska's appointed territorial governor, and Secretary of the Interior Franklin K. Lane. Riggs, formerly one of the three lead engineers in charge of constructing the Alaska Railroad, had long been considered by Wickersham to be in league with the hated Alaska Syndicate, and in the two latest elections Riggs had actively campaigned against him. Now Wickersham, "like the cur that he is" in Riggs's words,[38] accused Riggs of incompetence in his role as railroad construction engineer, and he blamed Lane for appointing this "menace" to the governorship. Such tirades did little to enhance Wickersham's reputation either in Washington or Alaska, and, knowing that an election campaign in 1920 would be as exhausting as all the others, he bowed out and gave his support to Dan Sutherland. Sutherland served until 1931, when

Wickersham ran for and won a seventh term in Congress. Following that term, he retired to his home in Juneau, where he died in 1939 at age eighty-two.

Wickersham was the most influential Alaskan of the first half of the twentieth century. His triumphs were all the more remarkable for the fact that he served as a lone territorial delegate to the House of Representatives, where he had no vote and therefore no bargaining power in the rough world of partisan politics. His success was due to his extensive and comprehensive knowledge of Alaska history and geography along with his obvious passion for the place and his persuasiveness in debate. He achieved major victories—the elective territorial legislature in 1912 and the Alaska Railroad two years later— but he was also instrumental in securing legislation for establishment of Mt. McKinley (now Denali) National Park and a federal land grant to form the beginnings of the University of Alaska. With significant accomplishments as both judge and politician, he was witness to the birth of modern-day Alaska as centers of population, systems of transportation, and the structures of government and the judiciary took shape, all with the help of the federal government in the age of Progressive democracy.

NOTES

INTRODUCTION

1. Diary of James Wickersham, January 1, 1914. James Wickersham's Diary (1900–1939) is available on the Alaska State Library website (library.alaska.gov).

2. *Congressional Record,* 63rd Cong. 2nd Sess. The Alaska Railway Bill, Speech of Hon. James Wickersham in the House of Representatives, January 14 and 28, 1914, 6–7.

3. *Congressional Record,* 63rd Cong. 2nd Sess. The Alaska Railway Bill, Speech of Hon. James Wickersham in the House of Representatives, January 14 and 28, 1914, 6–7.

4. William H. Dall, *Alaska and Its Resources* (New York: Arno & The New York Times, 1970), 4.

5. Dall, *Alaska and Its Resources,* 281.

6. Alfred Hulse Brooks, *Blazing Alaska's Trails* (Fairbanks: University of Alaska Press, 1973), 256, 272.

7. Robert Campbell, *In Darkest Alaska: Travel and Empire Along the Inside Passage* (Philadelphia: University of Pennsylvania Press, 2007), 61–62.

8. Frederick Schwatka, *A Summer in Alaska in the 1880s* (Secaucus, NJ: Castle Books, 1888).

9. William R. Hunt, *North of 53°: The Wild Days of the Alaska-Yukon Mining Frontier 1870–1914* (New York: Macmillan Publishing Co., Inc., 1974), 4–5.

10. Hunt, *North of 53°,* 4–5.

11. Brooks, *Blazing Alaska's Trails,* 332.

12. William Haskell, *Two Years in the Klondike and Alaskan Gold-Fields 1896–1898* (Fairbanks: University of Alaska Press, 1998), 249.

13. Melody Webb, *The Last Frontier* (Albuquerque: University of New Mexico Press, 1985), 121.

14. Frederick Jackson Turner, "The Significance of the Frontier in American History," in *The Frontier in American History* (New York: Henry Holt and Company, 1920).

15. Roxanne Willis, *Alaska's Place in the West: From the Last Frontier to the Last Great Wilderness* (Lawrence: University Press of Kansas, 2010), 14.

16. Susan Kollin, *Nature's State: Imagining Alaska as the Last Frontier* (Chapel Hill: The University of North Carolina Press, 2001), 24–25.

17. *Alaska-Yukon Magazine*, March 1908, 56–57.

18. *The Alaska Citizen* (Fairbanks), October 12, 1914.

19. Patricia Nelson Limerick, *The Legacy of Conquest: The Unbroken Past of the American West* (New York: W.W. Norton & Company, 1987), 322.

20. Limerick, *The Legacy of Conquest*, 26.

21. *Fairbanks Daily Times*, May 30, 1906.

22. Marion T. Bennett, *American Immigration Policies: A History* (Washington, DC: Public Affairs Press, 1963), 30–31.

23. Richard Hofstadter, *The Age of Reform: From Bryan to F.D.R.* (New York: Vintage Books, 1955), 23.

24. Richard Hofstadter, *The Progressive Historians: Turner, Beard, Parrington* (New York: Alfred A. Knopf, 1968), 154.

25. US Department of the Interior, *Annual Report of the Governor of Alaska, 1900*, 12.

26. US Department of the Interior, *Annual Report of the Governor of Alaska, 1901*, 11.

27. *Congressional Record*, 63rd Cong. 2nd Sess. The Alaska Railway Bill, Speech of Hon. James Wickersham in the House of Representatives, Wednesday, January 14 and 28, 1914, 86.

28. *Congressional Record*, 58th Cong. 1st and 2nd Sess. House of Representatives. Hearings Before the Committee on Territories, 116.

29. *The Daily Alaskan* (Skagway) May 14, 1906.

30. *Alaska-Yukon Magazine*, March 1908, 63.

31. Rex Beach, *The Iron Trail* (Sausalito, CA: A Comstock Edition, 1912), Chapter V.

32. Hunt, *North of 53°*, 256–257.

33. Ernest Gruening, *The State of Alaska: A Definitive History of America's Northernmost Frontier* (New York: Random House, 1954).

34. *Alaska's Struggle for Self Government: 83 Years of Neglect*, collected editorials, *Anchorage Daily Times* (March 24 to April 19, 1950).

35. Jeanette P. Nichols, *Alaska: A History of its Administration, Exploitation, and Industrial Development during its First Half Century under the Rule of the United States* (Cleveland: The Arthur H. Clark Company, 1924) 115, 408.

36. William H. Wilson, "The Alaska Railroad and Coal," *Pacific Northwest Quarterly* 73, no. 2 (April 1982), 66–67.

37. Stephen Haycox, *Alaska: An American Colony* (Seattle: University of Washington Press, 2002), 231.

38. Stephen Haycox, *Battleground Alaska: Fighting Federal Power in America's Last Wilderness* (Lawrence: University Press of Kansas, 2016), 18.

39. Ross Coen, "The Myth of Alaskan Exceptionalism," *Anchorage Daily News*, June 29, 2016.

CHAPTER 1: THE PROMINENCE OF GOLD IN 1890s AMERICA

1. *Seattle Post-Intelligencer*, July 10, 1896.

2. *New York Times*, July 10, 1896.

3. Robert H. Wiebe, *The Search for Order 1877–1920* (New York: Hill and Wang, 1967), 99.

4. Paul W. Glad, *McKinley, Bryan, and the People* (Philadelphia and New York: J.P. Lippincott Company, 1964), 76.

5. Sean Dennis Cashman, *America in the Gilded Age: From the Death of Lincoln to the Rise of Theodore Roosevelt* (New York and London: New York University Press, 1993), 328.

6. Cashman, *America in the Gilded Age,* 314.

7. Milton Friedman, *Money Mischief: Episodes in Monetary History* (New York: Harcourt Brace Jovanovich, 1992), 54.

8. Friedman, *Money Mischief,* 60, 105.

9. Friedman, *Money Mischief,* 68.

10. Hofstadter, *The Age of Reform,* 104.

11. Matthew Josephson, *The Politicos 1856–1896* (New York: Harcourt, Brace & World, Inc., 1938), 456–457.

12. Robert C. McMath, *American Populism: A Social History 1877–1898* (New York: Hill and Wang, 1993), 161.

13. Cashman, *America in the Gilded Age,* 324; Hofstadter, *The Age of Reform,* 105.

14. McMath, *American Populism,* 168.

15. Josephson, *The Politicos,* 476.

16. Friedman, *Money Mischief,* 76.

17. Jean Strouse, *Morgan: American Financier* (New York: Harper Perennial, 2000), 339.

18. McMath, *American Populism,* 184.

19. Cashman, *America in the Gilded Age,* 271.

20. *New York Times,* June 7, 1896.

21. Cashman, *America in the Gilded Age,* 272.

22. Josephson, *The Politicos,* 533.

23. William Hope Harvey, *Coin's Financial School* (Chicago: Coin Publishing Company, 1894), 43, 130.

24. Harvey, *Coin's Financial School,* 43, 112.

25. Harvey, *Coin's Financial School,* 43, 128.

26. Lewis Corey, *The House of Morgan: A Social Biography of the Masters of Money* (New York: AMS Press, 1969), 185.

27. *Scribner's Magazine,* 1896, 470.

28. Ron Chernow, *The House of Morgan: An American Banking Dynasty and the Rise of Modern Finance* (New York: Atlantic Monthly Press, 1990), 71.

29. Corey, *The House of Morgan,* 182.

30. Chernow, *The House of Morgan,* 71; Josephson, *The Politicos,* 601.

31. Thomas Beer, *Hanna* (New York: Alfred A. Knopf, 1929), 133.

32. *Congressional Record,* 53rd Cong. 3rd Sess. Vol. XXVII, 1958.

33. *Congressional Record,* 53rd Cong. 3rd Sess. Vol. XXVII, 2066.

34. *Congressional Record,* 53rd Cong. 3rd Sess. Vol. XXVII, 2188.

35. *Congressional Record,* 53rd Cong. 3rd Sess. Vol. XXVII, 2194.

36. *Congressional Record,* 53rd Cong. 3rd Sess. Vol. XXVII appendix, 287.

37. *New York Times,* February 9, 1895; February 7, 1895.

38. Michael Kazin, *A Godly Hero: The Life of William Jennings Bryan* (New York: Anchor Books, 2006), 52.

39. *New York Times,* June 10, 1896.

40. *New York Times,* June 11, 1896.

41. Josephson, *The Politicos,* 655.

42. *New York Times,* June 12, 1896.

43. Clarence Stern, *Resurgent Republicanism: The Handiwork of Hanna* (Ann Arbor, MI: Edwards Brothers, Inc., 1963), 20.

44. Josephson, *The Politicos,* 657.

45. William T. Horner, *Ohio's Kingmaker: Mark Hanna, Man and Myth* (Athens: Ohio University Press, 2010), 161, 182.

46. *New York Times,* June 16, 1896.

47. Charles W. Johnson, *Official Proceedings of the Eleventh Republican National Convention* (Minneapolis: James Francis Burke, stenographer, 1896), 86–90.

48. *New York Times,* June 16, 1896.

49. Johnson, *Official Proceedings of the Eleventh Republican National Convention,* 86–90.

50. Johnson, *Official Proceedings of the Eleventh Republican National Convention,* 100–101.

51. Stern, *Resurgent Republicanism,* 22.

52. *Alaska Searchlight,* June 6, 1896.

53. *Alaska Mining Record,* May 20, 1896.

54. Johnson, *Official Proceedings of the Eleventh Republican National Convention,* 79.

55. *Alaska Mining Record,* July 1, 1896.

56. Richard F. Bensel, *Passion and Preferences: William Jennings Bryan and the 1896 Democratic National Convention* (New York: Cambridge University Press, 2008), 41.

57. *New York Times,* July 1, 1896.

58. *Seattle Post-Intelligencer,* July 4, 1896.

59. Bensel, *Passion and Preferences,* 38.

60. *Seattle Post-Intelligencer,* July 4, 1896.

61. Edward B. Dickenson, *Official Proceedings of the Democratic National Convention* (Logansport, IN: Wilson, Humphreys & Co., 1896), 125–131.

62. *New York Times,* July 1, 1896.

63. *New York Times,* July 2, 1896.

64. Dickenson, *Official Proceedings of the Democratic National Convention,* 192.

65. Dickenson, *Official Proceedings of the Democratic National Convention,* 197–198.

66. Dickenson, *Official Proceedings of the Democratic National Convention,* 204–208.

67. Bensel, *Passion and Preferences,* 215; Kazin, *A Godly Hero,* 55.

68. Dickenson, *Official Proceedings of the Democratic National Convention,* 209.

69. Dickenson, *Official Proceedings of the Democratic National Convention,* 229.

70. *New York Times,* July 10, 1896.

71. *Seattle Post-Intelligencer,* July 11, 1896.

72. *Alaska Searchlight,* June 6, 1896.

73. Dickenson, *Official Proceedings of the Democratic National Convention,* 241, 249, 327, 375.

74. *The Alaska News,* August 6, 1896.

75. *New York Times,* July 11, 1896.

76. *New York Daily Tribune,* July 11, 1896.

77. Nell Irvin Painter, *Standing at Armageddon: A Grassroots History of the Progressive Era* (New York: W.W. Norton & Company, 2008), 136.

78. Gretchen Ritter, *Goldbugs and Greenbacks: The Antimonopoly Tradition and the Politics of Finance in America* (New York: Cambridge University Press, 1997), 206.

79. Stern, *Resurgent Republicanism,* 23.

80. Horner, *Ohio's Kingmaker,* 183.

81. Herbert Croly, *Marcus Alonzo Hanna: His Life and Work* (New York: The Macmillan Company, 1912), 209.

82. Paolo E. Coletta, *William Jennings Bryan: Vol. I. Political Evangelist 1860–1908* (Lincoln: University of Nebraska Press, 1964), 151.

83. Beer, *Hanna,* 153; Painter, *Standing at Armageddon,* 138.

84. Croly, *Marcus Alonzo Hanna,* 227.

85. *New York Times,* November 3, 1896.

86. *New York Times,* November 1, 1896.

87. Croly, *Marcus Alonzo Hanna,* 222.

88. *New York Times,* November 4, 1896

89. *The Alaska News,* August 6, 1896.

90. *Alaska Mining Record,* November 18, 1896.

CHAPTER 2: THE BEGINNINGS OF MODERN-DAY ALASKA

1. Pierre Berton, *Klondike: The Last Great Gold Rush 1896–1899* (Toronto: McClelland and Stewart Limited, 1972), 40.

2. Ken S. Coates and William R. Morrison, *Land of the Midnight Sun: A History of the Yukon* (Montreal: McGill-Queens University Press, 2005), 82.

3. Coates and Morrison, *Land of the Midnight Sun,* 49.

4. *Alaska Mining Record,* April 15, 1895.

5. US Department of the Interior, *Annual Report of the Governor of Alaska 1896.*

6. *Douglas Miner,* October 21, 1896.

7. *San Francisco Chronicle,* July 15, 1897.

8. *San Francisco Chronicle,* July 15, 1897.

9. *Seattle Post-Intelligencer,* July 17, 1897.

10. Berton, *Klondike,* 95.

11. Berton, *Klondike,* 103.

12. *Seattle Post-Intelligencer,* July 19, 1897.

13. *Seattle Post-Intelligencer,* July 23, 1897.

14. Berton, *Klondike,* 113, 116.

15. *Alaska Mining Record,* February 26, 1896.

16. Coates and Morrison, *Land of the Midnight Sun,* 87.

17. Hunt, *North of 53°,* 44.

18. *Alaska Mining Record,* November 13, 1895.

19. Coates and Morrison, *Land of the Midnight Sun,* 91.

20. Ted C. Hinckley, *The Americanization of Alaska, 1867–1897* (Palo Alto, CA: Pacific Books Publishers, 1972), 243.

21. Hinckley, *The Americanization of Alaska,* 239.

22. *Douglas Miner,* October 21, 1896.

23. Terris Moore, *Mt. McKinley: The Pioneer Climbs* (Fairbanks: University of Alaska Press, 1967), 14; Walter R. Borneman, *Alaska: Saga of a Bold Land* (New York: Harper Collins, 2003), 220.

24. Belmore Browne, *The Conquest of Mt. McKinley* (Cambridge, MA: The Riverside Press, 1956), 8; Donald J. Orth, *Dictionary of Alaska Place Names,* Geological Survey Professional Paper 567 (Washington, DC: United States Government Printing Office, 1967).

25. Eric Foner, *The Story of American Freedom* (New York: W.W. Norton and Company, 1998), 116.

26. Hofstadter, *The Age of Reform,* 110.

27. Hofstadter, *The Age of Reform,* 110.

28. Hofstadter, *The Age of Reform,* 111.

29. J. Leonard Bates, *The United States 1898–1928: Progressivism and a Society in Transition* (New York: McGraw-Hill Book Company, 1976), 11.

30. Jerome M. Mileur, "The Legacy of Reform: Progressive Government, Regressive Politics," in *Progressivism and the New Democracy,* ed. Sidney M. Milkis and Jerome M. Mileur (Amherst: University of Massachusetts Press, 1999), 260.

31. Sidney M. Milkis, "Progressivism Then and Now," introduction to *Progressivism and the New Democracy,* ed. Sidney M. Milkis and Jerome M. Mileur (Amherst: University of Massachusetts Press, 1999), 5.

32. Bates, *The United States 1898–1928,* 43.

33. Mileur, "The Legacy of Reform," 265.

34. Robert S. Maxwell, *La Follette and the Rise of the Progressives in Wisconsin* (Madison: State Historical Society of Wisconsin, 1956), 12.

35. Robert M. La Follette, *A Personal Narrative of Political Experience* (Madison, WI: The Robert LaFollette Co., 1911), 18.

36. La Follette, *A Personal Narrative of Political Experience,* 760.

37. David P. Thelen, *Robert M. La Follette and the Insurgent Spirit,* ed. Oscar Handlin (Boston: Little Brown and Company, 1976), 26.

38. Thelen, *Robert M. La Follette and the Insurgent Spirit,* 31.

39. US Department of the Interior, *Annual Report of the Governor of Alaska 1896,* 206.

40. *Alaska Mining Record,* April 13, 1898.

41. *Alaska Mining Record,* December 15, 1897.

42. *Congressional Record,* 55th Cong. 2nd Sess. Vol. XXXI, 3083.

43. *Congressional Record,* 55th Cong. 2nd Sess. Vol. XXXI, 3132.

44. *Congressional Record,* 55th Cong. 2nd Sess. Vol. XXXI, 3084.

45. Mary F. Ehrlander, "The Paradox of Alaska's 1916 Alcohol Reform Referendum: A Dry Vote Within a Frontier Alcohol Culture," *Pacific Northwest Quarterly* 102, no. 1 (Winter 2010/2011), 29–42.

46. *Alaska Mining Record,* April 20, 1898.

47. *Seattle Post-Intelligencer,* December 30, 1898.

48. *Congressional Record,* 55th Cong. 3rd Sess., 588.

49. *Congressional Record,* 55th Cong. 3rd Sess., 592.

50. *Congressional Record,* 55th Cong. 3rd Sess., 2702.

51. *Congressional Record,* 55th Cong. 3rd Sess., 2702.

52. *Congressional Record,* 55th Cong. 3rd Sess., 2704.

53. *Alaska Mining Record,* January 4, 1899.

54. *Congressional Record,* 55th Cong. 3rd Sess. House of Representatives Report No. 1807.

55. US Department of the Interior, *Annual Report of the Governor of Alaska to the Secretary of the Interior 1899,* 42–43.

56. *Congressional Record,* 56th Cong. 1st Sess. Vol. XXXIII, 4167–4168.

57. *Congressional Record,* 56th Cong. 1st Sess. Vol. XXXIII, 4712.

58. Hunt, *North of 53°,* 97.

59. *Congressional Record,* 56th Cong. 1st Sess. Vol. XXXIII, 4841.

60. *Congressional Record,* 56th Cong. 1st Sess. Vol. XXXIII, 4173.

61. *Congressional Record,* 56th Cong. 1st Sess. Vol. XXXIII, 4845.

62. For full accounts of the corruption and conspiracy in Nome and the roles played by Carter and Hansbrough et al., see Terrence Cole, *A History of the Nome Gold Rush: The Poor Man's Paradise* (PhD diss., University of Washington, 1983), 159 ff.; Hunt, *North of 53°,* 122 ff.; and Andrea R. C. Helms and Mary Childers Mangusso, "The Nome Gold Conspiracy," *Pacific Northwest Quarterly* 73, no. 1 (January 1982), 10–19.

63. Johnson, *Official Proceedings of the Eleventh Republican National Convention,* 85; Dickenson, *Official Proceedings of the Democratic National Convention,* 195.

64. *Congressional Record,* 56th Cong. 1st Sess. Vol. XXXIII, 5658–5659.

65. *Congressional Record,* 56th Cong. 1st Sess. Vol. XXXIII, 5658–5659.

66. *Skaguay News,* February 2, 1900.

67. *Alaska Record Miner,* March 24, 1900.

68. *Seattle Post-Intelligencer,* May 22, 1900.

69. *Congressional Record,* 56th Cong. 1st Sess. Vol. XXXIII, 5865.

70. Claus-M. Naske and Herman Slotnick, *Alaska: A History* (Norman: University of Oklahoma Press, 2011), 141.

71. *Seattle Post-Intelligencer,* May 6, 1900.

72. *Skaguay News,* March 30, 1900.

73. *Daily Alaskan,* May 9, 1900.

74. *Seattle Post-Intelligencer,* May 30, 1900.

CHAPTER 3: THE ROOTS OF PROGRESSIVISM

1. Shelton Stromquist, *Reinventing "The People": The Progressive Movement, the Class Problem, and the Origins of Modern Liberalism* (Urbana and Chicago: University of Illinois Press, 2006), 71; Sidney M. Milkis, "Progressivism Then and Now," 6.

2. Nichols, *Alaska,* 183.

3. William Mitchell, "Building the Alaskan Telegraph System," *National Geographic* XV, no. 9 (September 1904), 357–361; William Mitchell, *The Opening of Alaska,* ed. Lyman L. Woodman (Anchorage: Cook Inlet Historical Society, 1982).

4. Gruening, *The State of Alaska*, 115.

5. *The Skagway News*, June 1, 1900.

6. Foner, *The Story of American Freedom*, 117.

7. Bates, *The United States 1898–1928*, 41.

8. Haycox, *Alaska*, 229.

9. *Daily Alaskan*, June 14, 1900.

10. *Daily Alaskan*, June 14, 1900.

11. Nichols, *Alaska*, 205.

12. Haycox, *Alaska*, 226.

13. Terrence Cole, introduction to *Old Yukon: Tales, Trails, and Trials* by James Wickersham, ed. and abridged by Terrence Cole (Fairbanks: University of Alaska Press, 2009), xix.

14. *Congressional Record,* 58th Cong. 2nd Sess. *Conditions in Alaska*, 105.

15. Melody Webb Grauman, "Kennecott: Alaskan Origins of a Copper Empire, 1900–1938," *Western Historical Quarterly* 9, no. 2 (April 1978), 197–211; Robert Alden Stearns, *The Morgan-Guggenheim Syndicate and the Development of Alaska, 1906–1915* (PhD diss., University of California Santa Barbara, 1967), 253–254.

16. George E. Mowry, *The Era of Theodore Roosevelt, 1900–1912* (New York: Harper & Brothers, 1958), 121.

17. *New York Times*, December 4, 1901.

18. Edmund Morris, *Theodore Rex* (New York: The Modern Library, 2001), 65.

19. Morris, *Theodore Rex*, 65.

20. Morris, *Theodore Rex*, 60.

21. Painter, *Standing at Armageddon*, 176–179.

22. Mowry, *The Era of Theodore Roosevelt*, 88–89.

23. Hofstadter, *The Age of Reform*, 137.

24. Terrence Cole, *Crooked Past: The History of a Frontier Mining Camp: Fairbanks, Alaska* (Fairbanks: University of Alaska Press, 1991), 36–38; Naske and Slotnick, *Alaska*, 136.

25. Naske and Slotnick, *Alaska*, 137.

26. James Wickersham, *Old Yukon: Tales, Trails, and Trials*, ed. and abridged by Terrence Cole (University of Alaska Press, 2009), 109–123.

27. Diary of James Wickersham, August 17, 1904.

28. John Braeman, *Albert J. Beveridge: American Nationalist* (Chicago and London: University of Chicago Press, 1971), 72–74.

29. Douglas Brinkley, *The Wilderness Warrior: Theodore Roosevelt and the Crusade for America* (New York: Harper Collins, 2009), 527.

30. Brinkley, *The Wilderness Warrior*, 530.

31. *Seattle Post-Intelligencer*, May 23, 1903.

32. *Seattle Post-Intelligencer*, May 23, 1903.

33. Theodore Roosevelt, *Theodore Roosevelt: An Autobiography* (New York: Charles Scribner's Sons, 1922), 402.

34. Doris Kearns Goodwin, *The Bully Pulpit: Theodore Roosevelt, William Howard Taft, and the Golden Age of Journalism* (New York: Simon & Schuster, 2013), 279.

35. Timothy Egan, *The Big Burn: Teddy Roosevelt and the Fire that Saved America* (Boston: Houghton Mifflin Harcourt, 2009), 42, 45.

36. *Congressional Record,* 58th Cong. 2nd Sess. *Conditions in Alaska*, 2.

37. *Congressional Record,* 58th Cong. 2nd Sess., *Conditions in Alaska,* 13, 21.

38. *Congressional Record,* 58th Cong. 2nd Sess., *Conditions in Alaska,* 30.

39. *Congressional Record,* 58th Cong. 2nd Sess., *Conditions in Alaska,* 125.

40. *Congressional Record,* 58th Cong. 2nd Sess., *Conditions in Alaska,* 123.

41. *Congressional Record,* 58th Cong. 2nd Sess., *Conditions in Alaska,* 10.

42. *Congressional Record,* 58th Cong. 2nd Sess., *Conditions in Alaska,* 13–14.

43. *Congressional Record,* 58th Cong. 2nd Sess., *Conditions in Alaska,* 31–32.

44. *Congressional Record,* 58th Cong. 1st and 2nd Sess. Vol. II, 513.

45. *Congressional Record,* 58th Cong. 1st and 2nd Sess. Vol. II, 512.

46. *Congressional Record,* 58th Cong. 1st and 2nd Sess. Vol. II, 516.

47. *Congressional Record,* 58th Cong. 1st and 2nd Sess. Vol. II, 524–528, 538.

48. *Congressional Record,* 58th Cong. 2nd Sess. Vol. XXXVIII, 4394.

49. Elting E. Morison, ed., *The Letters of Theodore Roosevelt,* Vol IV (Cambridge, MA: Harvard University Press, 1954), 762.

50. Morison, *The Letters of Theodore Roosevelt,* 775.

51. Louis A. Coolidge, *An Old-Fashioned Senator: Orville H. Platt of Connecticut* (New York: G.P. Putnam's Sons, 1910), 309.

52. Gruening, *The State of Alaska,* 139.

53. Nichols, *Alaska,* 246.

CHAPTER 4: CONGRESS CONSIDERS THE NEEDS OF ALASKA

1. Diary of James Wickersham, April 4–12, 1904.

2. Diary of James Wickersham, April 12, 1904.

3. Diary of James Wickersham, May 31, 1904.

4. Diary of James Wickersham, July 8, 1904.

5. David M. Dean, *Breaking Trail: Hudson Stuck of Texas and Alaska* (Athens: Ohio University Press, 1988), 54.

6. Hudson Stuck to John Wood, September 1, 1904, Episcopal Church Records, Alaska and Polar Regions Archives, Rasmuson Library, University of Alaska Fairbanks.

7. Hudson Stuck to John Wood, September 7, 1904, Episcopal Church Records.

8. Hudson Stuck to John Wood, September 7, 1904, Episcopal Church Records.

9. Hudson Stuck to Manning, September 28, 1904, Episcopal Church Records.

10. Hudson Stuck to John Wood, September 7, 1904, Episcopal Church Records.

11. Hudson Stuck to John Wood, October 18, 1904, Episcopal Church Records.

12. Debbie Miller, "Tanana Valley Railroad," *Alaska Geographic: Alaska's Railroads* 9, no. 4 (1992), 33–39; Falcon Joslin, "Railroad Building in Alaska," *Alaska-Yukon Magazine* 7, no. 4 (January, 1909), 245–250.

13. Wickersham Collection, Alaska State Library, Juneau, Alaska.

14. Joslin, "Railroad Building in Alaska," 245–250.

15. Joslin, "Railroad Building in Alaska," 245–250.

16. Arthur Weinberg and Lila Weinberg, eds., *The Muckrakers* (Chicago: First Illinois paperback, 2001), 4–5.

17. Ray Stannard Baker, *American Chronicle: The Autobiography of Ray Stannard Baker* (New York: Charles Scribner's Sons, 1945), 169, 183–184.

18. James L. Aucoin, *The Evolution of American Investigative Journalism* (Columbia and London: University of Missouri Press, 2005), 32–33.

19. Aucoin, *The Evolution of American Investigative Journalism*, 28–31.

20. Steve Weinberg, *Taking on the Trust: The Epic Battle of Ida Tarbell and John D. Rockefeller* (New York: W.W. Norton & Company, 2008), 192, 198.

21. Harold S. Wilson, *McClure's Magazine and the Muckrakers* (Princeton, NJ: Princeton University Press, 1970), 147.

22. Kathleen Brady, *Ida Tarbell: Portrait of a Muckraker* (New York: Seaview/ Putnam, 1984), 140.

23. Hofstadter, *The Age of Reform*, 186–192.

24. Robert Harrison, *Congress, Progressive Reform, and the New American State* (Cambridge, UK: Cambridge University Press, 2004), 52.

25. Goodwin, *The Bully Pulpit*, 453–459.

26. Goodwin, *The Bully Pulpit*, 450, 455, 458.

27. Theodore Roosevelt, "Municipal Administration: The New York Police Force," *The Atlantic* LXXX (September 1897), 289–300.

28. Baker, *American Chronicle*, 201–204.

29. *Fairbanks Daily Times*, June 3, 1906.

30. Mark Neuzil, "Hearst, Roosevelt, and the Muckrake Speech of 1906: A New Perspective," *Journalism & Mass Communication Quarterly* 73, no. 1 (1996), 29–39.

31. Goodwin, *The Bully Pulpit*, 487.

32. *Fairbanks Sunday Times,* February. 18, 1906.

33. Diary of James Wickersham, December 8, 1904.

34. Thomas A. McMullin and David Walker, *Biographical Directory of American Territorial Governors* (Westport, CT: Meckler Publishing, 1984), 10.

35. Elizabeth Tower, "Captain David Henry Jarvis: Alaskan Tragic Hero— Wickersham's Victim," *Alaska History* 5, no.1 (Spring 1990), 1–21.

36. *Fairbanks Daily Times*, July 19, 1906.

37. *Fairbanks Daily Times*, July 18, 1906.

38. *Fairbanks Daily Times*, July 18, 1906.

39. *Fairbanks Daily Times*, July 21, 1906.

40. *Fairbanks Daily Times*, July 25, 1906.

41. *Daily Alaska Dispatch*, February 14, 1906.

42. *Daily Alaskan*, May 19, 1906.

43. *Daily Alaskan*, July 30, 1906.

44. *Daily Alaskan*, July 30, 1906.

45. *Fairbanks Daily Times*, July 21, 1906.

46. *Daily Alaska Dispatch,* May 11, 1906.

47. *Daily Alaska Dispatch,* August 6, 1906.

48. *Daily Alaska Dispatch,* August 13, 1906.

49. *Daily Alaska Dispatch,* August 16, 1906.

50. Wickersham, *Old Yukon*, 251–255; Elizabeth Tower, *Icebound Empire: Industry and Politics on the Last Frontier, 1898–1938* (Anchorage Publication Consultants, 1996), 69–80.

51. John M. Davis, *The Guggenheims: An American Epic* (New York: William Morrow and Company, Inc., 1978), 100.

52. *New York Times*, April 3, 1906.

53. *New York Times*, September 3, 1906.

54. *New York Times*, April 4, 1906.

55. *Wall Street Journal,* September 27, 1930, quoted in Davis, *The Guggenheims,* 102.

56. Davis, *The Guggenheims,* 102.

57. Tower, *Icebound Empire,* 113–114.

58. Lone E. Janson, *The Copper Spike* (Anchorage: Alaska Northwest Publishing Company, 1975), 32; Tower, *Icebound Empire,* 114–115; Melody Webb Grauman, "Big Business in Alaska: The Kennecott Mines, 1898–1938," Anthropology and Historic Preservation Cooperative Park Studies Unit, Occasional Paper #1 (University of Alaska Fairbanks, 1977), 9.

59. Grauman, "Big Business in Alaska," 8–9.

60. Robert Alden Stearns, *The Morgan-Guggenheim Syndicate and the Development of Alaska, 1906–1915* (PhD diss., University of California Santa Barbara, 1967), 92–93.

61. John S. Whitehead, *Completing the Union: Alaska, Hawai'i, and the Battle for Statehood* (Albuquerque: University of New Mexico Press, 2004), 41.

62. Nancy J. Taniguchi, *Necessary Fraud: Progressive Reform and Utah Coal* (Norman: University of Oklahoma Press, 1996), 3–8.

63. Roosevelt, *Theodore Roosevelt: An Autobiography,* 361, 407.

64. *Alaska Prospector,* January 3, 1907.

65. Janson, *The Copper Spike,* 110.

CHAPTER 5: THE ALASKA SYNDICATE EMERGES
AS AN ECONOMIC AND POLITICAL FORCE

1. *Daily Alaska Dispatch,* February 5, 1907.

2. *Daily Alaska Dispatch,* February 5, 1907.

3. Gifford Pinchot, *Breaking New Ground* (New York: Harcourt, Brace and Company, 1947), 324, 326.

4. *Valdez News,* February 17, 1906.

5. *The Alaskan,* February 9, 1907.

6. *Fairbanks Evening News,* December 12, 1906.

7. *Alaska Prospector,* August 15, 1907.

8. Diary of James Wickersham, August 10–11, 1907.

9. *Alaska Prospector,* August 15, 1907.

10. *Cordova Alaskan,* August 31, 1907.

11. *Alaska Prospector,* September 5, 1907.

12. *Cordova Alaskan,* September 4, 1907.

13. *Cordova Alaskan,* September 14, 1907.

14. *Seattle Post-Intelligencer,* September 26, 1907.

15. *Seattle Post-Intelligencer,* September 28, 1907.

16. *Alaska Prospector,* October 17, 1907.

17. *Cordova Alaskan,* October 19, 1907.

18. *Seattle Post-Intelligencer,* September 4, 1907.

19. *Cordova Alaskan,* November 9, 1907.

20. *Seattle Post-Intelligencer,* November 7, 1907.

21. *Seattle Post-Intelligencer,* November 15, 1907.

22. *Seattle Post-Intelligencer,* November 17, 1907.

23. *New York Times*, December 4, 1907.

24. *Seattle Post-Intelligencer*, December 4, 1907.

25. Nelson to James Wickersham, January 30, 1906, Wickersham Collection MS 107 Box 60, Alaska State Library, Juneau.

26. Diary of James Wickersham, September 10, 1907.

27. *The Letters of Theodore Roosevelt*, Vol. 6, 1409.

28. *The Letters of Theodore Roosevelt*, Vol. 7, 323–324.

29. Theodore Roosevelt to James Wickersham, Wickersham Collection.

30. *Seattle Post-Intelligencer*, September 28, 1907.

31. Diary of James Wickersham, July 1, 1907.

32. *Seattle Post-Intelligencer*, November 17, 1907.

33. *Fairbanks Daily Times*, October 18, 1907.

34. James Wickersham to Stephen Birch, February 1, 1908, Wickersham Collection.

35. Diary of James Wickersham, April 6, 1908.

36. Diary of James Wickersham, April 8, 1908.

37. Stephen Birch to James Wickersham, May 6, 1908, Wickersham Collection.

38. Diary of James Wickersham, June 8, 1908.

39. *Fairbanks Daily News*, June 5, 1908.

40. *Fairbanks Daily News*, June 8, 1908.

41. Diary of James Wickersham, May 14, 1908.

42. *Fairbanks Daily News*, June 18, 1908.

43. *Fairbanks Daily News*, June 25, 1908.

44. *Fairbanks Daily Times*, July 2, 1908.

45. *Fairbanks Daily Times*, July 6, 1908.

46. Diary of James Wickersham, July 3, 4, 1908.

47. *Fairbanks Daily Times*, July 22, 1908.

48. Diary of James Wickersham, July 17, 1908.

49. Tower, "Captain David Henry Jarvis," 11.

50. *Fairbanks Daily Times*, July 9, 1908.

51. *Fairbanks Daily Times*, July 23, 1908.

52. *Fairbanks Daily Times*, August 13, 1908.

53. A. E. Light to James Wickersham, December 15, 1908, Wickersham Collection.

CHAPTER 6: ALASKANS FIGHT FOR TERRITORIAL SELF-GOVERNMENT

1. *Collier's*, November 13, 1909, 9, 15.

2. Claus-M. Naske and Don Triplehorn, "The Federal Government and Alaska's Coal," *The Northern Engineer,* Geophysical Institute, University of Alaska, 12, no. 3 (Fall 1980), 11.

3. *Collier's*, November 13, 1909, 15–19.

4. Pinchot, *Breaking New Ground*, 427.

5. Herman Slotnick, "The Ballinger-Pinchot Affair in Alaska," *Journal of the West* 10, no. 2 (1971), 339.

6. Irwin Unger and Debi Unger, *The Guggenheims: A Family History* (New York: Harper Collins, 2005), 106.

7. Pinchot, *Breaking New Ground*, 429.

8. Pinchot, *Breaking New Ground*, 447.

9. Pinchot, *Breaking New Ground*, 440, 453.

10. *Congressional Record*, 61st Cong. 2nd Sess., *Government of Alaska*, Senate Committee on Territories, 14–15.

11. *Congressional Record*, 61st Cong. 2nd Sess., 1019.

12. Leonard Schlup, "Coe I. Crawford and the Progressive Campaign of 1912," South Dakota Historical Society, 1979.

13. *Congressional Record*, 61st Cong. 2nd Sess., 1838.

14. *Congressional Record*, 61st Cong. 2nd Sess., 1019–1027.

15. *Congressional Record*, 61st Cong. 2nd Sess., *Government of Alaska*, Senate Committee on Territories, 18.

16. *Congressional Record*, 61st Cong. 2nd Sess., *Government of Alaska*, Senate Committee on Territories, 28.

17. Claus-M. Naske, *Paving Alaska's Trails: The Work of the Alaska Road Commission*, Alaska Historical Commission Studies in History No. 152 (Lanham, MD: University Press of America), 40.

18. *Congressional Record*, 61st Cong. 2nd Sess., *Government of Alaska*, Senate Committee on Territories, 42–43.

19. *Congressional Record*, 61st Cong. 2nd Sess., *Government of Alaska*, Senate Committee on Territories, 46.

20. *Congressional Record*, 61st Cong. 2nd Sess., *Government of Alaska*, Senate Committee on Territories, 68–69.

21. *Seattle Post-Intelligencer*, January 26, 1910; *Seattle Post-Intelligencer*, February 1, 1910.

22. *Seattle Post-Intelligencer*, January 18, 1910.

23. Nichols, *Alaska*, 353.

24. *The Outlook*, February 26, 1910, 436, 437.

25. *The Outlook*, February 26, 1910, 413–414.

26. *Hampton's*, April 1910, 460.

27. *Hampton's*, April 1910, 467, 468.

28. *Hampton's*, May 1910, 645–646.

29. *Congressional Record*, 61st Cong. 2nd Sess., *Government of Alaska*, House of Representatives Committee on Territories, 9.

30. *Congressional Record*, 61st Cong. 2nd Sess., *Government of Alaska*, House of Representatives Committee on Territories, 9–11.

31. *McClure's*, January 1910, 444–445.

32. *McClure's*, January 1910, 352, 355.

33. Pinchot, *Breaking New Ground*, 475.

34. Nelson M. McGeary, *Gifford Pinchot: Forester, Politician* (Princeton, NJ: Princeton University Press, 1960), 166.

35. McGeary, *Gifford Pinchot*, 166.

36. McGeary, *Gifford Pinchot*, 491, 497.

37. Slotnick, "The Ballinger-Pinchot Affair in Alaska," 344.

38. *Alaska-Yukon Magazine*, May, 1910, 394, 396.

39. *Congressional Record*, 61st Cong. 2nd Sess., House of Representatives, "A National Coal Monopoly in Alaska, Speech of Hon. James Wickersham," February 23, 1911, 33.

40. *Congressional Record,* 61st Cong. 2nd Sess., "A National Coal Monopoly," February 23, 1911, 58–60.

41. *Congressional Record,* 61st Cong. 2nd Sess., "A National Coal Monopoly," February 23, 1911, 55–57.

42. *Congressional Record,* 61st Cong. 2nd Sess., "A National Coal Monopoly," February 23, 1911, 71.

43. *New York Times,* February 24, 1911.

44. Diary of James Wickersham, February 14, 1911.

45. Nichols, *Alaska,* 390.

CHAPTER 7: A WIN FOR SELF-GOVERNMENT

1. Rex Beach, "What Is the Matter With Alaska?," *Saturday Evening Post* 183, no. 35 (February 25, 1911), 3.

2. Abe C. Ravitz, *Rex Beach,* ed. James H. Maguire (Boise: Boise State University, 1994), 5.

3. Rex Beach, *Personal Exposures* (New York: Harper & Brothers Publishers, 1940), 32.

4. Rex Beach, "The Looting of Alaska: The True Story of a Robbery by Law," *Appleton's Booklovers Magazine* VII, nos. 1–5 (January, February, March, April, May 1906), 12.

5. Beach, "The Looting of Alaska," 133.

6. Beach, "The Looting of Alaska," 138.

7. Beach, "The Looting of Alaska," 612.

8. Elizabeth Tower, "Rex Beach's Alaska: Novels and Autobiography," *Alaska History News* 20, no. 4 (October, 1989), 7.

9. Beach, *Personal Exposures,* 30.

10. Tower, "Rex Beach's Alaska," 7.

11. Ravitz, *Beach,* 23.

12. Beach, "What Is the Matter With Alaska?," 3.

13. Beach, "What Is the Matter With Alaska?," 4.

14. Beach, "What Is the Matter With Alaska?," 40.

15. Beach, "What Is the Matter With Alaska?," 41.

16. *Alaska-Yukon Magazine,* April 1911, 54–55.

17. *Cordova Daily Alaskan,* May 2, 1911.

18. *Cordova Daily Alaskan,* May 4, 1911.

19. *Seattle Post-Intelligencer,* May 5, 1911.

20. *Seattle Post-Intelligencer,* May 7, 1911.

21. *Cordova Daily Alaskan,* May 10, 1911.

22. *Cordova Daily Alaskan,* May 13, 1911.

23. *Congressional Record,* 61st Cong. 2nd Sess., Senate Committee on Territories, *Civil Government in Alaska,* May 23, 1911, 58–59.

24. Theodore Roosevelt, "Alaska—It Must be Developed," *The Outlook* (July 22, 1911), 614, 615; Theodore Roosevelt, "Alaska Again," *The Outlook* (August 12, 1911), 821, 822.

25. *Congressional Record,* 62nd Cong. 1st Sess. Vol. XLVII, Part V, 4264.

26. *Congressional Record,* 62nd Cong. 1st Sess. Vol. XLVII, Part V, 4266.

27. Charles Sulzer, "What Alaska Needs," *Alaska-Yukon Magazine* XI, no. 4 (May,

1911), 21.

28. W. D. Hulbert, "What Is Really Going on in Alaska," *The Outlook*, December 23, 1911, 950, 951.

29. Hulbert, "What Is Really Going on in Alaska," 962.

30. *Congressional Record*, 62nd Cong. 2nd Sess. Vol. XLVII, Part II, 4935.

31. *Congressional Record*, 62nd Cong. 2nd Sess. Vol. XLVII, Part II, 4940.

32. *Congressional Record*, 62nd Cong. 2nd Sess. Vol. XLVII, Part II, 4943.

33. *Congressional Record*, 62nd Cong. 2nd Sess. Vol. XLVII, Part II, 4951.

34. *Congressional Record*, 62nd Cong. 2nd Sess. Vol. XLVII, Part II, 5267.

35. *Valdez Daily Prospector* February 7, 1912.

36. US Department of the Interior, *Reports of the Department of the Interior for the Fiscal Year Ended June 30, 1911*, 496–499.

37. *Congressional Record*, 62nd Cong. 2nd Sess. Vol. XLVII, Part II, 5268.

38. *Congressional Recor,d* 62nd Cong. 2nd Sess. Vol. XLVII, Part II, 5273.

39. *Congressional Record*, 62nd Cong. 2nd Sess. Vol. XLVII, Part II, 5285.

40. *Seattle Post-Intelligencer*, April 14, 1912.

41. Diary of James Wickersham, April 24, 1912.

42. Gruening, *The State of Alaska*, 152, 153.

CHAPTER 8: FRONTIER POLITICS IN 1912

1. Eugene H. Rosebloom, *A History of Presidential Elections: From George Washington to Richard M. Nixon* (New York: The Macmillan Company, 1970), 358.

2. Herbert Croly, *The Promise of American Life* (Boston: Northeastern University Press, 1989), 274–275.

3. Croly, *The Promise of American Life*, 145, 169.

4. William Manners, *TR and Will: A Friendship that Split the Republican Party* (New York: Harcourt Brace & World, Inc., 1969), 178–179.

5. John Allen Gable, *The Bull Moose Years: Theodore Roosevelt and the Progressive Party* (Port Washington, NY: Kennikat Press, 1978), 11.

6. Gable, *The Bull Moose Years*, 14.

7. Goodwin, *The Bully Pulpit*, 713.

8. Gable, *The Bull Moose Years*, 17.

9. Painter, *Standing at Armageddon*, 268.

10. Painter, *Standing at Armageddon*, 269.

11. Scott Berg, *Wilson* (New York: G.P. Putnam's Sons, 2013), 231.

12. Richard Hofstadter, ed., *Great Issues in American History*, Vol. 2 (New York: Random House, 1958), 244.

13. Berg, *Wilson*, 240.

14. Richard Hofstadter, *The American Political Tradition and the Men Who Made It* (New York: Alfred A. Knopf, 1948), 253.

15. Woodrow Wilson, *The New Freedom: A Call for the Emancipation of the Generous Energies of a People* (New York: Doubleday, Page and Company, 1913), 165, 180, 190.

16. Goodwin, *The Bully Pulpit*, 727.

17. Woodrow Wilson, *The Papers of Woodrow Wilson*, Vol. 25, ed. Arthur S. Link (Princeton, NJ: Princeton University Press, 1979), 350.

18. Wilson, *The Papers*, 397.

19. Diary of James Wickersham, March 9, 1912.

20. *Daily Alaska Dispatch*, March 20, 1912.

21. *Daily Alaska Dispatch*, March 5, 1912.

22. *Daily Alaska Dispatch*, April 1, 1912.

23. *Valdez Daily Prospector*, March 30, 1912.

24. *Daily Alaska Dispatch*, May 9, 1912.

25. Diary of James Wickersham, April 4, 1912.

26. *Valdez Daily Prospector*, March 26, 1912.

27. *Daily Alaska Dispatch*, April 2, 1912.

28. *Valdez Daily Prospector*, April 12, 1912.

29. *Valdez Daily Prospector*, April 12, 1912.

30. *Daily Alaska Dispatch*, June 7, 1912.

31. *Valdez Daily Prospector*, April 5, 1912.

32. *Valdez Daily Prospector*, April 11, 1912.

33. *Daily Alaska Dispatch*, May 10, 1912.

34. *Nome Daily Nugget*, June 29, 1912.

35. *Nome Daily Nugget*, July 25, 1912.

36. *Daily Alaska Dispatch*, June 19, 1912.

37. Joseph Sullivan, "Sourdough Radicalism: Labor and Socialism in Alaska, 1905–1920," *Alaska History* 7, no. 1 (1992), 5.

38. Sullivan, "Sourdough Radicalism," 1.

39. *Alaska Citizen*, May 6, 1912.

40. *Alaska Citizen*, July 15, 1912.

41. Diary of James Wickersham, August 3, 4, 5, 1912.

42. *Fairbanks Daily News-Miner*, August 5, 1912; August 7, 1912.

43. *Cordova Daily Alaskan*, August 8, 1912.

44. *Nome Daily Nugget*, July 12, 1912.

45. *Fairbanks Daily Times*, August 14, 1912.

46. *Tanana Valley Socialist*, October 15, 1912.

CHAPTER 9: PROGRESSIVISM AND THE ALASKA RAILROAD

1. Harold W. Currie, *Eugene V. Debs,* Twayne's United States Authors Series 267, ed. Sylvia E. Bowman (Boston: Twayne Publishers, 1976), 44.

2. *Fairbanks Daily Times*, August 14, 1912.

3. *Saturday Evening Post*, May 11, 1912, 24.

4. US Department of the Interior, *Reports for the Fiscal Year Ended June 30, 1911*, 52.

5. *Congressional Record*, 62nd Cong. 2nd Sess. Vol. XLVII Part II, 1717–1718.

6. *Congressional Record*, 62nd Cong. 2nd Sess. Senate Committee on Territories, Hearings on Railroads for Alaska, March 5, 1912, 12, 14.

7. *Congressional Record*, 62nd Cong. 2nd Sess. House Committee on Territories, Hearings on Transportation for Alaska, April 5, 1912, 38.

8. *Congressional Record*, 62nd Cong. 2nd Sess. Senate Committee on Territories, Hearings on Railroads for Alaska, March 5, 1912, 31.

9. *Congressional Record,* 62nd Cong. 2nd Sess. House Committee on Territories, Hearings on Transportation for Alaska, April 5, 1912, 42.

10. William H. Wilson, *Railroad in the Clouds: The Alaska Railroad in the Age of Steam* (Boulder, CO: Pruett Publishing Company, 1977), 7.

11. *Congressional Record,* 62nd Cong. 3rd Sess. U.S, House of Representatives, Document No. 1346 "Railway Routes in Alaska," January 20, 1913, 35.

12. Wilson, *Railroad in the Clouds,* 8.

13. *Congressional Record,* 62nd Cong. 3rd Sess., "Railway Routes in Alaska," January 20, 1913, 18–22.

14. *Congressional Record,* 62nd Cong. 3rd Sess., "Railway Routes in Alaska," January 20, 1913, 141, 135.

15. *Congressional Record,* 62nd Cong. 3rd Sess., "Railway Routes in Alaska," January 20, 1913, 141, 135.

16. *Congressional Record,* 62nd Cong. 3rd Sess. Vol. XLIX Part III, 2660–61.

17. *Congressional Record,* 62nd Cong. 3rd Sess. Vol. XLIX Part V Appendix, 106.

18. *Congressional Record,* 63rd Cong. 1st Sess., House of Representatives Report No. 92, "Construction of Railroads in Alaska," 3–4.

19. *Literary Digest,* May 31, 1913, 1212.

20. *Seattle Post-Intelligencer,* August 17, 1913.

21. *New York Times,* August 21, 1913.

22. *The Nation,* January 1, 1914, 7–8.

23. *Congressional Record,* 63rd Cong. 1st Sess., Hearings before the House Committee on Territories, July 9–30, 1913, 411.

24. *Congressional Record,* 63rd Cong. 1st Sess., Senate Committee on Territories, "Construction of Railroads in Alaska," May 2, 1913, 36–37.

25. Wilson, *Railroad in the Clouds,* 15–16.

26. *Congressional Record,* 63rd Cong. 1st Sess, "Construction of Railroads in Alaska," May 2, 1913, 19–21.

27. Wilson, *The Papers,* Vol. 29, 9.

28. *Congressional Record,* 63rd Cong. 2nd Sess. Vol. LI Part IV, 1513.

29. James Gordon Steese, "Transportation Conditions in Alaska," *The American Review of Reviews* XLIX (January 1914), 58–64.

30. *Congressional Record,* 63rd Cong. 2nd Sess., 1627.

31. *The Literary Digest,* January 31, 1914, 193.

32. *Congressional Record,* 63rd Cong. 2nd Sess., 1634–1641.

33. *Congressional Record,* 63rd Cong. 2nd Sess., 1893.

34. *Congressional Record,* 63rd Cong. 2nd Sess., 1646.

35. *Congressional Record,* 63rd Cong. 2nd Sess., 1660–1661.

36. *Congressional Record,* 63rd Cong. 2nd Sess., 1687.

37. *Congressional Record,* 63rd Cong. 2nd Sess. Appendix, 91.

38. *Congressional Record,* 63rd Cong. 2nd Sess. Appendix, 94, 96.

39. *Congressional Record,* 63rd Cong. 2nd Sess. Appendix, 109.

40. *Congressional Record,* 63rd Cong. 2nd Sess. Appendix, 158.

41. Wilson, *The Papers,* Vol. 29, 332.

42. *Fairbanks Daily News-Miner,* January 22, 1914.

43. W. F. Thompson to James Wickersham, January 28, 1914, Wickersham Collection Ms. 107, Alaska State Library, Box 60, Folder 1.

44. James Wickersham to W. F. Thompson, February 24, 1914, Wickersham Collection Ms. 10,7 Alaska State Library, Box 60, Folder 1.

45. Diary of James Wickersham, April 1, 1914.

46. *American Review of Reviews*, April 1914, 397.

47. *The Outlook*, February 7, 1914, 278; *Literary Digest*, February 28, 1914, 418.

CHAPTER 10: THE NEW LAND OF OPPORTUNITY

1. *Alaska-Yukon Gazetteer and Business Directory 1915–1916*, 196ff.

2. *Fairbanks Daily News-Miner*, January 2, 1915.

3. Margaret E. Murie, *Two in the Far North*, 2nd ed. (Anchorage: Alaska Northwest Publishing Company, 1978), 16.

4. Murie, *Two in the Far North*, 17; Terrence Cole, *Ghosts of the Gold Rush: A Walking Tour of Fairbanks* (Fairbanks: Tanana Yukon Historical Society, 1978), 4.

5. Murie, *Two in the Far North*, 53–72.

6. *Fairbanks Daily News-Miner*, April 17, 1915.

7. Diary of James Wickersham, April 16, 1915.

8. *Alaska Citizen*, October 12, 1914.

9. *Descriptive of Fairbanks "Alaska's Golden Heart,"* The Fairbanks Commercial Club, 1916, 7.

10. Alfred H. Brooks, "The Development of Alaska by Government Railroads," *The Quarterly Journal of Economics* 28, no. 3 (May 1914), Oxford University Press, 586–596.

11. Katharine Carson Crittenden, *Get Mears! Frederick Mears: Builder of the Alaska Railroad* (Portland, OR: Binford & Mort Publishing, 2002), 53.

12. *Congressional Record*, 64th Cong. 1st Sess., House of Representatives Document No. 610, Reports of the Alaskan Engineering Commission, March 12, 1914 to December 31, 1915, 84.

13. Wilson, *Railroad in the Clouds*, 27.

14. *Fairbanks Daily Times*, March 26, 1915.

15. Crittenden, *Get Mears!*, 80.

16. Michael Krauss, "Na-Dene," *Current Trends in Linguistics* 10 (1973), 903–978; James Kari, "The Athabaskan Language Family and the Koyukon Language Area," in *Koyukon Athabaskan Dictionary*, comp. Jules Jette and Eliza Jones (University of Alaska Fairbanks: Alaska Native Language Center), xlvi.

17. Frederica De Laguna, *Travels Among the Dene: Exploring Alaska's Yukon Valley* (Seattle: University of Washington Press, 2000), 36.

18. James W. VanStone, *Athabaskan Adaptations: Hunters and Fishermen of the Subarctic Forests* (Arlington Heights, IL: Harlan Davidson, Inc., 1974), 97.

19. Robert A. McKennan, "Tanana," in *Handbook of North American Indians*, Vol. 6, *Subarctic*, ed. William C. Sturtevant, volume editor June Helm (Washington, DC: Smithsonian Institution, 1981); Wallace M. Olson, "Minto, Alaska," in *Handbook of North American Indians*, Vol. 6, *Subarctic*.

20. Matthew K. Sniffen and Thomas Spees Carrington, *The Indians of the Yukon and Tanana Valleys of Alaska* (Philadelphia: Indian Rights Association, 1914), 5.

21. Diary of James Wickersham, May 22, 1915.

22. *Alaska Citizen*, July 12, 1915.

23. *Proceedings of a Council held in the library room at Fairbanks, Alaska*, on July

5, 1915. Alaska Digital Archives (vilda.alaska.edu).

24. Peter Trimble Rowe to James Wickersham, November 22, 1908, Episcopal Church Records, Box 102, Alaska and Polar Regions Archives, Rasmuson Library, University of Alaska Fairbanks; James Wickersham to Peter Trimble Rowe, December 18, 1908, Box 102, Alaska and Polar Regions Archives, Rasmuson Library, University of Alaska Fairbanks.

25. Diary of James Wickersham, January 16, 1912.

26. Michael McGerr, *A Fierce Discontent: The Rise and Fall of the Progressive Movement in America 1870–1920* (New York: Free Press, 2003), 202; Francis Paul Prucha, *The Great Father: The United States Government and the American Indians,* 2 vols. (Lincoln: University of Nebraska Press, 1984), 759.

27. Hudson Stuck to John Woods, June 19, 1909, Episcopal Church Records.

28. Alaska Digital Archives (vilda.alaska.edu).

29. McGerr, *A Fierce Discontent,* 215.

30. Berg, *Wilson,* 309; Painter, *Standing at Armageddon,* 279.

31. *Congressional Record,* 63rd Cong. 1st Sess., House of Representatives Report No. 92, "Construction of Railroads in Alaska," November 26, 1913.

EPILOGUE

1. *Congressional Record,* 68th Cong. 2nd Sess., "Alaska Railroad," Senate Document No. 175, The Report of the Alaska Railroad from January 1 to December 31, 1923, 2, 8, 9.

2. Edwin M. Fitch, *The Alaska Railroad* (New York: Frederick A. Praeger, 1967), 55.

3. Anne Wintermute Lane and Louise Herrick Wall, eds., *The Letters of Franklin K. Lane: Personal and Political* (Boston and New York: Houghton Mifflin Company, 1922), 290.

4. *Congressional Record,* 66th Cong. 1st Sess., 8896-8897.

5. *Congressional Record,* 66th Cong. 1st Sess., 4977.

6. *Congressional Record,* 66th Cong. 1st Sess., 4985, 4986.

7. *Congressional Record,* 67th Cong. 1st Sess., House Committee on Territories, "Construction of the Alaskan Railroad," October 7, 1921, 13–20.

8. *Congressional Record,* 69th Cong. 1st Sess., House of Representatives Document No. 255, "The Alaska Railroad," The Report of the Alaska Railroad covering the Period from July 1, 1924, to June 30, 1925, 2, 3.

9. *Congressional Record,* 64th Cong. 1st Sess., House of Representatives Document No. 610, Reports of the Alaskan Engineering Commission for the Period from March 12, 1914, to December 31, 1915, 84.

10. US War Office, Annual Report of the Board of Road Commissioners for Alaska 1917, 10.

11. Brooks, "The Development of Alaska by Government Railroads," 586.

12. *The Weekly Northwestern Miller* (Indianapolis, Indiana), November 11, 1903, 1059.

13. Michael P. Malone, *James J. Hill: Empire Builder of the Northwest* (Norman: University of Oklahoma Press, 1996), 152.

14. Fitch, *The Alaska Railroad,* 67.

15. Wilson, *Railroad in the Clouds,* 180, 203, 238.

16. *Congressional Record,* 66th Cong. 1st Sess., 4981, 4987.

17. Vincent W. Ponko, "The Alaskan Coal Commission 1920 to 1922," *The Alaska Journal: History and Arts of the North* 8, no. 2 (Spring 1978), 119.

18. Wilson, "The Alaska Railroad and Coal," 67.

19. Fitch, *The Alaska Railroad,* 69; Ponko, "The Alaskan Coal Commission 1920 to 1922," 125.

20. US War Office, Annual Report of the Board of Road Commissioners for Alaska 1917, 10.

21. *Congressional Record,* 63rd Cong. 2nd Sess, Vol. LI, Part IV, 3622.

22. Josephine E. Papp and Josie A. Phillips, *Like a Tree to the Soil: A History of Farming in Alaska's Tanana Valley, 1903 to 1940* (Fairbanks: School of Natural Resources and Agricultural Sciences, University of Alaska Fairbanks, 2007), 21.

23. Papp and Phillips, *Like a Tree to the Soil,* 43, 49.

24. Donald Craig Mitchell, *Sold American: The Story of Alaska Natives and Their Land 1867–1959* (Hanover, NH: University Press of New England, 1997), 176–177.

25. Alfred H. Brooks, *Mineral Resources of Alaska,* Bulletin 714, Department of the Interior, United States Geological Survey (Washington: US Government Printing Office, 1919), 9.

26. Edwin Walter Kemmerer, *Gold and the Gold Standard: The Story of Gold Money Past, Present and Future* (New York: McGraw-Hill Book Company, Inc., 1944), 103.

27. Philip S. Smith, *Mineral Resources of Alaska: Report of Progress of Investigations in 1928,* Bulletin 813, Department of the Interior, United States Geological Survey (Washington: US Government Printing Office, 1930), 6.

28. Milton Friedman and Anna Jacobson Schwartz, *A Monetary History of the United States 1867–1960* (Princeton, NJ: Princeton University Press, 1963), 465–471.

29. La Follette, *A Personal Narrative,* 760; Daniel Levine, *Varieties of Reform Thought* (Madison: The State Historical Society of Wisconsin, 1964), 68.

30. Haycox, *Alaska,* 214–231.

31. William E. Brown, *Denali: Symbol of the Alaskan Wild* (Virginia Beach, VA: The Donning Company/Publishers, 1993), 88–91.

32. Gable, *The Bull Moose Years,* 239.

33. William E. Leuchtenburg, "Tired Radicals," in *The Progressive Era: Liberal Renaissance or Liberal Failure?,* ed. Arthur Mann (New York: Holt Rinehart and Winston, 1963), 95.

34. Arthur S. Link, *Wilson: The New Freedom,* 2 vols. (Princeton, NJ: Princeton University Press, 1956), 468.

35. Evangeline Atwood, *Frontier Politics: Alaska's James Wickersham* (Portland, OR: Binford & Mort, 1979), 230.

36. Atwood, *Frontier Politics,* 307–335.

37. Atwood, *Frontier Politics,* 323.

38. Diary of Thomas Riggs, March 31, 1918, Alaska State Library (library .alaska.gov).

REFERENCES CITED

NEWSPAPERS AND MAGAZINES

Alaska Citizen (Fairbanks)
Alaska Mining Record (Juneau)
Alaska Monthly (Seattle)
Alaska News (Juneau)
Alaska Prospector (Valdez)
Alaska Record-Miner (Juneau)
Alaska Searchlight (Juneau)
Alaska-Yukon Magazine
American Review of Reviews
Anchorage Daily Times
Appleton's Booklovers Magazine
Collier's
Cordova Alaskan
Cordova Daily Alaskan
Daily Alaska Dispatch (Juneau)
Daily Alaskan (Skagway)
Daily Nugget (Nome)
Douglas Miner
Fairbanks Daily News
Fairbanks Daily News-Miner
Fairbanks Daily Times
Fairbanks Evening News
Fairbanks Sunday Times
Hampton's
Literary Digest
McClure's
New York Daily Tribune
New York Sun
New York Times
The Outlook

Quarterly Journal of Economics
San Francisco Chronicle
Saturday Evening Post
Scribner's Magazine
Seattle Post-Intelligencer
Skaguay News
Tanana Valley Socialist (Fairbanks)
The Alaskan (Cordova)
The Atlantic
Valdez Daily Prospector
Valdez News
Weekly Northwestern Miller (Indianapolis, Indiana)

CONGRESSIONAL RECORDS AND GOVERNMENT DOCUMENTS

Congressional Record, 53rd Congress. 3rd Sess. Volume XXVII. Washington: Government Printing Office, 1895.

———, 55th Cong. 2nd Sess. Vol. XXXI. Washington: Government Printing Office, 1898.

———, 55th Cong. 3rd Sess. House of Representatives. Report No. 1807, Committee on Territories. Civil Government for Alaska. January 23, 1899.

———, 58th Cong. 2nd Sess. Hearings Before Subcommittee of Committee on Territories Appointed to Investigate Conditions in Alaska. *Conditions in Alaska*. January 12, 1904. Washington: Government Printing Office.

———, 58th Cong. 2nd Sess. Report of Subcommittee of Committee on Territories Appointed to Investigate Conditions in Alaska. *Conditions in Alaska*. January 12, 1904. Washington: Government Printing Office.

———, 58th Cong., 1st and 2nd Sess. House of Representatives. Hearings Before the Committee on Territories. Vol. II. Washington: Government Printing Office, 1904.

———, 61st Cong. 2nd Sess. *Government for Alaska*. Statement of Mr. Falcon Joslin, March 22, 1910, House of Representatives Committee on the Territories. Washington: Government Printing Office, 1910.

———, 61st Cong., 2nd Sess. Hearing before the Senate Committee on Territories, May 23, 1911. *Civil Government in Alaska*. Washington: Government Printing Office, 1911.

———, 61st Cong., 2d Sess. Proceedings in the House of Representatives (February 23, 1911). *A National Coal Monopoly in Alaska. Speech of Hon. James Wickersham*. Washington: Government Printing Office, 1911.

———, 61st Cong., 2d Sess. *Government of Alaska*. Statements Before the Committee on Territories, United States Senate on the bill S. 5436 to Create a Legislative Council in the District of Alaska. Washington: Government Printing Office, 1910.

———, 61st Cong., 2d Sess., Vol. XLV, Part 1. Washington: Government Printing Office, 1910.

———, 62nd Cong., 1st Sess., Vol. XLVII, Part 5. Washington: Government Printing Office, 1911.

———, 62nd Cong. 2nd Sess. House of Representatives Committee on Territories. Hearings on Transportation in Alaska. April 5, 1912. Washington: Government Printing Office, 1912.

———, 62nd Cong. 2nd Sess. Senate Committee on Territories. Hearings on Railroads for Alaska. March 5 and April 12, 1912. Washington: Government Printing Office, 1912.

———, 62nd Cong. 2nd Sess. Vol. XLVII, Part II. Washington: Government Printing Office, 1912.

———, 62nd Cong. 3rd Sess. House of Representatives. Report of the Alaska Railroad Commission January 20, 1913. "Railway Routes in Alaska." Document No. 1346. Washington: Government Printing Office, 1913.

———, 62nd Cong. 3rd Sess. Vol. XLIX, Part III. Washington: Government Printing Office, 1913.

———, 62nd Cong. 3rd Sess. Vol. XLIX, Part V Appendix. Washington: Government Printing Office, 1913.

———, 62nd Cong., 2nd Sess., Vol. XLVIII, Parts 5, 6. Washington: Government Printing Office, 1912.

———, 63d Cong. 1st Sess. House of Representatives. Report No. 92, Committee on Territories "Construction of Railroads in Alaska." November 26, 1913. Washington; Government Printing Office, 1913.

———, 63rd Cong. 1st Sess. House of Representatives. "The Building of Railroads in Alaska" Hearings before the Committee on Territories. July 9–30, 1913. Washington: Government Printing Office, 1913.

———, 63rd Cong. 1st Sess. House of Representatives. Report No. 92 "Construction of Railroads in Alaska." November 26, 1913. Washington: Government Printing Office, 1913.

———, 63rd Cong. 1st Sess. Senate Committee on Territories. "Construction of Railroads in Alaska." May 2, 1913. Washington: Government Printing Office, 1913.

———, 63rd Cong. 2nd Sess. The Alaska Railway Bill, Speech of Hon. James Wickersham in the House of Representatives, Wednesday, January 14 and 28, 1914. Washington: Government Printing Office.

———, 63rd Cong. 2nd Sess. Vol. LI, Part IV. Washington, DC: Government Printing Office.

———, 63rd Cong. 2nd Sess. Vol. LI, Part XVII Appendix. Washington: Government Printing Office, 1914.

———, 63rd Cong. 2nd Sess. Vol. LI, Parts I, II, III. Washington: Government Printing Office, 1914.

———, 64th Cong. 1st Sess. House of Representatives. Document No. 610. Reports of the Alaskan Engineering Commission for the Period from March 12, 1914, to December 31, 1915. Washington: Government Printing Office, 1915.

———, 64th Cong. 1st Sess. House of Representatives. Reports of the Alaskan Engineering Commission for the Period from March 12, 1914, to December 31, 1915. Document 610. Washington: Government Printing Office, 1916.

———, 67th Cong. 1st Sess. House of Representatives. Committee on Territories. "Construction of the Alaskan Railroad." October 7, 1921. Washington, DC: Government Printing Office, 1921.

———, 68th Cong. 2nd Sess. Senate Document No. 175. "Alaska Railroad."

The Report of the Alaska Railroad from January 1 to December 31, 1923. Washington, DC: Government Printing Office, 1925.

———, 69th Cong. 1st Sess. House of Representatives Document No. 255. "The Alaska Railroad." The Report of the Alaska Railroad Covering the Period from July 1, 1924, to June 30, 1925. Washington, DC: Government Printing Office, 1925.

United States of America War Office. *Annual Report of the Board of Road Commissioners for Alaska*. Washington: Government Printing Office, 1917.

US Department of the Interior. *Annual Report of the Governor of Alaska to the Secretary of the Interior*. Washington: Government Printing Office, 1900, 1901.

———. *Reports of the Department of the Interior for the Fiscal Year Ended June 30, 1911*. "Report of the Governor of the District of Alaska" Vol. II. Washington: Government Printing Office, 1912.

———. *Report of the Secretary of the Interior for the Fiscal Year Ended June 30, 1911*. Washington: Government Printing Office, 1912.

SECONDARY AND PRIMARY SOURCES

Abercrombie, W.R. "Into the Copper River Valley, Alaska." In *Compilation of Narratives of Explorations in Alaska*. Washington, DC: Government Printing Office, 1900.

Alaska-Yukon Gazetteer and Business Directory 1915–1916. Seattle: R.L. Polk and Company, Inc.

Allen, Henry T. *Report of an Expedition to the Copper, Tanana, and Koyukuk Rivers, Territory of Alaska in the Year 1885*. Washington, DC: Government Printing Office, 1887.

Atwood, Evangeline. *Frontier Politics: Alaska's James Wickersham*. Portland, OR: Binford & Mort, 1979.

Aucoin, James L. *The Evolution of American Investigative Journalism*. Columbia and London: University of Missouri Press, 2005.

Baker, Ray Stannard [David Grayson]. *American Chronicle: The Autobiography of Ray Stannard Baker*. New York: Charles Scribner's Sons, 1945.

Bates, J. Leonard. *The United States 1898–1928: Progressivism and a Society in Transition*. New York: McGraw-Hill Book Company, 1976.

Beach, Rex. "The Looting of Alaska: The True Story of a Robbery by Law." *Appleton's Booklovers Magazine* VII, no. 1, "The Golden Opportunity" (January 1906); no. 2, "A Suborned Judiciary" (February 1906); no. 3, "The Receivership Business" (March 1906); no. 4, "The Reign of Terror" (April 1906); no. 5, "Aftermath and Retrospect" (May 1906).

———. "What Is the Matter With Alaska?" *Saturday Evening Post* 183, no. 35 (February 25, 1911): 3–5, 40–41.

———. *The Iron Trail*. Sausalito, CA: A Comstock Edition, 1912.

———. *Personal Exposures*. New York: Harper & Brothers Publishers, 1940.

Beer, Thomas. *Hanna*. New York: Alfred A. Knopf, 1929.

Bennett, Marion T. *American Immigration Policies: A History*. Washington, DC: Public Affairs Press, 1963.

Bensel, Richard F. *Passion and Preferences: William Jennings Bryan and the 1896 Democratic National Convention*. New York: Cambridge University Press, 2008.

Berg, A. Scott. *Wilson*. New York: G.P. Putnam's Sons, 2013.

Berton, Pierre. *Klondike: The Last Great Gold Rush 1896–1899*. Toronto: McClelland and Stewart Limited, 1972.

Borneman, Walter R. *Alaska: Saga of a Bold Land*. New York: Harper Collins, 2003.

Brady, Kathleen. *Ida Tarbell: Portrait of a Muckraker*. New York: Seaview/ Putnam, 1984.

Braeman, John. *Albert J. Beveridge: American Nationalist*. Chicago and London: University of Chicago Press, 1971.

Brinkley, Douglas. *The Wilderness Warrior: Theodore Roosevelt and the Crusade for America*. New York: Harper Collins, 2009.

Brooks, Alfred Hulse. "The Development of Alaska by Government Railroads." *The Quarterly Journal of Economics* 28, no. 3 (May 1914): 586–596.

———. *Mineral Resources of Alaska*. Bulletin 714, Department of the Interior, United States Geological Survey. Washington: US Government Printing Office, 1919.

———. *Blazing Alaska's Trails*. Fairbanks: University of Alaska Press, 1973.

Brown, William E. *Denali: Symbol of the Alaskan Wild*. Alaska Natural History Association. Virginia Beach, VA: The Donning Company/Publishers, 1993.

Browne, Belmore. *The Conquest of Mt. McKinley*. Cambridge, MA: The Riverside Press, 1956.

Campbell, Robert. *In Darkest Alaska: Travel and Empire Along the Inside Passage*. Philadelphia: University of Pennsylvania Press, 2007.

Cashman, Sean Dennis. *America in the Gilded Age: From the Death of Lincoln to the Rise of Theodore Roosevelt*. 3rd ed. New York and London: New York University Press, 1993.

Chernow, Ron. *The House of Morgan: An American Banking Dynasty and the Rise of Modern Finance*. New York: Atlantic Monthly Press, 1990.

Coates, Ken S., and William R. Morrison. *Land of the Midnight Sun: A History of the Yukon*. Montreal: McGill-Queens University Press, 2005.

Coen, Ross. "The Myth of Alaskan Exceptionalism." *Anchorage Daily News* online (June 29, 2016). https://www.adn.com/commentary/article/myth-alaskan-exceptionalism/2010/03/20/

Cole, Terrence. *Ghosts of the Gold Rush: A Walking Tour of Fairbanks*. Fairbanks: Tanana Yukon Historical Society, 1978.

———. *A History of the Nome Gold Rush: The Poor Man's Paradise*. PhD diss., University of Washington, 1983.

———. *Crooked Past: The History of a Frontier Mining Camp: Fairbanks, Alaska*. Fairbanks: University of Alaska Press, 1991.

———. Introduction. In *Old Yukon: Tales, Trails, and Trials* by James Wickersham, edited and abridged by Terrence Cole. Classic Reprint Series No. 10. Fairbanks: University of Alaska Press, 2009.

Coletta, Paolo E. *William Jennings Bryan: Vol I. Political Evangelist 1860–1908*. Lincoln: University of Nebraska Press, 1964.

Coolidge, Louis A. *An Old-Fashioned Senator: Orville H. Platt of Connecticut*. New York: G.P. Putnam's Sons, 1910.

Corey, Lewis. *The House of Morgan: A Social Biography of the Masters of Money*. New York: AMS Press, 1969.

Crittenden, Katharine Carson. *Get Mears! Frederick Mears: Builder of the Alaska Railroad*. Portland, OR: Binford & Mort Publishing, 2002.

Croly, Herbert. *Marcus Alonzo Hanna: His Life and Work*. New York: The Macmillan Company, 1912.

———. *The Promise of American Life*. Boston: Northeastern University Press, 1989.

Currie, Harold W. 1976. *Eugene V. Debs*. Twayne's United States Authors Series 267. Edited by Sylvia E. Bowman. Boston: Twayne Publishers, 1989.

Dall, William H. *Alaska and Its Resources*. American Environmental Studies. New York: Arno & The New York Times, 1970.

Davis, John M. *The Guggenheims: An American Epic*. New York: William Morrow and Company, Inc., 1978.

de Laguna, Frederica. *Travels Among the Dena: Exploring Alaska's Yukon Valley*. Seattle: University of Washington Press, 2000.

Dean, David M. *Breaking Trail: Hudson Stuck of Texas and Alaska*. Athens: Ohio University Press, 1988.

Dickinson, Edward B. (comp.). *Official Proceedings of the Democratic National Convention*. Logansport, IN: Wilson, Humphreys & Co., 1896.

Egan, Timothy. *The Big Burn: Teddy Roosevelt and the Fire that Saved America*. Boston: Houghton Mifflin Harcourt, 2009.

Ehrlander, Mary F. "The Paradox of Alaska's 1916 Alcohol Reform Referendum: A Dry Vote Within a Frontier Alcohol Culture." *Pacific Northwest Quarterly* 102, no. 1 (Winter 2010/2011): 29–42.

Episcopal Church Records. Correspondence, Bishop Rowe, Box 102, Alaska and Polar Regions Archives, Rasmuson Library, University of Alaska Fairbanks.

———. Correspondence, Box 105, Alaska and Polar Regions Archives, Rasmuson Library, University of Alaska Fairbanks.

Fitch, Edwin M. *The Alaska Railroad*. New York: Frederick A. Praeger, 1967.

Foner, Eric. *The Story of American Freedom*. New York: W.W. Norton and Company, 1998.

Friedman, Milton. *Money Mischief: Episodes in Monetary History*. New York: Harcourt Brace Jovanovich, 1992.

Friedman, Milton, and Anna Jacobson Schwartz. *A Monetary History of the United States 1867–1960*. Princeton, NJ: Princeton University Press, 1963.

Gable, John Allen. *The Bull Moose Years: Theodore Roosevelt and the Progressive Party*. Port Washington, NY: Kennikat Press, 1978.

Glad, Paul W. *McKinley, Bryan, and the People*. Philadelphia and New York: J.P. Lippincott Company, 1964.

Goodwin, Doris Kearns. *The Bully Pulpit: Theodore Roosevelt, William Howard Taft, and the Golden Age of Journalism*. New York: Simon & Schuster, 2013.

Grauman, Melody Webb. "Big Business in Alaska: The Kennecott Mines, 1898–1938." Anthropology and Historic Preservation Cooperative Park Studies Unit, Occasional Paper #1. University of Alaska Fairbanks, 1977.

———. "Kennecott: Alaskan Origins of a Copper Empire, 1900–1938." *Western Historical Quarterly* 9, no. 2 (April 1978): 197–211.

Gruening, Ernest. *The State of Alaska: A Definitive History of America's Northernmost Frontier*. New York: Random House, 1954.

Harrison, Robert. *Congress, Progressive Reform, and the New American State.* Cambridge, UK: Cambridge University Press, 2004.

Harvey, William Hope. *Coin's Financial School.* Chicago: Coin Publishing Company, 1894.

Haskell, William B. *Two Years in the Klondike and Alaskan Gold-Fields 1896–1898.* Fairbanks: University of Alaska Press, 1998. First published 1898 by Hartford Publishing Company.

Haycox, Stephen. *Alaska: An American Colony.* Seattle: University of Washington Press, 2002.

———. *Battleground Alaska: Fighting Federal Power in America's Last Wilderness.* Lawrence: University Press of Kansas, 2016.

Helms, Andrea R. C., and Mary Childers Mangusso. "The Nome Gold Conspiracy." *Pacific Northwest Quarterly* 73, no. 1 (January 1982): 10–19.

Hinckley, Ted C. *The Americanization of Alaska, 1867–1897.* Palo Alto, CA: Pacific Books, 1972.

Hofstadter, Richard. *The American Political Tradition and the Men Who Made It.* New York: Alfred A. Knopf, 1948.

———. *The Age of Reform: From Bryan to F.D.R.* New York: Vintage Books, 1955.

———. *The Progressive Historians: Turner, Beard, Parrington.* New York: Alfred A. Knopf, 1968.

———, ed. *Great Issues in American History.* Vol. 2 1864–1957. New York: Random House, 1958.

Horner, William T. *Ohio's Kingmaker: Mark Hanna, Man and Myth.* Athens: Ohio University Press, 2010.

Hulbert, W.D. "What Is Really Going on in Alaska." *The Outlook.* "Wanted: a New Deal in the Coal Fields" (December 23, 1911); "Bringing the Coal to the Sea" (January 20, 1912); "Fish, Fur and a Forest—And a Few Other Things" (March 23, 1912); "In the Haunts of the Syndicate" (April 20, 1912).

Hunt, William R. *North of 53°: The Wild Days of the Alaska-Yukon Mining Frontier 1870–1914.* New York: Macmillan Publishing Co., Inc., 1974.

Janson, Lone E. *The Copper Spike.* Anchorage: Alaska Northwest Publishing Company, 1975.

Johnson, Charles W., comp. *Official Proceedings of the Eleventh Republican National Convention.* James Francis Burke, stenographer. Minneapolis, 1896.

Josephson, Matthew. *The Politicos 1856–1896.* New York: Harcourt, Brace & World, Inc., 1938.

Joslin, Falcon. "Railroad Building in Alaska." *Alaska-Yukon Magazine* VII, no. 4 (January 1909): 245–250.

Kari, James. "The Athabaskan Language Family and the Koyukon Language Area." In *Koyukon Athabaskan Dictionary* by Jules Jetté and Eliza Jones, ed. James Kari. University of Alaska Fairbanks: Alaska Native Language Center, 2000.

Kazin, Michael. *A Godly Hero: The Life of William Jennings Bryan.* New York: Anchor Books, 2006.

Kemmerer, Edwin Walter. *Gold and the Gold Standard: The Story of Gold Money Past, Present and Future.* New York: McGraw-Hill Book Company, Inc., 1944.

Kollin, Susan. *Nature's State: Imagining Alaska as the Last Frontier.* Chapel Hill: The University of North Carolina Press, 2001.

Krauss, Michael E. "Na-Dene." *Current Trends in Linguistics* 10 (1973): 903–978.

LaFollette, Robert M. *A Personal Narrative of Political Experience*. Madison, WI: The Robert LaFollette Co., 1911.

Lane, Anne Wintermute, and Louise Herrick Wall, eds. *The Letters of Franklin K. Lane: Personal and Political*. Boston and New York: Houghton Mifflin Company, 1922.

Leuchtenburg, William E. "Tired Radicals." In *The Progressive Era: Liberal Renaissance or Liberal Failure?*, ed. Arthur Mann. New York: Holt Rinehart and Winston, 1963.

Levine, Daniel. *Varieties of Reform Thought*. Madison: The State Historical Society of Wisconsin, 1964.

Limerick, Patricia Nelson. *The Legacy of Conquest: The Unbroken Past of the American West*. New York: W.W. Norton & Company, 1987.

Link, Arthur S. *Wilson: The New Freedom*. 2 vols. Princeton, NJ: Princeton University Press, 1956.

Malone, Michael P. *James J. Hill: Empire Builder of the Northwest*. Norman: University of Oklahoma Press, 1996.

Manners, William. *TR and Will: A Friendship That Split the Republican Party*. New York: Harcourt Brace & World, Inc., 1969.

Maxwell, Robert S. *La Follette and the Rise of the Progressives in Wisconsin*. Madison: State Historical Society of Wisconsin, 1956.

McGeary, Nelson M. *Gifford Pinchot: Forester, Politician*. Princeton, NJ: Princeton University Press, 1960.

McGerr, Michael. *A Fierce Discontent: The Rise and Fall of the Progressive Movement in America, 1870–1920*. New York: Free Press, 2003.

McKennan, Robert A. "Tanana." In *Handbook of North American Indians*. Vol. 6, *Subarctic*, edited by William C. Sturtevant, volume editor June Helm. Washington, DC: Smithsonian Institution, 1981.

McMath, Robert C., Jr. *American Populism: A Social History 1877–1898*. New York: Hill and Wang, 1993.

McMullin, Thomas A., and David Walker. *Biographical Directory of American Territorial Governors*. Westport, CT: Meckler Publishing, 1984.

Mileur, Jerome M. "The Legacy of Reform: Progressive Government, Regressive Politics." In *Progressivism and the New Democracy*, ed. Sidney M. Milkis and Jerome M. Mileur. Amherst: University of Massachusetts Press, 1999.

Milkis, Sidney M. "Progressivism Then and Now." Introduction to *Progressivism and the New Democracy*, ed. Sidney M. Milkis and Jerome M. Mileur. Amherst: University of Massachusetts Press, 1999.

Miller, Debbie S. "Tanana Valley Railroad." *Alaska Geographic: Alaska's Railroads* 19, no. 4 (1992): 33–39.

Mitchell, Donald Craig. *Sold American: The Story of Alaska Natives and Their Land 1867–1959*. Hanover, NH: University Press of New England, 1997.

Mitchell, William. "Building the Alaskan Telegraph System." *National Geographic* XV, no. 9 (September 1904): 357–361.

———. *The Opening of Alaska*. Ed. Lyman L. Woodman. Anchorage: Cook Inlet Historical Society, 1982.

Moore, Terris. *Mt. McKinley: The Pioneer Climbs*. Fairbanks: University of Alaska Press, 1967.

Morison, Elting E., ed. *The Letters of Theodore Roosevelt.* 8 vols. Selected and edited by Elting E. Morison. Cambridge, MA: Harvard University Press, 1954.

Morris, Edmund. *Theodore Rex.* New York: The Modern Library, 2001.

Mowry, George E. *The Era of Theodore Roosevelt, 1900–1912.* New York: Harper & Brothers, 1958.

Murie, Margaret E. *Two in the Far North.* 2nd ed. Illustrated by Olaus J. Murie. Anchorage: Alaska Northwest Publishing Company, 1978.

Naske, Claus-M. *Paving Alaska's Trails: The Work of the Alaska Road Commission.* Alaska Historical Commission Studies in History No. 152. Lanham, MD: University Press of America, 1986.

Naske, Claus-M., and Herman E. Slotnick. *Alaska: A History.* Norman: University of Oklahoma Press, 2011.

Naske, Claus-M., and Don M. Triplehorn. "The Federal Government and Alaska's Coal." *The Northern Engineer.* Geophysical Institute, University of Alaska 12, no. 3 (Fall 1980).

Neuzil, Mark. "Hearst, Roosevelt, and the Muckrake Speech of 1906: A New Perspective." *Journalism & Mass Communication Quarterly* 73, no. 1 (1996): 29–39.

Nichols, Jeannette P. *Alaska: A History of its Administration, Exploitation, and Industrial Development during its First Half Century under the Rule of the United States.* Cleveland: The Arthur H. Clark Company, 1924.

Olson, Wallace M. "Minto, Alaska." In *Handbook of North American Indians.* Vol. 6, *Subarctic*, ed. William C. Sturtevant, volume editor June Helm. Washington, DC: Smithsonian Institution, 1981.

Orth, Donald J. *Dictionary of Alaska Place Names.* Geological Survey Professional Paper 567. Washington, DC: United States Government Printing Office, 1967.

Painter, Nell Irvin. *Standing at Armageddon: A Grassroots History of the Progressive Era.* New York: W.W. Norton & Company, 2008.

Papp, Josephine E., and Josie A. Phillips. *Like a Tree to the Soil: A History of Farming in Alaska's Tanana Valley, 1903 to 1940.* Fairbanks: School of Natural Resources and Agricultural Sciences, University of Alaska Fairbanks, 2007.

Patty, Stanton H. "A Conference with the Tanana Chiefs." *Alaska Journal: History and Arts of the North* 1, no. 2 (Spring 1971): 2–18.

Pinchot, Gifford. *Breaking New Ground.* New York: Harcourt, Brace and Company, 1947.

Ponko, Vincent W., Jr. "The Alaskan Coal Commission 1920 to 1922." *The Alaska Journal: History and Arts of the North* 8, no. 2 (Spring 1978): 118–129.

Proceedings of a Council held in the library room at Fairbanks, Alaska, on July 5, 1915. Alaska Digital Archives (vilda.alaska.edu).

Prucha, Francis Paul. *The Great Father: The United States Government and the American Indians,* 2 vols. Lincoln: University of Nebraska Press, 1984.

Ravits, Abe C. *Rex Beach.* Boise State University Western Writers Series Number 113. Edited by James H. Maguire. Boise, ID: Boise State University, 1994.

Riggs, Thomas. Diary. Online at library.alaska.gov/hist_docs/asl_ms273_2_1918-1919_transcript.pdf.

Ritter, Gretchen. *Goldbugs and Greenbacks: The Antimonopoly Tradition and the Politics of Finance in America.* New York: Cambridge University Press, 1997.

Roosevelt, Theodore. "Municipal Administration: The New York Police Force." *The Atlantic* LXXX (September 1897): 289–300.

———. "Alaska—It Must Be Developed." *The Outlook* (July 22, 1911): 612–615.

———. "Alaska Again." *The Outlook* (August 12, 1911): 821–822.

———. *Theodore Roosevelt: An Autobiography*. New York: Charles Scribner's Sons, 1922.

Rosebloom, Eugene H. *A History of Presidential Elections: From George Washington to Richard M. Nixon*. New York: The Macmillan Company, 1970.

Schlup, Leonard. "Coe I. Crawford and the Progressive Campaign of 1912." South Dakota Historical Society, 1979.

Schwatka, Frederick. *A Summer in Alaska in the 1880s*. Secaucus, NJ: Castle Books, 1888.

Sherwood, Morgan B. *Exploration of Alaska 1865–1900*. New Haven and London: Yale University Press, 1992.

Slotnick, Herman. "The Ballinger-Pinchot Affair in Alaska." *Journal of the West* 10, no. 2 (1971): 337–347.

Smith, Philip S. *Mineral Resources of Alaska: Report of Progress of Investigations in 1928*. Bulletin 813, Department of the Interior, United States Geological Survey. Washington: U.S. Government Printing Office, 1930.

Sniffen, Matthew K., and Thomas Spees Carrington. *The Indians of the Yukon and Tanana Valleys, Alaska*. Philadelphia: Indian Rights Association, 1914.

Stearns, Robert Alden. *The Morgan-Guggenheim Syndicate and the Development of Alaska, 1906–1915*. PhD diss., University of California Santa Barbara, 1967.

Steese, James Gordon. "Transportation Conditions in Alaska." *The American Review of Reviews* XLIX (January 1914): 58–64.

Stern, Clarence A. *Resurgent Republicanism: The Handiwork of Hanna*. Ann Arbor, MI: Edwards Brothers, Inc., 1963.

Stromquist, Shelton. *Reinventing "The People": The Progressive Movement, the Class Problem, and the Origins of Modern Liberalism*. Urbana and Chicago: University of Illinois Press, 2006.

Strouse, Jean. *Morgan: American Financier*. New York: Harper Perennial, 2000.

Sullivan, Joseph. "Sourdough Radicalism: Labor and Socialism in Alaska, 1905–1920." *Alaska History* 7, no. 1. (1992): 1–15.

Sulzer, William. "What Alaska Needs." *Alaska-Yukon Magazine* XI, no. 4 (May 1911): 20–21.

Taniguchi, Nancy J. *Necessary Fraud: Progressive Reform and Utah Coal*. Norman: University of Oklahoma Press, 1996.

Thelen, David P. *Robert M. La Follette and the Insurgent Spirit*. Boston: Little Brown and Company, 1976.

Tower, Elizabeth A. "Rex Beach's Alaska: Novels and Autobiography." *Alaska History News* 20, no. 4 (October 1989): 7.

———. "Captain David Henry Jarvis: Alaskan Tragic Hero—Wickersham's Victim." *Alaska History* 5, no.1 (Spring 1990): 1–21.

———. *Icebound Empire: Industry and Politics on the Last Frontier 1898–1938*. Anchorage: Publication Consultants, 1996.

Turner, Frederick Jackson. "The Significance of the Frontier in American History." In *The Frontier in American History*. New York: Henry Holt and Company, 1920.

Unger, Irwin, and Debi Unger. *The Guggenheims: A Family History.* New York: Harper Collins, 2005.

VanStone, James W. *Athabaskan Adaptations: Hunters and Fishermen of the Subarctic Forests.* Arlington Heights, IL: Harlan Davidson, Inc., 1974.

Webb, Melody. *The Last Frontier.* Albuquerque: University of New Mexico Press, 1985.

Weinberg, Arthur, and Lila Weinberg, eds. *The Muckrakers.* Chicago: First Illinois Paperback, 2001. First published 1961 by Simon and Schuster (New York).

Weinberg, Steve. *Taking on the Trust: The Epic Battle of Ida Tarbell and John D. Rockefeller.* New York: W.W. Norton & Company, 2008.

Whitehead, John S. *Completing the Union: Alaska, Hawai'i, and the Battle for Statehood.* Albuquerque: University of New Mexico Press, 2004.

Wickersham, James. *Old Yukon: Tales, Trails, and Trials.* Edited and abridged by Terrence Cole. Fairbanks: University of Alaska Press, 2009.

Wiebe, Robert H. *The Search for Order 1877–1920.* New York: Hill and Wang, 1967.

Willis, Roxanne. *Alaska's Place in the West: From the Last Frontier to the Last Great Wilderness.* Lawrence: University Press of Kansas, 2010.

Wilson, Harold S. *McClure's Magazine and the Muckrakers.* Princeton, NJ: Princeton University Press, 1970.

Wilson, William H. *Railroad in the Clouds: The Alaska Railroad in the Age of Steam.* Boulder, CO: Pruett Publishing Company, 1977.

———. "The Alaska Railroad and Coal." *Pacific Northwest Quarterly* 73, no. 2 (April 1982).

Wilson, Woodrow. *The New Freedom: A Call for the Emancipation of the Generous Energies of a People.* New York: Doubleday, Page and Company, 1913.

———. *The Papers of Woodrow Wilson.* Edited by Arthur S. Link. 68 vols. Princeton, NJ: Princeton University Press, 1979.

ACKNOWLEDGMENTS

As both student and career employee at the University of Alaska Fairbanks, I have had the great fortune to have benefited from the influence of a number of teachers, mentors, colleagues, and friends. Going back to 1970, some of the most memorable teachers were Claus-M. Naske, Herman Slotnick, and Charles Keim. In my years as editor at the Alaska Native Language Center at UAF, I worked with some of the world's leading scholars of Eskimo and Athabascan languages. I am grateful to have known and learned from Michael Krauss, Lawrence Kaplan, Steven Jacobson, Jim Kari, Walkie Charles, and a large number of others who were not only linguists but also experts in the history and anthropology of the Alaska Native peoples. From them and the many speakers of Alaska Native languages, I learned to appreciate the vital connection between language and culture. Others at UAF who have had a strong positive influence on my life and career include Terrence Cole and Judith Kleinfeld.

As this book came together over the past five years, I benefited from the help of many people who showed a continued interest in its progress. Among them are Rose Speranza, of the Rasmuson Library Alaska and Polar Regions Collections and Archives, and Bill Schneider, retired Rasmuson Library professor of library science, who offered valuable advice and encouragement along the way. Stephen Haycox and Ross Coen carefully read the manuscript and supplied many thoughtful suggestions for additions and improvements. Nate Bauer and Krista West of the University of Alaska Press guided the book through to publication, and Rachel Fudge edited the manuscript with expertise and care. Thank you to all.

And finally I thank my family for their constant interest and encouragement: Amanda, whose courage and determination are an inspiration to me; Jack, whose love of knowledge and learning have brought success to him as a father and a professional; and, above all, Kathy, who makes everything possible.

INDEX

Page numbers with an *f* refer to a figure or a caption; *n* indicates a footnote.